D1488089

Midnight Calling

A Memoir of a
Drug Smuggler's Daughter

LYNN WALKER

MZW
PUBLISHING
Seattle WA
USA

The author is grateful for permission to reprint lyrics from "Mariner's Song" by Michael Timmins © Paz Junk Music Inc. The author also wishes to thank Eileen Pollack for editing this book.

Library of Congress Control Number: 2021918368
ISBN: 978-1-7378955-0-3

MZW Publishing
Washington USA
www.MZWPublishing.com

For Mom, who gave me life and saved my life.

The last of man's great unchained beast
lies lappin' at my door
An' I'd be happy to give it what it wants
But I do know it would just ask for more

I search for you with every crest I ride
In every trough I travel through

I didn't mean to leave you
I unfurled my sail and the wind did blow
Why? Oh, why I did not drop my anchor
Oh Lord, I will never know

From "Mariner's Song"
By Michael Timmins

FINGERPRINTS

*W*e were walking behind the hedge that screened our house from the street. That hedge was my castle wall, my hiding place, my brother's source of ammunition—wormy berries that exploded red on impact. I had just glanced at Mom, when Dad jerked his hand out in front of her. In the space between them, I could see our front door. It was open a crack.

Dad spun around to face us, serious and focused. "Back to the car. Lay down on the floor and *don't* move 'til I come back." Looking down at Ricky and me, he pressed his finger to his pursed lips.

Mom hurried us into the car and scrambled in behind us. Ricky and I hunkered under the glove box while she leaned over and rested her arm across us. It was a warm day, but a shiver ran down my back. Afraid I would see a bad guy reaching in for us, I kept my sights off the windows. I tried not to move, just like Daddy told me, even when my feet prickled with pins and needles. When my neck ached from being wedged in there, I rested my chin on the seat. I stared at the creases in the upholstery that were supposed to make it look like real leather. Up close, I could see tiny cracks branching out from some of the creases; those were from our car baking in the Miami sun day after day.

After several minutes, Mom shifted around in her seat and fumbled to put the keys in the ignition while peeking over the dashboard. Her face had gone pale.

I whispered, "Can we get out now?"

She shook her head and leaned back over us. "Let's wait another minute for your daddy."

A rapping on the car roof made me flinch, but it was one of those involuntary movements (as Mommy would call it), because in the split second after I heard that drumming noise above us, I knew it was only Dad. No criminal would tap on the roof of a car where a family was hiding; he would sneak up slow and quiet. As Mom straightened up, Dad leaned in the window and pecked her on the cheek. He grinned at Ricky and me. "Okay kiddos, coast is clear."

We tumbled out of the passenger door, and I smoothed the wrinkles from my dress while Ricky ran around the front of the car, bouncing all over. "Did you have to shoot anyone, Daddy? Huh? Was there any bad guys in there? Any robbers?" That was a dumb question because Dad wouldn't tell us we could go inside if crooks were in there, but I paused my dress-smoothing and peered over the hood at Dad.

Circles of sweat darkened his shirt around the armpits, his tie was loose and he had that line between his eyebrows that showed up sometimes. "Not a one," he said.

"Awww," Ricky groaned then pushed his glasses back up since they had inched down from all that bouncing. Mom sat motionless in the car. Her frowning lips were still frosted Glitter-sweet Pink, but her hair, which she had styled for church by sleeping in springy curlers, was now limp. No amount of hairspray could hold up against crouching in a muggy car like that.

"Guess we didn't pull the door shut all the way when we left for church," Dad said.

She finally stepped out of the car, letting out a long breath, her hand on her chest. "Whew. That was scary."

We all walked toward the house again, Ricky with a pretend

gun—finger pointed, thumb up—twisting to the left, to the right, then poking in the hedge for robbers. "Naw. It was cool. I wasn't scared one bit."

"I'm *sure* I pulled that door shut. Could you tell if anything's missing or bothered?" Mom asked. That got me imagining a burglar lurking in our house with a black mask stretched tight over his face.

I stopped walking.

"Nothing's out of place, and I checked the entire house." He swept his arm in an arc. "No one's been in there. You probably just didn't pull it 'til it latched, then a breeze blew it open. Everything's alright inside." They all continued toward the door, and Dad slid his hand across the small of Mom's back to her hip. She was all slim and hourglass-shaped there, especially in that polka dot dress she had made. I noticed Dad's pistol tucked in the waistband of his slacks. He looked over his shoulder, came back, scooped me up and carried me inside. His neck had a whiff of the aftershave that he had let me pat on his face that morning—I had picked English Leather because it reminded me of Grandma and Grandpa's cabin, like pine trees and smoke from the chimney and a piecrust in the oven all swirled together.

Mom directed Ricky toward his room to change out of his church clothes, then lifted me out of Dad's arms. "Come here, sweetie. Let's get you in some play clothes too." As she carried me down the hall, Dad flashed his big, easy smile after me. The wrinkle between his eyebrows was gone now. But I knew for sure the house was safe because he was removing the bullets from his gun. He always did that before he put it away, right next to his silver badge and handcuffs in the lockbox in his bedroom closet.

I changed out of my Sunday school dress and was headed to the kitchen for one of the donuts we had picked up on our way home, when Dad called out from his bedroom. "Wanna help clean my guns today, darlin'?" That chocolate cake donut popped right out of my mind, and I made an about-face in the hallway. Dad had introduced us to guns right along with teaching us to tie our shoes and ride bicycles. He would haul us out to the junkyard where I aimed at a busted-up refrigerator, television or paint can while he kneeled behind me with his hands wrapped around mine. Nestled against him, I would giggle with the anticipation and fear of that CRACK! as I squeezed the trigger, his finger right below mine. But I had never been allowed to clean the guns.

Skidding into their bedroom, I said, "Really? I can clean them today? Can I take them apart too? And put them all back together?"

"Yeah, I think five is old enough to clean a gun. Let's take 'em all to the table." Reaching into his lockbox, he removed his revolver and offered it to me. I hesitated. I had never shot that gun because Dad always said it would knock me clean over. It was long and sleek and shiny as a brand-new nickel. He tipped his chin at it still in his outstretched hand. "Go on. It's not loaded. Just remember how to hold it." The gun was heavier than I thought it would be as I wrapped both hands around it and carried it, barrel down, to the dining room. Behind me, Dad let out a soft chuckle.

Dad spread the usual towel on the table with his three guns, cleaning fluid, a stack of swabs, cleaning rods and brushes laid out in rows. I pointed at the gun I always shot. "This one's the PPK, right?" It was his smallest gun, blocky and solid black, with a short barrel and a checkered, rubbery grip.

"Very good! A Walther PPK. Remember what these are called?"

I glanced back and forth between the silver gun and his biggest gun: black, all squared angles and boxy, with a wooden grip screwed on each side of the handle. Tapping the table in front of the big, black one, I said, "I remember this one. It's a brownie."

He tossed his head back and laughed. "That's right. A Browning. It's a Browning nine-millimeter. And this one's a three-fifty-seven Magnum. I wear it with the handle pointing front-wards, so I can grab it real fast if I'm chasin' a crook." He slid the .357 alongside his left hip where his holster usually hung, then whipped it out in front of him so fast I barely kept the gun in my sights. "That also makes it hard for anyone to sneak up behind me and take it."

He held the .357 in front of me, the cylinder popped out to the side. "Now, with the barrel pointing away from you always"—he looked me in the eyes, waiting until I nodded—"check those chambers and tell me if you see any bullets."

I peeked into each of the six openings. "No. No bullets in the chambers." My stomach fluttered with excitement.

"Good. Now slide one of these cleaning cloths through the slot on this rod and squirt some oil on it."

I didn't need those instructions because I had watched him do this dozens of times. Though it was much harder than I thought to get the swatch through that little hole. I pushed and pulled and wiggled the cloth. "Like that?"

He gave the cloth a tug until it was wedged tight through the top of the cleaning rod. "Perfect." He pointed to the Hoppe's No. 9 oil. I tipped and squeezed the tin, the liquid streaming onto the cloth. "Now shove the rod all the way through the barrel. That's good, keep going 'til it comes out the other end." The swab squeaked as I pushed it through. "See how it comes out gray? That's all the gunpowder from the last time I shot it. We have to get all that out, so pull that dirty swab off, put on a clean one, oil it and run it through again. Keep that up 'til the swab comes out clean. Then do the same thing in each bullet chamber."

Next to me, Dad took apart the PPK and Browning, piece by piece, laying each part on the towel so he didn't lose any and naming each one for me: magazine, slide, barrel, recoil spring, spring guide and slide stop.

When I finished the .357, I twisted around to show him how clean it was.

"Whoa there." He pushed the barrel away from him, his face stern. "Remember, even when you know it's not loaded, always keep the gun pointed away from you or anyone else. Unless you plan on shootin' someone."

My cheeks grew hot. I swung the barrel away from us then angled the back of the gun toward him so he could peek through it.

Inspecting the gun, he whistled. "Cleaned like a pro. That might be the cleanest that Magnum's ever been."

Something swelled inside me, like a huge smile starting in my belly, spreading through my middle, then breaking out on my face. "Can I do another one?"

"Go on." He pointed his finger back and forth between the Browning and PPK barrels. I cleaned the insides of the barrels while he soaked and scrubbed the small parts. Any fear I had left over from the morning drifted away as the sweet, metallic smell of Hoppe's No. 9 enveloped us. After he reassembled the guns, we polished the outsides, holding each one with a clean rag so we didn't leave so much as a smudge. Not a single fingerprint anywhere.

Not this time. Our fingerprints, and our crimes, would come a decade later.

Over the next several years, my childhood would unravel as Dad deteriorated from undercover narcotics agent to drug smuggler, from protective father to monster—a very charming monster. This transformation occurred right before my eyes, even as Mom and I continued pasting into a scrapbook all the newspaper articles about drug busts Dad made, one was the largest in Miami's history, and awards he received for outstanding narcotics work. With only a child's-eye view, I couldn't fathom my father was waging an internal battle against the allure of Miami's drug smuggling scene of the 1970s with its free-flowing drugs and booze and women and money. Easy money. And lots of it. The thrill and extravagance were calling to him. There was no way our family—church on Sundays, Dad teaching Sunday school, our modest house with a small pool in a blue-collar suburb—could compete with the opulent smuggling world in which Dad worked every day. Our family was going to lose. But all I knew was my daddy was drifting further and further from me until one night he disappeared, leaving a note in the mailbox.

I didn't know fathers ever left their families. To my thinking, daddies took care of their families, especially their daughters, and daddies who were cops were the best at it.

Without Dad's larger-than-life presence, I tried anything and everything to stabilize my wobbling world. I analyzed every past interaction with my father to determine what I had done to make him leave and what I could do to bring him home again. I became ever vigilant of my mother's whereabouts and state of mind, for she now offered my only security; though it was clear to me that my mother's world was also wobbling. She was lost and devastated. I tried to steady my brother and tiptoe around his anger, but there wasn't much I could do to settle him down.

I turned eight, and Ricky was eleven, the summer Mom explained Dad wasn't coming back to live with us. Ricky bolted for his room. Mom caught up with him in the hallway and pulled him to her, rocking him in her arms. "Honey, this doesn't have anything to do with you. Sometimes mommies and daddies just can't live together anymore." As I walked up to them, she put her arm around me too. Tears began rolling down her face. "Your daddy still loves you both very much, and you'll see him every weekend." The image of that moment is etched in my memory as if I were looking down from the ceiling at the three of us huddled in the dim hallway, hanging onto each other like we were in a lifeboat. Perhaps because on that summer day, I couldn't imagine how our family would survive without my father.

I never understood what had happened to Dad until I was in high school, and he was in prison—for smuggling 12,000 pounds of marijuana. He and his partners had loaded half the bales into a cargo truck from speed rollers jutting out from the belly of a Convair 440 airplane. Dad was inching the first truck down a gravel road, headlights off in the pitch-black night, when lights blasted on, blinding him momentarily. Then, plain as day, he saw the blue lights swirling from atop a police car.

By the time my father had been arrested, I was already filling the void he had left in my life with an insatiable compulsion for the attention of men and a massive drug and alcohol habit of my own. This was a perfect setup for me to latch on to the only connection to Dad that remained once he was released from prison four years later—cocaine. My father met his big connection in prison. A few months after he was paroled, Dad waltzed back into my life dishing out his pure Colombian cocaine to me and launching my brother's coke-dealing career. After a few years of abusing coke with Dad, I would lose everything and everyone I cared about and be forced to choose between my life and my father.

Only I had no idea how *I* could walk away from *Dad* this time. Or if I would ever find my way back to him.

2

DEEP END OF THE POOL

*D*ad stopped wearing his police uniform to work the year I started school. Gone was his bright silver badge pinned over his heart, protecting it, I thought, in case a criminal shot at him. No more handcuffs hooked on his belt or crisp creases that Mom ironed in his pants every Sunday evening. Instead, he wore regular clothes to work, but not *his* regular clothes. These were button-down shirts, bell-bottomed jeans and ankle-high boots, or some days it was Converse basketball shoes, ratty jeans and his old Marine Corps utility shirt with the long sleeves cut off raggedy. He grew a mustache and sideburns down to his jaw and his hair long enough that it became wavy, all of it the exact color of a milk-chocolate bar. He wore sunglasses in which I could see my reflection and a miniature silver spoon, an inch long, on a chain around his neck. I asked if I could use that spoon to play with my baby doll, but he laughed and said it was only for work. Instead of a holster on his belt, he wore a hidden one strapped under his left arm and a second one around his right calf for his PPK. Sometimes he drove home from work in a new car—Ricky called it a hot rod—with the Roadrunner cartoon character on the steering wheel. Its engine had a loud rumble I could hear even before he rolled into the driveway. Mostly that car was kept at work.

Dad had a new partner too: Carl. They were best friends; I could tell by the way they knew with a glance what the other was thinking and how they razzed each other about things that made no sense to me but made Mom and Carl's wife, Beth, tsk their tongues in pretend disgust.

Our family often went boating in the Keys with Carl, Beth and their two boys. At the marina, Ricky and I ran ahead to the exact spot where our favorite boat was moored, the sound of our feet pounding on the dock and echoing up from the water under-neath. Everything about the marina was bump and sway, the clang of rigging against masts, the thud of boats against the dock. The first thing Carl and Dad did when we climbed into a boat was stash their guns in one of the compartments, warning us kids to stay out of that one. Ricky and Carl's boys would look at each other with sly grins, but they didn't dare touch those guns.

The grown-ups let us take turns steering with the tiller, but we never got to mess with the sails—too complicated, they said. Dad and Carl taught us how to fish in the ocean, which I only liked if we released the fish. When we kept the red snappers for dinner, I hated to see them helpless, gasping for air with their pink frowny lips opening and closing and their scaly gills pulsing. Plus, I didn't even like fish except fish sticks from the freezer.

On one of our trips, Ricky caught a hammerhead shark, which looked like it swallowed a huge blade that got stuck sideways in its mouth, leathery gray skin stretched tight around it. The shark was about as long as I was tall and twisted and flopped all over the boat as I squealed and jumped out of its way. Ricky stepped back, still clutching his pole, while Dad and Carl struggled to remove the hook from its mouth.

"Shit. I can't get the hook out. He swallowed the whole damn thing," Carl said. Dad grabbed his fishing knife.

"No, don't!" Ricky yelled just as Dad slit the shark's throat.

Blood pooled underneath the slippery, limp shark as Carl cut the line and chucked the shark into the ocean. Ricky dropped his fishing pole and turned his face away, toward Mom, his eyes frantic with the horror of the killing. He had a great, big soft spot for animals, any kind, and filled our house with stray cats, box turtles, lizards, snakes, injured birds. "Why'd they have to kill it? I wanted to turn it loose."

Mom pulled Ricky and me up to the bow of the boat away from the bloody mess. "They couldn't get the hook out, and if they left it in, the shark would've died anyway."

After splashing water over the blood, Dad came over to us. "We tried to save it but couldn't get that hook out. He swallowed it. Would've been cruel to cut the line and set him free with a big hook stuck down his throat. He wouldn't have been able to eat and would have starved to death."

Ricky nodded and swiped the snot off his nose with the back of his hand.

With a loud clap, Carl tried to snap us out of our misery. "Hey, that's enough fishing for the day. Who wants to go swimming?" He climbed down the ladder and fell backwards into the water. The boys followed, launching themselves off the ladder so hard the boat rocked. Mom and Beth slipped in last. I stayed put near the bow, avoiding the pink, watery area where the shark died.

"I don't want to go in," I said to Dad.

"What? You always swim out here. Come on. I'll stay right there next to you in the water." We were in the Keys where the water was so clear and shallow, I could see the ocean floor, and the water was calm, barely swaying the boat. Normally, I was in and out of the water so many times my skin would be sticky and parched from saltwater by lunchtime. But the image of that shark was still in my mind.

I shook my head.

Mom was floating on her back, making angel wings with her arms to keep afloat. Course, she didn't look like an angel down

there with her tanned skin and her lean body all curvy underneath her bikini, which was magically held on by a few bows.
More like a Barbie Doll than an angel. "Sure you don't want to
swim with Mommy? It's *fuunnn*. You can use the backstroke
you're so good at now." Between her coaxing and the boys
goofing off in the water, I was tempted. If I didn't jump in soon,
they might be ready to get out just when I was finally ready to get
in. Then I wouldn't get to swim at all, which was my most
favorite thing to do in the whole world. But the bloody shark was
down there somewhere. I glanced at Dad. His lanky legs were
stuck out in front of him, ankles crossed, and his arms were
stretched across the edge of the boat. He was taking in the sea
around us. No pressure there; he was fine staying on the boat
with me.

Suddenly, he jumped up, cupped his hands around his mouth
and yelled, "Everyone, back to the boat. Now! Stay real calm, no
splashing. Boys, swim back here now without any splashing."

He lurched to the compartment that held the guns, pulled his
out and jammed in the magazine. All the while, he looked back
and forth from the water behind me, to where everyone was
swimming. He racked the slide of his gun, leaving the hammer
cocked. Ready to fire. In two long strides, he was at the ladder. I
looked behind me where Dad kept glancing. A dark shadow
glided under the surface of the water—a huge shark, half the size
of our boat—circling the area where the hammerhead had been
tossed. While Dad was in full motion, I froze, my nerves thrum-
ming with fear. Silently, I shot up a pleading prayer that the shark
wouldn't notice my family.

As everyone came closer to the boat, Dad reached his hand
down the ladder, gun in his other hand with the barrel pointing
toward the sky. Continuously, he scanned the water. "Carl, get
those kids out first." As soon as each boy touched the ladder, Dad
yanked them onto the boat, popping them out of the water like
they were bobbers on a fishing line.

Once the boys were on board, Dad mumbled, "There's a big

shark over by the hammerhead." Then Carl began scanning the water around him while he pushed Beth and Mom up the ladder. Once everyone was back on board, Dad pointed to the shark, which by then was thrashing over the hammerhead's body. A thick ribbon of blood drifted toward our boat.

"Guess that's enough swimming for the day too," Carl said. A nervous laugh passed between the adults. Dad ejected the magazine from his gun, pulled the slide back and shook the bullet loose from the chamber. He even peered in the chamber, just like he taught me, to be extra sure it was empty before putting the gun back in the compartment. Then he let a rush of air out of his lungs.

Back at home, Dad read me a bedtime story. While I listened to his voice, I noticed the sensation of rolling on the waves still in my body. I closed my eyes and felt the sea swelling underneath me as I recalled the day: steering the boat, the hot sun on my skin, the fishy-salt tang of the ocean, the huge shark devouring the hammerhead then Dad pulling everyone to safety.

I thought all fathers kept their families safe but figured we were extra safe because mine was a policeman. Everywhere we went, Dad took his pistol. It was either in the glovebox or his jacket pocket; rarely was it in his holster, not when he was off-duty. I never saw other fathers, except Carl, carry guns. But Dad's PPK was so much a part of our life that I never questioned why he brought it. Though I did wonder how other daddies kept *their* families safe when they ran into bad guys.

I was also unaware of just how much those bad guys were becoming part of my father's life and, by extension, mine. They were seeping in around the edges of his life, pressing in on him. But as a child, I was mostly sheltered from the seedy underworld he conned his way into every day. There were a few instances when his undercover work spilled over into our lives. At first, my father was frantic to keep his two worlds from colliding. Later, he walked his undercover world right through our patio door.

Strolling down the midway of the county fair one sweltering day, the sticky-sweet scent of cotton candy mingling with the musky odor of the horses and donkeys, Dad suddenly steered us behind a game booth. His smile was gone. He looked all around us while he slid his gun out of Mom's purse. "Linda, listen." He tucked the gun in the waistband of his jeans, yanking his t-shirt over it. "I want you to walk with the kids towards the carousel and meet me at the car in five, ten minutes."

"John! We just got here. You know the kids want to go on all the rides. Why don't we just go to another part of the fair? I'm sure those men aren't going to the kiddie ride section."

"Too risky."

"I'm getting so fed up with your job. It's taking over our life."

Dad glanced over his left, then right, shoulder. "If these guys see me with a family, my cover's blown."

She glared at him with her stubborn look. "How about the animal barns? That's clear on the other side of the fair. You don't think they're going to see the bunnies, do you?"

Please, oh please, let Mommy win this one so we can go on the rides.

"I can *not* risk blowing my cover. That wouldn't be good." He tucked his chin down, lowering his head so his eyes were more lined up with Mom's. "It'd be dangerous." He said this in his adults-only whisper, but I heard loud and clear. I looked at Ricky and could tell from his wide eyes that he had heard too. With that, she caved in, puffing her cheeks out with a big exhale and shaking her head.

Mom shuffled us into a stream of people walking by, while Dad walked around the other end of the game booth to reenter the midway without us. When I looked back at him, he was giving high-fives and funny handshakes to three men: one had dark, slicked-back hair and a thick gold chain around his neck and two other men had long hair like women's—the kind of men Dad called hippies. They all clustered into a circle, the men smiling as Dad talked to them. That was how my father was with everyone. Even in a room full of people, like after church, he would be the one with a group standing around him howling in laughter.

My legs cramped from trotting to keep up with Mom, and my hand ached where she clutched it. The music from the carousel grew louder. With each ride we passed, my disappointment grew. Dad was nowhere in sight as we neared the exit gate and still nowhere to be seen as we fanned the car doors back and forth to let the heat out. Then, out of nowhere, he was there, scooting in behind the steering wheel and telling us to get in. Ricky and I slid into the back seat, the upholstery blistering hot under my legs and sticking to my thighs. Dad didn't even roll down his window before starting the engine. He kept looking at the exit gate while he drove out of the parking lot.

I was crushed about missing the rides, but I didn't dare cry because Dad was tense and silent, his concern so great it filled our car until I could almost feel it pressing against my chest. Before we were halfway home though, something in him shifted, and he stopped checking the rearview mirror every few seconds and seemed relaxed again.

"I wanted to go on the rides." Once I said that, I couldn't hold back my crying any longer.

Mom reached back and rubbed my knee, the wind whipping her hair around her face. "We'll go again. The fair's here all weekend." She patted my knee again before reaching her hand to the back of Dad's neck, fingering his hair there.

"But why? Why did we have to leave? I didn't go on any rides or have cotton candy or anything."

He glanced at Mom then eyes back to the road. "Bad guys. There were some bad guys at the fair. And I'm not chasin' them today. I'm playing with my *kids*." He tipped the rearview mirror down so he could see Ricky and me. "Who wants to go swimming when we get home?"

"Meeee," Ricky and I yelled in unison.

As soon as we arrived home, Dad went straight to his bedroom. I got my swimsuit on and was walking toward the sliding glass door when I heard Dad dive in the pool. I marveled to see him swim the entire length, underwater, before shooting to the surface. His back to me, he let out a long, deep sigh. He ran a hand over his face, wiping away the water, then stood staring at the sky.

After a moment, he noticed me and motioned me toward him. "Come on. Let's practice your diving today." He backed up to the edge of the pool and patted his shoulder. "Climb on my shoulders and grab my hands." He held his arms up over his head.

Clutching his hands, I teetered with one foot on each of his shoulders while he waded toward the deep end. The water rose above his waist.

"Just remember what I told you. Bend your knees and push into the air with your legs. Push as hard as you can."

"Wait, wait! Not yet." I had been trying to dive for months but could never tuck soon enough, doing belly flops instead.

"You can do it. As soon as you jump, put your hands over your head, pressed together, like you're praying, then bend at your waist and push your legs toward the sky. It helps if you keep your toes pointed." The water was now at his chest. "On the count of three, okay? You ready?"

The image of the drain at the bottom of the deep end shimmered under the rippling water. I set my sights on the drain. "Okay, okay, I'm ready."

"One, two"—I bent my knees, still gripping his hands—"and three," he shouted.

Reaching as high as I could, I propelled myself into the air, bent over and, to my amazement, plunged into the water hands first, toes last. In seconds, I reached the bottom of the pool. Just like Ricky always did when he dove, I touched the drain with my hand. My cheeks hurt from smiling and holding my breath. As I neared the top of the water, my giggles bubbled to the surface ahead of me. I popped out of the water and twirled around to see Dad's expression. He was looking at the sky again, but this time his head was thrown back in laughter, hooting and clapping for me.

Dad always returned his attention to me and our family. It's where he wanted to be once he shook off work: his guns, his concealed holsters, his hippie clothes, the crooks. I could always pull him back to me, like reeling in, inch-by-inch, a giant red snapper. Or, if Dad had a really tough day, more like reeling in a shark. The secret was to be patient and to never, ever let the line go slack.

3

GONE

A couple of years after Dad went undercover, something in him changed, and with it, my whole world. He was always thinking about something else—something not us. Instead of being smack-dab in the middle of everything and all of us, he hung around the edges. When Dad lounged around our pool, Ricky and I begged him to do a cannonball to make a tidal wave of water wash over us, but he only took another sip of iced tea and promised to swim with us later. We skittered near him and teased him to try and catch us, hoping he would toss us, kicking and screaming, into the deep end, but he only gave us a weak smile and swiped at us, not really trying to catch us.

On a long, slow summer day, Ricky and I were splashing around in the pool while Mom stretched out on a lounge chair, tanning, when we heard Dad's car pull up in the driveway. He never came home in the middle of the day. We stopped playing and turned to see Dad walking through the patio door with a man following close behind. The man had dried blood caked on the side of his face with sweat trickling through the crusty blood.

Mom jumped out of the chair, her magazine flopping to the floor. "John! What are you doing?"

He stopped and so did the man behind him, though the

stranger continued to sway slightly. Pointing his thumb toward the laundry room off the patio, Dad said, "I'm just gonna let him clean up a little."

"What? Why? Why'd you bring him here?"

"I didn't think you'd all be out here. We'll just be a few minutes. We'll use the sink in the laundry room."

She glanced at us and inched closer to the pool where we stood motionless in the water.

"And maybe you could take a look, see if it's serious."

She shook her head. "I can't do that. I'm a nurse not a doctor."

"Can't you just, I don't know, feel his jaw, see if it seems like it's broken?"

"I'm *not* a doctor. For God's sake, take him to the ER." Now at the edge of the pool, she stepped directly between us and the stranger.

"Cool it! I'm just letting him get cleaned up. We'll be in the laundry room for a few minutes. It's no big deal."

"John! The kids are here. What the hell are you doing?" She gestured in our direction, palm facing up, fingers spread. Dad's eyes followed her hand but stopped there; they didn't continue out to take in Ricky and me in the water. If he looked at me, I would know if he should take that man away or if Mom should cool it. But he never looked at me, only back to Mom. The space between them was like an overfilled balloon still being pumped with air. Her face was harsh, her usually smiling, bright green eyes now glaring furious and dark. He stared back, his face rigid and stubborn. That balloon couldn't take much more pressure.

The stranger had his eyes trained in Mom's direction too, but he didn't seem to be focusing on her. If I didn't move at all, I thought, or if I slipped silently under the water, maybe the man wouldn't turn his blank stare to me.

Finally, Dad took a few faltering steps backwards, almost bumping into the man. "Ah, fuck it. Let's split, man." He turned abruptly and, mumbling that Mom was making a big deal out of nothing, nudged the bloody stranger back out through the screen door.

For a few seconds, Mom stared at the screen door.

Ricky broke the silence. "Can we play now?"

His words propelled her into action. She rushed to the screen door and locked it, something we never did. A year earlier, when we had the patio screened in to keep out the mosquitos, Dad had laughed about the absurdity of a flimsy screen door with a lock on it. Her hand remained on the latch while the Roadrunner's engine started and remained there while the engine rumble faded down the driveway.

"Mom," he said again. "Can we play now?"

She nodded.

We resumed our game of Marco Polo, and each of us finished a turn as the tagger before she finally picked up her magazine and sank back down in the lounge chair. She never opened the magazine, she only held it in her lap and kept her eyes on us until we were ready to get out of the pool.

*S*hortly after New Year's, my best friend, Diana, and I made our usual Saturday plan to ride our bikes to McDonald's as soon as we finished our chores. I helped Mom take the clothes off the line while babbling about what I was going to order for lunch. Squinting against the sun, I reached up to take a towel from her, bringing the stiff cloth to my face. It smelled like an ice cream parlor: sweet and a little fruity and vanilla-y at the same time. That got me to figuring if I would have enough chore money to get a milkshake too.

After we folded all the whites, I picked up the basket and followed her into her bedroom. She opened one of the dresser drawers and paused, staring down into it, opened a second drawer then yanked open a third. All empty. When she opened the closet door, there was a gaping space on Dad's side of the closet—a tooth knocked out of the smile that had been my parents' closet, source of play-dress-up clothes, full length mirrors and all things mysteriously adult. She stood in front of it for so long my arms began aching from the weight of the laundry basket.

I set the basket down on the edge of their bed. "Can I go to McDonald's now?"

She turned away from the closet, glanced at the phone on the nightstand and again at those yawning drawers. "What?"

"Can I go now? With Diana . . . to McDonald's."

She began calling someone on the phone, her fingers forcefully spinning the dial. "This is Linda Walker. Is John Walker in his office?" She'd called the police station. As soon as she hung up, I was going to ask again, but she only pressed the phone hook down before dialing another number. This time it was to Beth and Carl to see if they knew where Dad was. She listened for a few seconds, then said, "No. All of his things are gone. All of his clothes. Not just a few days' worth." She paused again. "No, it's— No, really. It's okay. Thanks though—I know, but I want the kids here right now."

I slipped out of the bedroom, but Mom stayed in there for a long time, muttering into the phone or blowing her nose. I paced around the living room waiting for her to come out so I could ask again about McDonald's. When there were no sounds from her bedroom for several minutes, I tiptoed down the hall and knocked gently on the door. No response. I nudged the door open, peeking in to see her still sitting on the edge of the bed near the nightstand and phone. Her nose was shiny and pink and her eyes red. I had seen her cry a few times before when something bad happened— like the time Daddy accidentally slammed her fingers in the car door—so I knew something was wrong. But Diana was waiting for me, and my stomach was growling for that Big Mac and milk-shake, so as polite as could be, I said, "Can I please go now? Diana's done with her chores too, and she's waiting for me."

"Not today."

"Why?" My politeness disappeared and my voice came out in the tone that I knew she didn't like, the one she always called whining, but I didn't care. Riding to McDonald's with Diana, only the two of us with no parents or older brothers, was our weekend tradition.

"We need to stay at home right now. In case we have to go, or . . . "

"Why do *I* have to stay?"

"Because I might have to leave while you're away, and then you'd be here alone."

"Where do you have to go?" My stubbornness was settling in. I planted myself in front of her.

She shook her head. "I just want you to stay close to home right now."

I pestered her until she finally gave up and drove us to McDonald's for carry-out. It wasn't as fun as riding our bikes, but at least Diana and I had our Big Mac, Quarter Pounder and fries— that's what we always ordered unless we went on a Friday in the summer, then she had to get the Filet O' Fish because she was Catholic.

On the way back into the house, Ricky plucked a sheet of yellow legal paper out of the mailbox, read it then handed it to Mom. His face looked like he'd just been smacked. Right away, I recognized Dad's tight, swirly handwriting. Her eyes darted back and forth across the page, then she stomped back to her bedroom.

At dinnertime, Mom kept a smile pasted on her face but only nudged the food around on her plate while Ricky and I ate. Her eyelids were puffy, and she looked like it was one of those days when she would tell us to go outside and play so she could have some peace and quiet. I knew how to give her some peace.

When I finished eating, I dragged a chair over to the sink and started filling it with soapy water. Mom came in the kitchen with the dirty dishes as the suds were rising up the side of the sink.

She slid the dishes in the water then hugged me. "You don't

have to do the dishes. I'm alright. I'm just a little sad because Daddy's away for a while."

"When's he coming back?"

She took a sharp inhalation, and I could tell she was holding back a sob, one of those that catch in your throat and make your breath jerky. "I'm not sure." She stroked my hair. "Soon, I hope."

I knew he would be back; he always came back. Even though he hadn't been home much lately, his presence was everywhere: the aroma of his pipe, his huge slippers on my feet when I flopped around in them, his half-empty packs of Rolaids with the foil paper curling away from the open ends. He was probably just away a few days for work. Not that long ago, he had been gone two days before he finally burst into the house with a big grin on his face, picked me up and towed Mom and Ricky outside behind us. There was the bulk of his concealed holster under his arm, the scrape of his whiskers on my face, the cinnamony hint of his Old Spice (underneath that was a hint of something else, on his breath, like Listerine but stronger and bitter, not minty at all). His Roadrunner was parked at the curb, facing the wrong direction, Carl in the passenger seat, grinning and waving at us. As we neared the car, I knew Daddy was going to show us something terrific. My skin tingled with excitement as I imagined puppies and toys. He set me down, popped open the trunk, stepped back and gestured for us to take a look. On my tiptoes, I peered in the trunk and frowned to see several dirt-caked plastic bags that looked like they were full of brown sugar. Talking a mile-a-minute, he said, "Eight pounds of heroin. Eight pounds! I just had to show you before we took it in. We've been workin' this case for months. It's uncut, which means we're on to something big. A big smuggling ring. Maybe the biggest one in Miami." His happiness was bubbling over, and everything about him was so strong and true and good that I forgot all about any puppies. The next morning, Mom and I had snipped an article out of the *Miami Herald*—"Million-Dollar Drug Operation Smashed"—and pasted it in our scrapbook.

That's where I guessed Dad was this time too, on another big case. He'd be home soon to swoop us up in his arms, everything normal again.

But when Diana came over that evening to see if I could go to the bowling alley with her family—another thing we did most weekends, roaming around the alley and ordering Shirley Temples and popcorn from the bar while her parents bowled—it started to sink in that everything wasn't normal. When Mom said she wanted me there at home still, a darkness seemed to descend over us, giving me a twinge of sadness or fear in my chest. All the whining in the world wasn't getting me out of our house that night.

A week passed and then another. Mom hardly ate anything, and slept, or at least lay down, whenever she could. Even when she was moving around the house, she looked sleepy: hair uncombed, grayish color under her eyes. The house was still when I came home from school each day, and I would find her curled up in bed. She sat up, her clothes wrinkled, patting the mattress for me to sit down beside her. In a groggy voice, she asked how school was then pulled herself up to make me a snack.

I started making my own cinnamon-sugar toast when I came home from school.

A few weeks after he left, Dad came back—without his suitcase. Ricky was outside playing, and Mom suggested I go watch after-school cartoons. I clicked on the TV but turned the volume up only enough that they would hear the cartoons, but low enough that I could hear them talk if I sat on the end of the couch closest to the kitchen.

"I don't believe in divorce," she said, and I heard a tissue being plucked from the box.

I knew what divorce was, but I knew of exactly zero kids whose parents were divorced. An uneasiness sprouted somewhere inside me and began to unfurl. From the TV, Scooby-Doo was slurping his slobbery chops and sniffing for food, as usual.

"I'm not asking for a divorce. I just need a break," he said, and something else about getting his head straightened out and the job being too much.

She blew her nose. "The pastor recommended a counselor we could—"

He made a grunting sound. "You think I'm gonna talk to some counselor about my life? About the work I do? I don't talk to anyone 'bout that."

"No kidding! *I* don't even know what's going on with you anymore. I don't even know who you *are* anymore."

"Nobody does. And they never will."

I held my breath and listened to another long silence in the kitchen. From the TV, Scooby-Doo said, "Ruh-roh." I heard the metal lid of Dad's lighter flipping open and closed, open, closed, open, closed.

"Do you have to smoke that cigarette in the house? I can't breathe with all that stinky smoke," she said.

"Want me to leave?"

"No, I want you to stop blowing that damn smoke in my face." The smoke that wafted into the living room *was* gross, nothing like his sweet pipe tobacco. The sink water turned on, and a cupboard door opened and closed, hopefully the one with the trashcan where he, hopefully, threw out that stinky cigarette.

"When are you coming back?"

"I don't know. Few weeks, a month."

I began chewing on my thumbnail. This didn't sound like an undercover case. He had been gone too long, and there was no excitement in his voice. But I was sure he wouldn't leave us; he loved us. But their discussion gave me a sinking feeling in my gut.

After that conversation, I started saving anything and everything associated with Dad: photos, notes, old birthday cards, even the stem from a candied cherry he had plucked out of a fancy drink and given to me. Every couple of weeks, he stopped by to visit but was always in a hurry and never brought his suitcase. During one visit, I offered him some chocolate chip cookies I had helped make. He looked at the plate of cookies, and his face seemed to collapse with sadness. Pulling me onto his lap, he nibbled on a cookie and said they were delicious. I grinned and nodded, but as I sat there in his lap and ate my cookie, I noticed he didn't take a second one. Usually, we ate a half-plate of cookies together.

As he prepared to leave that day, I stood behind Mom and Dad when they hugged goodbye. When she began to cry, he patted her on the back and, as he did, looked down at me and rolled his eyes.

In that gesture, I saw everything. He was gone. Gone for good.

4

ADRIFT

*W*ithin a month of my parents' divorce, Dad introduced Ricky and me to his new wife, Laura. We had met her a few months before, but he had told us then she was a neighbor who came over to his apartment and cooked for him. I had thought that was odd because Mommy never cooked in high-heels and tight white jeans rolled up into wide cuffs. Laura wore red lipstick with matching nail polish and spoke with a syrupy-sweet Southern accent.

After our first weekend spent with Dad and his new wife, we set our overnight bags down in the living room while Mom stood with her arms crossed over her chest. "So, how was your weekend?" It was the matter-of-fact tone she used when she wanted to hide that she was, actually, concerned about something.

"It was fun. Laura makes really good fried shrimp. And look, she painted my fingernails." I wiggled my pearly pink nails in front of her.

Her eyes fluttered closed for a few seconds, then a smile stretched across her face, but her lips stayed in a straight line, so I knew the smile was fake. "That's nice." I wasn't sure if she meant it was nice that Laura made good fried shrimp or had painted my fingernails, but I wasn't going to ask because anger was radiating right out through that smile of hers.

"And she's got big boobies," Ricky said, cupping his hands out in front of his chest.

That took the fake smile right off her face. "I don't want to hear any more of that language coming out of your mouth." Usually when Ricky used words like boobies, she just explained what the proper word was, or at least the words that nurses used, like "breasts." We knew all the right words, because we had Invisible Man and Invisible Woman dolls that showed all the parts, inside and out, and a brochure with the organs and privates labeled. But I was pretty sure the boobie talk wasn't what she didn't want to hear any more of, it was the Laura talk. So, I didn't bother telling her that Laura wore those stewardess uniforms, exactly like the ones in the TV commercials, with a blazer, slim skirt, silky blue scarf and even the pin that read *I'm Laura. Fly Me.* Plus, before I could think of anything else to tell Mom about our weekend, she lugged our overnight bags down the hall to our bedrooms. She took forever to unpack them.

After Dad remarried, Mom's bursts of sadness were replaced by bursts of anger, especially when she had to talk to him about child support or a big expense for the house or how Ricky was misbehaving (which he was doing more and more). I preferred the anger; it made her seem less helpless. Still, I worried about Mom if I was away for long or was more than a stone's throw from our house. That was the distance she had always told us to keep when dinner was almost ready so we could hear her call. A stone's throw away from our house was not very far and did not include Dad's apartment, where we now went every weekend. When I was that far away from Mom, I no longer felt anchored to the world.

One night at Dad's place, I lay in my bed—the only piece of furniture in an otherwise empty bedroom—trying to stop my mind from latching on to what would happen to me if Mom also walked away from us. Through my open door I could see Ricky's bedroom door across the hall, and even though he kept it closed, knowing he was in there linked me to our home, our real home, and what was left of our family. My mind flashed on a memory of Dad checking on Ricky and me when we were so young that we still slept in the same room in bunk beds. Daddy had not come home before our bedtime because he was searching for a missing girl that day. In the middle of the night, I woke to find him standing there in his police uniform staring at Ricky and me. The house was dark and silent, except for the thrum of frogs outside. In my groggy half-sleep, his face looked crumpled and tired. "Did you find the little girl?" I whispered. He knelt under the top bunk and hugged me. "We did. Now go back to sleep. Everything's fine." Then he had tucked the blankets around me, did the same for Ricky, and tiptoed out of the room.

I didn't have that father anymore, a father whose priority was protecting Ricky and me, and children who were lost or in danger. My perception of Dad was so enmeshed with him being a policeman, those two identities had been inseparable. But with Dad—cop and father—no longer part of our daily life, the world became a scary place. And this I sensed without any comprehension of how truly dangerous Miami was at the time: the city had the highest crime rate in the country, largely due to drug trafficking; and an acquaintance of Mom's, who lived right down the street from us, had been murdered. But as an eight-year-old, all I knew was that my family was falling apart, and I wasn't sure who would take care of us now that Dad was gone.

As I stared at Ricky's closed door across the hall, it seemed I was so alone that I could drift into nothingness—no family, no friends, not even Jesus, who my Sunday school teacher said would always be there for me—only black, silent outer space. The fear grew wild in my chest until I almost couldn't catch my breath. I slinked across the hall to Ricky's door and slowly opened it.

He rolled over and looked at me, all annoyed. "What?"

"Can I leave your door open?"

"You're a little old to still be afraid of the dark, aren't you?"

I jiggled my legs, trying to fend off the outer space expanding all around me. "I'm not scared of the dark. I just . . . want to be at home."

He sighed disgustedly and rolled back over. "Whatever."

Leaving his door open, I tiptoed back to my bed and curled up on my side, staring at the dark shape I knew was Ricky in the bed across the hall. Still, that dark loneliness engulfed me, and I covered my head with the pillow to muffle my crying.

"Not again. You're such a baby," Ricky said from across the hall. I heard him walk down the hall and mumble something to Dad.

After a minute, I felt the weight of Dad sitting down on the edge of my bed. He lifted my pillow. "What's up, darlin'?"

As I peeked up at him from under my pillow, a small bubble formed between us, pushing back some of the emptiness that had been surrounding me. "I don't feel so good."

"Homesick again?

I nodded. "It feels like something bad's going to happen. Something really bad."

A crease formed between his eyebrows. "I'm not gonna let anything bad happen to you. Ever."

He rubbed my back for a few minutes. The bubble of safety surrounding us now. As long as Dad was there, I would be okay. But if the line that was now stretched taut between us snapped, then what would become of me? And I wasn't certain he even had ahold of the line anymore.

"Hey, you're not still afraid of the boogeyman, are you?"

I shook my head.

"I better check anyway." He slid off the bed onto his knees and, with great caution, peered under the bed then popped back up. "Phew! Nothin' under there." I couldn't help smiling at his goofy antics. Still on his knees, he propped his forearms on the bed, his fingers interlaced. That reminded me of how Diana always said her bedtime prayers, kneeling, elbows on her mattress, fingers intertwined in front of her face. Thinking of her, and having Dad there next to me, I was no longer drifting into black outer space.

"You want to talk to Laura?"

That meant he didn't know what else to say to me, which never happened when he had lived at home. I did *not* want to talk to Laura. I wanted him to leave her and move back home. "No. Can you just stay here for a while?" I slid my hand between his.

He gave my hand a squeeze. "Sure."

Drained, I relaxed into the weight and warmth of his hands around mine. Before sleep finally overcame me, I forced my eyelids open twice. Through the gauze of my eyelashes, he looked all fuzzy and blotchy, as if he were far, far away.

5

THE GREEN TUNNEL

*W*hile Mom searched for a full-time job, her brother, Floyd, flew down to stay with us for a week. Uncle Floyd was quiet and steady, the opposite of Dad in every way, even in appearance. Where Dad was tall and lean, with a full head of dark hair, Floyd was short, stocky and balding on top of his head, with a half-circle of blond hair around the sides and back. Floyd had a way of listening to me intently for as long as I talked. No other adult in my life listened to me that way except my Sunday school teacher, but even he couldn't pay attention to me for as long as Floyd could, what with all the other students he needed to teach. When I talked, Floyd stopped what he was doing, asked me questions, nodded and focused his eyes on mine until I finished what I was saying. And he played with us—well, with me, because Ricky said he was too big to be tickled or thrown in the pool. But I knew for a fact that Ricky would still do those things if it was Dad playing with us.

After Mom took a job at a hospital and Floyd went back home to Ohio, I dreaded the empty hour each day after I came home from school and before Mom came home. I noticed the silence more than anything. Most days, I went to Diana's house since she and I walked home together, but sometimes her mom couldn't watch me. On those days, Ricky was supposed to stay with me. Those were the worst, because he grumbled that he had better things to do than babysit me, then ignored me and wouldn't even let me pick any cartoons to watch.

When Ricky and I were alone, our arguments escalated, sometimes turning physical. I scratched him so deeply that both of us paused our shouting and watched as three long, dark red, parallel lines of blood emerged on his forearm. He stared at his arm, then back at me, his mouth hanging open, his eyes wide with shock. "You little bitch," he said, punching me in the gut so hard his fist forced the air out of my lungs.

After that, on any day he was supposed to watch me, I walked home from school as slowly as I could, lingering to pet every dog or cat I passed or splashing in puddles or climbing trees. That was why I was so happy one Friday afternoon to come home and find Laura sitting in her car in the driveway. I didn't even think about why she was there on Friday instead of Saturday morning, the usual day we were picked up for weekend visits.

"Hi, sweetheart," she said. "Where's Ricky?"

I shrugged. "Not home yet, I guess."

"Hmm." She shut off the ignition. "Well, let's get your things packed for the weekend. Maybe he'll be home by then."

Laura followed me into the house, pausing just inside the front door while I scooted over a pile of junk on the dining room table to make room for my school bag. As I trotted down the hall to my bedroom to pack, I noticed Laura hadn't followed me. I peeked out my bedroom door and saw she still stood in the same spot barely inside the front door. It dawned on me then that this was the first time she had been inside our home, and if Mom were here, Laura wouldn't be inside the house at all. She was glancing around our living and dining rooms. Thinking of the stacks of mail and school papers sliding toward the edges of the table and the dirty bowls, now coated with crusty cereal, we left there when we rushed out of the house that morning, I blushed with embarrassment. As quickly as I could, I shoved clothes into my overnight bag, including Dad's tattered gray t-shirt, which I'd slept in every night since he'd left, then walked back to Laura at the front door. Ricky still wasn't home.

She looked at her watch. "Why don't we wait in the car? We can turn the AC on in there." I followed her to the car through the green tunnel, which is what I now called our front hedge, because instead of being a squared, well-trimmed castle wall, it had grown bushy and scrubby with branches arching over the sidewalk.

Laura and I sat in her car and watched for Ricky. With both her hands wrapped around the steering wheel, she asked me how school was. Fine, I told her. I fidgeted with the hem of my shirt and wished Dad were there, because I didn't always know what to say to her. I glanced down the road. Still no sign of Ricky.

"What would you like for dinner, fried shrimp or fried chick—"

"Shrimp."

Laura laughed softly.

"Shrimp, please."

I was starting to worry Mom would come home while we were sitting in the driveway. That would not be good. There hadn't been much interaction between her and Laura, and I sensed both of them wanted to keep it that way. The air conditioner hummed as we both watched down the sidewalk for Ricky.

"Well, I suppose your daddy can come back over later and get Ricky."

I looked one more time down the street for him as she backed the car out of the driveway. By the time she picked up speed on Dixie Highway, I forgot all about Ricky because that's when she told me she had a little surprise for me.

Shortly after we arrived at their apartment, the phone rang. Dad wasn't there yet, and Laura was preparing dinner while I played with the Barbie Doll she had just given me. I had been wanting my own ever since Diana got both Barbie and Ken Dolls and their camper. Laura propped the phone against her ear with her shoulder while she dried her hands. "Yes, she is." She glanced at me, then turned her back to me. "Well, John was supposed to—"

I could hear Mom's voice coming through the earpiece. I stopped dressing my doll and listened. This didn't sound good. I realized then that I didn't usually come over to Dad's until Saturday morning. And I hadn't left Mom a note. *Uh-oh. I am in deep doo-doo.*

"Yes, of course, Linda. You can—Yes. Okay. I am so sorry." Laura gently placed the phone back on its hook.

Her face was rosy pink when she turned to face me. She knelt and put her hands on my shoulders. "Sweetheart, your mama's coming to get you. Let's get your things together."

"Am I in trouble?" I asked, placing the Barbie and her clothes back in the carry case exactly the way they came.

Her voice was higher and more sugary than usual. "Nooo. Your mama and daddy just need to talk some more about the weekend plans."

"Am I coming back?"

"I hope so." She looked at me with a smile on her face that led me to believe I would not be coming back.

She helped me zip up my overnight bag and carried it out of the apartment, while I carried my Barbie Doll, who was all snug in her case. We waited behind the glass door of the apartment lobby until we saw Mom's car pull up. Laura took my hand and started walking me toward the car. Ricky sat in the passenger seat, staring straight ahead, not looking at us.

We walked halfway to the car before Mom cranked the window down, her eyes wild. "If you come one—step—closer to this car, I will scratch your fucking eyes out."

Laura stopped walking and released my hand.

I climbed in the back seat without saying a word and glanced back to see Laura standing where she had stopped. The frown on her face was more dramatic because of her red lipstick. Ricky looked over his shoulder at me and grimaced, his teeth clinched together and his mouth stretched wide, a look I knew meant *Yikes!*

Having never heard Mom talk that way before, neither of us dared to say a word the entire drive home.

Later that evening, Mom yelled into the phone at Dad. "You're not supposed to take them on Fridays. Her little purse was on the table. She was nowhere to be found. Ricky had no idea where she was. Laura could've left a note! Called. Something—anything." She paused her tirade for a moment, listening, but still marched back and forth across the floor, back and forth, as far as the phone cord would reach. "How could you forget to tell me? How? Just explain that to me." Another long pause. "No. I don't care. No way. You can't have them this weekend."

That night, as I slipped on Dad's t-shirt carefully—I didn't want to tear open any of the tiny holes stretched across the back like Swiss cheese—I was actually relieved I wouldn't be going back to his apartment. This way, I could do what I always did on the weekends: play with Diana, explore the neighborhood on our bikes, go to church with Mom, have Sunday donuts, swim in our pool or go to the beach. As much as I longed for Dad to be part of our life again, for him to adore me the way he used to, I couldn't capture his attention. When I was at his place for the weekend, Laura, for the most part, took care of me, and she was nice, but I hardly knew her. Or he hauled Ricky and me around while he ran errands for her. Or we sat around and watched TV. Sometimes he took us to a movie, but it wasn't the same. *He* wasn't the same. We rattled around his apartment having short, polite conversations with each other about what I had done that week in school, how Diana was and how the dog and cat were doing. It was like we weren't attached anymore, like the glue that held us together had dried up and flaked away.

After that clash with Laura, Mom arranged for a babysitter to come to our house after school. Ricky insisted the babysitter was there for me because I was a big baby, and he didn't need no sitter. The way our first babysitter sat in front of the television eating entire bags of our potato chips and rolling her eyes any time I asked for help with anything, I wasn't sure she was there for me either.

With Mom working full-time, our lawn grew shaggy and tall, creeping onto the sidewalk and driveway and itching my ankles. I tried to do more chores around the house but couldn't keep up with the stacks of dirty dishes and the rumpled clothes spilling out of the hamper. If our house was super messy, I even had Diana wait on the porch while I hollered to Mom that I was going outside to play. If we wanted to swim, I took her around the side of the house and through the patio door, instead of through the house, pretending I wanted to show her something on the way like a puddle of tadpoles. After rainstorms, Diana and I always checked puddles for tadpoles. Each day, we would peer into the toady-smelling water as the polliwogs sprouted legs and grew fatter and rounder, their tails shrinking away. When the puddles began shrinking, I prayed for those tadpoles to hurry and turn into frogs. Sometimes, we scooped up the wiggly things and relocated them to bigger puddles. Sometimes, we stood at the edge of a mud slick, the edges having dried and cracked overnight and the tadpoles having shriveled up, and I wondered why those stupid frogs left their babies all alone in mud puddles.

That's what I thought was going to happen to me when Dad told us he had quit the police force and was moving to North Carolina to find a better job: I would shrivel up. Despite his promise to fly us up there for visits, I was afraid I would never see him again. I had watched what became of Mom after Dad left; she was never the same. She had lost part of herself and was unable to become whole again. My world had already been ripped in half. I couldn't afford to lose part of myself too.

Ricky and I spent that summer in North Carolina, though we only saw Dad on weekends and occasional evenings when he came over to Grandma and Grandpa's house, which is where we stayed. Dad said we couldn't stay at his apartment, because it was too small, he worked all day and Laura was too tired to watch us because she was going to have a baby soon. Weren't we excited about that, he wondered. I was not the least bit excited about that. The thought of me being replaced by another child made my stomach hurt.

Grandpa had recently retired from being a preacher and now liked to nap or fuss over his African violets, not over his grand-children. I think he'd fussed over people long enough. Grandma preferred to pray and watch frenzied preachers on television pray. She wouldn't let us watch TV shows like *Happy Days*, which she said weren't proper for Christian children. We didn't bother telling her that Mom let us watch that show every week and even watched it with us sometimes.

We were afraid to tell our grandparents anything. Even Ricky wasn't brave enough to talk back to a preacher. It was a summer of secrets.

Grandma bought us our own milk instead of the blueish, watery skim milk they drank, and after a few days of being there, our milk tasted sour. I told her I didn't like milk, but she insisted we drink it because our bones were still growing.

"But it doesn't taste good," Ricky said.

"Well, it's not skim milk, its whole milk. I bought it just for you two." She stood and cleared the table, her frown deepening. "Go on. Drink it up."

Wondering when Dad would come to rescue us, I pinched my nose and gulped the spoiled milk until my tongue pushed against the roof of my mouth, not letting any more bitter milk down my throat. Grandma wiped the table, circling our cups with the rag. We watched her wipe, wipe, wipe, her arms jiggling faster and harder as our milk glasses sat half full on the table in front of us. With hands on her hips, rag dangling, she said, "You know, our missionaries work in villages in India that don't even have clean running water to drink. What do you think those kids would do with a glass of cold milk?" If I could have given those poor kids in India my milk, I would have, but I didn't think they would drink it either.

Grandpa chimed in from his recliner, where he was

surrounded by his dark purple violets staring at him with their silent, sad faces. "You kids can leave the table when you finish your milk. And Lynn, you need to drink it like a lady." I wasn't sure what that meant but assumed it involved me not pinching my nose first, so I held my breath and swallowed as much as I could before my tongue clamped shut my throat again. Ricky asked for instant chocolate powder to add to his milk, and we dumped heaping spoonfuls in our cups.

We had one more long meal after that, gagging down soured chocolate milk, before Ricky finally told Mom that Grandma was making us drink rotten milk. He hollered down the hall, "Grandma. Mom wants to talk to you." As soon as he passed the phone to her, we dashed outside.

Ricky and I spent more time together that summer than we had in a long time and hardly bickered, mostly because we didn't want Grandpa's lecture again about what the heavenly Father thought about brothers and sisters who screamed at and hit each other. Plus, there wasn't anything else to do but hang out together. I was glad for Rick's company, until he began sneaking cigarette butts out of Dad's truck ashtray.

We were way down the railroad tracks, far out of Grandpa's view, when Ricky pulled a stinky butt out of his pocket, lit it, took a puff and coughed, waving the smoke out of his face.

"You're gonna get in big trouble. You better get rid of that nasty thing."

"Who's gonna find out? You better not tell Dad." He shrugged. "Besides, he don't care anyway." He took another puff and coughed, puffed, coughed.

"You shouldn't do it. It's making you cough, and it really stinks. What if Grandma smells it on you?"

"She won't smell it. She couldn't even smell our rotten milk. Just don't tell anyone." He took another puff and released the smoke with a forced, angry laugh. He saw me watching him still and poked the ashy, glowing end toward me, laughing maniacally now.

"Yuck. Get it away." I hurried back to the house, his cackle growing more and more faint behind me.

If I told on him, he would be grounded and not allowed out of the house for sure, and I would be hanging out on the train tracks alone for the rest of our visit. So, each time Dad came over and Ricky went outside to "check on something," I kept my mouth shut. Part of me hoped Dad would catch him so Ricky wouldn't be smoking those nasty butts, but he never did. Or if Dad did know what Ricky was up to, he never said anything.

Partway through the summer, Ricky and I befriended a neighborhood girl who was his age. Sara had the same twangy accent as Laura and paid very little attention to me when Ricky was around. She had wavy auburn hair, peachy skin and large eyes framed by thick, dark lashes. Sara also had curvy hips and breasts that were big enough she wore a bra. I could barely take my eyes off Sara. Ricky clearly had the same struggle, as did any other boy or man who walked or drove by her. Those looks reminded me of the way Dad looked at Laura sometimes. When Sara noticed a boy looking at her, she glanced away, the corners of her lips turning up into the slightest of smiles, as if she were inviting them to go on and have a good, long look.

For the rest of the summer, Ricky cajoled me in to visiting Sara, combing his hair and checking in the mirror before we went looking for her. I didn't mind because I was on a mission to figure out her secret, to figure out how to be more like her so I could capture the attention of boys. More than anything I had ever wanted—a ten-speed bicycle, a pure white Bible with gold lettering on the cover that was awarded for perfect Sunday school attendance, a turntable—I wanted boys to look at me the way they looked at Sara. The same way Dad looked at Laura.

6

NO-SHOW SATURDAYS

I was thrilled the following year when Dad and Laura moved back to Miami, though a little less thrilled about my new half-sister, Julie. They bought a house with two extra bedrooms, one for Ricky and one for me, and Dad insisted we shop for new bedroom furniture, which I was sure cost a pretty penny, so I guessed he had found a good job. This new furniture was supposed to make his house more like home for me. It didn't. His house was too full of his other family to be a home for me. And Ricky could barely tolerate being there; every gesture and every word out of his mouth carried a hint of rudeness. Weekend visits became a rollercoaster: I craved Dad's attention but hated sharing it with Julie; I appreciated Laura's mothering but felt disloyal to Mom; I wanted Ricky there for company but dreaded his brooding.

One morning, I flopped onto the sofa and peered out the window, waiting for Dad to pick us up, the mix of anticipation and angst already rolling around inside me, rising and falling. My chin resting in my hands, I watched down the street for his truck. For hours. Late in the morning, long after Ricky had stormed out of the house, Mom coaxed me away from the window.

"When is he coming?" I asked.

"I don't know. I just don't know. Why don't you go see if Diana can play? I'll call you if . . . when he gets here."

Thrilled, I busted out of the house and ran across the street. I played with Diana all day because Mom never called.

After a few more no-shows, I came to dread our weekend visits and how they pitched me about. If Dad's planned arrival time came and went and he had not shown up, I wandered the house teary-eyed because he had forgotten about me. But as I unpacked my overnight bag, relief washed over me. With each article of clothing I placed back in my drawer, I became more settled. By the time I unpacked everything, I was bouncing down the hall hollering to Mom that I was going to Diana's to see if she could play.

Ricky showed no jumbled feelings on these topsy-turvy weekends, just pure anger. Mom's feelings were clear too. Right before Dad was supposed to pick us up, she straightened things around the house, her movements forceful, tossing shoes in closets and hanging up damp towels. After a few of his no-shows, she even stopped trying to explain his erratic behavior. He gave us all kinds of different reasons, like he worked for a construction company and got called in to cover for another worker, to which Mom let out a scoffing grunt. Later, he told us he was selling real estate and had to show a house. Next, he was grading and selling diamonds—I had no clue what that was or why selling diamonds required unplanned weekend work.

When weekend visits did go as planned, Dad was more exuberant than ever, determined to entertain Julie, Laura, Ricky and me. Our weekends now were manic with amusement parks, movies, Harlem Globetrotter games, shopping at big malls, fancy dinners out or special Southern meals Laura cooked. When Dad said, "Put on something nice, ladies, we're going out," I knew we'd be going to a dark restaurant with too many forks and spoons, or to the noisy Hialeah Race Tracks or Jai Lai games, where he was more interested in betting on the races and games than talking to me. And he had a new zest for shopping that animated him like nothing I had seen before: toy stores, department stores, jewelry stores, furniture stores. Laura said he didn't need to buy her this or that, but she always left with a bagful. When we were out shopping, she draped her arm through one of his, and he held Julie in his other arm, so he never had a free hand for me to hold.

On my eleventh birthday, when Dad suggested just the two of us go shopping for a gift, I couldn't help but get excited. Not about the shopping—I was getting real tired of that—but about us being alone.

As we pulled up to the department store, he said, "I reckon eleven is old enough to pick out your own gifts, don't you?"

"Sure. I have a couple of things on my list that Mom ca—won't be getting me."

He clapped and rubbed his hands together. "Alright. Let's do it."

We walked into the store, and he swept his arms out, hands high in the air. "You can buy anything you want in here. Anything at all. You just name it, and it's yours."

I described the turntable Diana had gotten for Christmas, and he said that would be great. Or some jewelry, he suggested. We checked out the turntables, and I was shocked to see that the cheapest one was around three hundred dollars, so I suggested we look at some clothes. That lasted about ten minutes before he steered me to the jewelry counter.

While I was perusing the racks of small, silver trinkety earrings I usually wore, Dad said to the man behind the counter, "What's the birthstone for this month?"

"Emerald."

"Show us your emeralds then."

The store clerk pointed us to a glass-topped counter. Dad motioned me to follow him and started pointing at different emerald earrings, most of them gold, and with diamonds in them. The only diamond jewelry Mom had was her old engagement ring that she kept in a small box in her top drawer under her bras and underwear. Dad had me trying on all different kinds of earrings, each pair too big or too dangly for my taste, all the while chatting with the clerk and making him crack up. Finally, the clerk handed me a dainty pair: gold post earrings shaped like a flower with a round emerald in the middle and five diamonds for the petals. They were marquise-cut diamonds the clerk told us, whatever that meant. When I put them on, Dad took one look and pointed at them. "Those are the ones, darlin'. They match those beautiful eyes of yours." He looked at the clerk. "Don't they?"

"They sure do." The clerk nodded vigorously, but Dad had that guy so charmed by then that he would have agreed to just about anything Dad asked.

"We'll take 'em," he said to the clerk and asked me if I wanted the matching necklace. With that, the clerk reached into the glass counter then slid a display with the matching necklace toward me. Having already seen the price tag on the earrings, I didn't dare ask for a necklace too.

I slid the necklace back to the clerk. "No necklace. They always get tangled up in my hair and give me a big rat's nest back there." I patted the hair at the back of my neck. "And I'm not sure about the earrings yet. I was still thinking about some clothes." Mom had a limited budget for back-to-school clothes, and I never asked her for more than she could afford, so this was my chance.

"Well, sure. Let's get the earrings, the necklace and the clothes."

The clerk smiled, likely wishing he could follow Dad over to the clothes section.

"I mean instead of the earrings. I was thinking the clothes instead of the earrings. And not the necklace."

"Why don't we just get 'em all? You're eleven today. Let's throw the turntable in too!"

The clerk unclasped the necklace, extending it to me.

It was too much; too much money, too much jewelry, too much —Dad. Overwhelmed, I agreed to let Dad buy me the earrings. The clerk frowned as he placed the necklace back under the glass and took forever to ring up the earrings, no doubt hoping Dad would talk me into the necklace. As soon as Dad paid, in cash, I made a beeline for the door, all the while refusing to stop and look at any more stuff.

Dad couldn't wait to show Laura and Julie my new earrings. I knew Laura would gush over them, but I was pretty sure Julie, who was eighteen months old, wouldn't be too interested in them. Good thing I hadn't gotten a stuffed animal, because Julie would have wanted one of those too, and Dad would've run right out and bought her one.

Julie wanted everything I had. Being the big sister, I was supposed to share. And I did try, though always with a lump in my throat. If she saw me sitting near Dad, she scampered into his lap, pushed me away and said, "*My* daddy." He chuckled and wrapped his arms around both of us. Being the big sister, I was supposed to understand. I didn't. I hated that he chose this girl over me, this girl who resembled me but with huge chocolatey eyes instead of green. I hated that he chose Laura, with her tight jeans and clicky high heels, over Mom, with her cut-offs and flip-flops.

Despite Dad's new family, I continued to fantasize my parents would get back together. It would be simple. One day, Laura and Julie would wake up and Dad would have disappeared; he would be back in our home. *They* would now have a hole in *their* lives the exact shape and size of Dad. On the rare occasion when Mom and Dad interacted—usually he waited in the car and she in the house for pick-ups and drop-offs—I watched for hints that he still loved her, or that she was softening toward him. I scanned their faces and bodies for any sign: her jaw not being so tight that I could see the tension in her muscles there; him making eye contact with her instead of looking only at Ricky or me or the floor; her offering him a glass of homemade limeade; him lingering in the house for a few extra minutes. I scrutinized their every exchange.

Right up until Mom invited a man over for dinner.

She dropped the news, like a bomb, right on the breakfast table. "I'm having a friend over for dinner tonight."

"Betty?" I asked. Diana's mom hadn't been over for dinner since the divorce.

"No. A friend from the hospital. You haven't met him yet. David. He's a doctor there."

Her words hung between the three of us. Ricky and I glanced at each other, and I could see he was not happy about this news. This was not good, I thought. This will destroy any chance of Dad ever coming back home.

Ricky finally blurted out, "I don't want any strange man sleeping over here."

With that, Mom's mouth actually fell open. "That's enough of that, young man! He's just coming for dinner." We all sat there eating in silence, the only sound the crunching of our cereal. Ricky slurped the last of his cereal milk, then pounded his empty bowl down on the table. A green, four-leaf clover marshmallow still clung to the inside of his bowl, though it didn't seem like anything lucky was going to happen that day.

"Do I *have* to be here for dinner?" he said.

"Yes. I want you to meet him, and he wants to meet you. Both of you. After school, I need you two to pick up all your things from the dining and living rooms. I left a note for the babysitter—"

"Aaahh. I'm not a *baby*," he said.

"The *sitter*. I left a note for the *sitter* to help you two tidy up the house."

As we cleaned the living room that afternoon, Ricky mumbled about having to pick up the house for some weirdo guy, all the while shoving papers into the trash without even looking to see what they were. Some of those may have been my A+ tests from school that I was saving to show Dad, but I didn't dare get between Ricky and the trashcan.

"How do you know he's a weirdo?"

"It's just weird. The whole thing is fucked-up. Having some strange guy over here."

I nodded as I stacked books to return to the library. "I don't think Dad's coming back home now."

"Hah! Dad's not comin' back. You can just forget about that. That ain't never happening. Never."

I turned as quickly as I could, hoping he wouldn't notice the tears welling up in my eyes, wouldn't notice what a big baby I was being, again.

Mom started dinner while still wearing her nurse uniform and cap, then went to change. When she returned to check on the spaghetti sauce, she was wearing a skirt and blouse, plus a sweep of pale blue eyeshadow and her favorite Glittersweet Pink lipstick. I liked that color so much better than Laura's dark red lipstick.

When David arrived with flowers and a half-gallon brick of Neapolitan ice cream, Mom's face was practically glowing, and I had a hunch it wasn't from cooking over the hot stove. They beamed at each other, and he helped her carry the serving dishes to the table.

As the four of us sat down to a full homemade meal and Mom chatted and smiled, I couldn't help but grin. I used my best manners, asking if someone could please pass the salad or the garlic bread, which made Ricky roll his eyes. David asked us all questions. Ricky wolfed down his spaghetti and answered bluntly that he was in seventh grade and no, he didn't like school or sports, he liked fishing and animals. You could practically see Mom's attention to David, her eyes were glued to him, and everything else in the room, including Ricky and me, seemed like a distraction for her.

After we finished eating, David leaned back in his chair. "I wasn't sure what flavor ice cream you kids liked, so I brought Neapolitan, the one with vanilla, chocolate and strawberry sections. That way you can pick whichever flavor you like. Hope that's okay?"

"We love all three flavors. Together," I said, nodding and smiling at Ricky.

Ricky shrugged like he didn't care, but I knew he was only being stubborn because I noticed he scooped out the ice cream, so he had some of each flavor in his dish.

I was happy to see Mom cheerful, but I couldn't break through her intense focus on David. Her interest in him reminded me of Sara, the girl in North Carolina, trying to capture a boy's gaze. Mom was consumed with hooking David's attention, to the exclusion of paying much mind to Ricky or me. This singular focus on a man was something I never saw her attempt with Dad. Maybe she should have, I thought. Maybe then Dad wouldn't have left. When Dad had still lived at home, my parents had always left enough room between them for me. But I could find no space for myself between David and my mother. There was only the two of them smiling at each other across the dinner table and brushing against each other here and there—their fingers when he passed a dish to her, their arms when she leaned into him in laughter, his hand on her shoulder when he told her to relax while he cleared the dishes. I tried to join their conversation and talk about things David might be interested in, but he only smiled at me politely until I finished talking. Clearly, I had much to learn about how to entertain a man. Maybe I could learn from watching this strange, new woman—my mother.

David was still there, waiting in the living room, while Mom tucked me into bed that night. I fell asleep to the murmur of their conversation in the other room. Ricky was wrong though. David wasn't there in the morning.

Several months later, Mom dated a different man from church who had three kids. Later, there was a man with no kids from the Positive Christian Singles group. If Mom had planned a dinner out when we were supposed to be at Dad's for the weekend and Dad didn't show up, she scrambled to find a sitter. Or, if she couldn't find one on such short notice, she invited her date to our house instead. That always resulted in a flurry of agitated house-cleaning, Mom angry at Dad, Ricky mad at the world and me all mixed up—bracing myself for Mom to be absorbed by her date all evening and devastated that Dad forgot about me again.

On an increasingly rare Saturday morning when Dad did pick me up—Ricky refused to go that time—he asked if I had a boyfriend yet. I had friends who were boys but knew that was not what he meant. No girls in my grade had boyfriends yet; we were only eleven. Though I did have a poster on my bedroom door of David Cassidy from *The Partridge Family* and often had dreamy conversations with him.

I shook my head.

"Well, if *I* was your age, I'd make you my girlfriend. You gotta be the prettiest girl at school!"

Heat flashed into my cheeks. *Pretty? He thinks I'm pretty? The prettiest girl at school! Maybe he thinks I'm prettier than Julie.* She was only a little girl. Little girls were cute, not pretty. Pretty was Sara, the girl who Ricky followed around in North Carolina. Pretty was what captured men's attention. Pretty was probably what drew Dad to Laura (though that confused me because Mom was also pretty).

That innocent comment from my father was a turning point for me, the point at which I understood, or thought I understood, what men wanted from women. From that moment on, I began seeking my father's approval of my appearance. My pursuit of his admiration would eventually color all of my relationships with men.

Packing for weekend visits, I began taking my pretty church dresses and shoes, though Dad never took us to church anymore. I grew my hair longer, like Laura's, and brushed it often, fretting because it was blond and straight, not dark and wavy like hers. When Laura was painting her nails, I asked her to do mine, but she only used pink or frosty pearl on my nails, never her cherry-red polish. Every time Dad commented on how I looked, or even seemed to notice my appearance, I received a jolt of happiness, a boost of hope, a tiny promise.

7

LEAVING MIAMI

$\mathcal{N}$ear the end of my sixth-grade year, Mom mentioned she was thinking of moving us to a small, safe town in Ohio where Uncle Floyd lived, the schools were good and nurses made more money. Ricky said there was no way he was moving; he'd rather stay in Miami with Dad. Mom didn't respond, but I could tell from how she held her lips tightly closed that *that* would never happen.

By summer, our house had been sold and our belongings packed into a moving truck. Mom had bought a new van to replace our dented, rusty Valiant. The day before we were to leave, Ricky was arrested for shoplifting.

Mom brought him home from the police station, slammed the front door behind her and followed him to his bedroom, screaming all the while. He yelled back that he had told her he wasn't leaving Miami. Their voices echoed through the empty house, as only our mattresses, the kitchen table and three chairs remained for the movers to put in the truck.

We had to stay in Miami until Ricky's hearing because Mom couldn't afford to fly or drive back to Miami later. But our house had sold already, so we moved in with Mom's friend Lucy to wait for the hearing. Lucy had a son and a daughter about the same ages as Ricky and me, but they went to a different school, so we had never met them. We lived out of our suitcases, and each night Lucy and Mom spread blankets and pillows on the living room floor where we slept. Each morning, we piled the bedding into the corner of the living room out of the way. Mom and Ricky hardly spoke to each other, but he wasn't allowed to leave the house. Plus, if she found any more marijuana in his things, Mom swore she would report it to the police. *Pot?* I knew Ricky still smoked cigarettes because Diana and I had found a pack in our brothers' hiding place—an empty coffee can in the fort they had built in the huge tree in the middle of our court. That was our go-to meeting place, "the circle," under the tree's massive branches arching over the road that encircled it. Hanging down from the tree were clusters of tiny, thin vines, hundreds of them stuck together like clumps of undercooked spaghetti. Diana and I always tried to swing from the chunky vines, but they were stiff and unyielding and left our hands sticky and stained. We checked the coffee can once in a while to see what those boys were up to—always no-good stuff like *Playboy* magazines and slingshots and now cigarettes. But smoking pot! I couldn't even fathom where Ricky would get pot. I wondered what Dad thought of this news, since that was exactly what he had fought against at work for years.

As the days went by, I was embarrassed to be stranded at Lucy's, sleeping on makeshift beds on the floor. To make matters worse, one night I was startled awake to find Lucy's son kneeling over me. My blankets had been pulled down to my thighs and he was staring at my body.

I yanked the blankets back up to my neck. "What? What do you want?"

He grinned then, without saying a word, stood and hurried out of the room.

Glancing over at Ricky then Mom, I couldn't see if either of them were awake or even facing me. "Ricky?" I whispered. No answer. "Mom?" Still nothing. I lay there a long time, listening for the boy's footsteps before finally falling back to sleep.

The next day, I waited for the right time to tell Mom, when Lucy and her kids weren't around, but she was either arguing with Ricky or on the phone with the moving company, Uncle Floyd or the public defender. Once, I was sure she was talking to Dad. The one moment when no one else was around and she wasn't on the phone, she looked exasperated—forehead resting in her palms, fingers laced through her hair. I hated to bother her with one more problem, and I wasn't sure where we would go if we left, so I didn't tell her. I set up my bedding next to Mom that night and lay awake as long as I could.

A week passed, and the court still hadn't set a hearing date. Still, we slept on Lucy's floor. All our belongings were due to arrive in Ohio without us. Ricky suggested Mom and I leave without him, asking to stay with Dad. As much as I hated sleeping on Lucy's floor, the idea of leaving Miami without Ricky felt like our life was unraveling.

Then late one morning, Mom hung up the phone, released a big sigh I knew meant good news and said, "Okay. We can go. Get your stuff in your suitcases and get in the van."

"What about my trial or hearing . . . whatever it's called?" Ricky asked.

"I called your father a couple of days ago and told him that he owed us big time and asked him to get us out of Miami. Then, out of the blue, an attorney called this morning. He was a friend of your dad's, I guess. Called and said it was okay for us to leave. He arranged a plea bargain for you and your dad signed all the paperwork."

"What's a plea bargain?"

"Basically, the judge lowered the charge to a misdemeanor and will allow you to serve probation in Ohio."

"That's it? No time in juvey?"

"Nope. Just probation."

"That's cool."

"It's not cool. It's lucky. You're lucky. Very lucky. The attorney pulled some strings or something. But *you* better be cool. You'll have to report to a probation officer every few weeks or so in Ohio. And you'll have to do whatever he says, or you will go to a detention center." She flicked a glance in his direction. "It's jail, basically, for teenagers. Do you realize how serious this is?"

"I know. I know."

"We'll contact your probation officer when we get to Ohio."

Ricky nodded and acted like being on probation was no big deal. It sounded scary to me, and I hoped he would stay out of trouble, so he didn't have to go to a jail. That would take Mom over the edge for sure.

Mom called Lucy at work to tell her we were leaving and thank her and her kids for their hospitality. Yeah, and your son is a pervert, I imagined saying. As we shoved things in our suitcases, I kept scanning Lucy's house thinking I was forgetting something. After being in limbo for a week, the reality came rushing at me from all directions: we were leaving Miami, the only home I'd ever known.

With our suitcases and a few boxes packed into our van, we were on the road by noon. The van was quiet as we drove out of Miami. Ricky sat scowling in the passenger seat, Mom drove in silence, and I sat on a box and stared out the back window, certain I would never see Diana or Dad again. The finality of our departure sank in as we left the familiar streets and buildings of southern Miami behind us. All I could see were parts of Florida I didn't recognize.

Until we found a house in Ohio, we moved in with Uncle Floyd and Aunt Sandy. They were exact opposites. Where he was patient and relaxed, she was nervous and always moving, cooking, wiping counters, straightening couch cushions, reorganizing magazines and coasters on the coffee table, sipping wine, picking up toys. She was striking to look at, with her hair cut to follow her jaw line perfectly, and her eyes were so dark they looked almost black. Those dark eyes were constantly darting about to see what was out of order or needed cleaning. Within an hour of our arrival, after a three-day drive and staying at dive motels, Sandy walked us into the living room, pointed to her white carpet, a smile pasted on her face, and told us to please remember to remove our shoes before coming in there. Compared to the mangy shag—in three shades of green—in our old house, her plush carpet seemed too pristine to walk on, so I avoided it when I could, tiptoed through with bare feet when I couldn't.

My cousin Nicole, who was four years younger than me, gave us a much warmer welcome and took me all around the neighborhood to meet her friends. That evening, Floyd played a hilarious game with us kids where we made up silly words and pretend definitions. He tried to coax Rick—as we had been instructed by Ricky to now call him because Ricky was a little boy's name—to join us, but Rick refused, saying he was too old for games like that.

Floyd worked with troubled kids—kids with *big* troubles like using drugs, getting arrested, going to juvenile detention—and I figured that could come in real handy with Rick. His job would explain why Floyd was so calm when Rick showed up one afternoon with droopy eyelids, slurring his words. Floyd and Mom sat him down at the kitchen table. Mom suggested I go play, so Nicole and I went into the living room, the plush, white carpet springy under my feet.

I heard Rick say, "I don't wanna be here and go to a new school. I wanna go back home."

"That's not going to happen," Floyd said. "Your mom needed to find a better place to raise you and your sister. And the schools here are very good. You'll make friends—"

"You crazy? This's high school. Everybody has friends already."

The other room was quiet for a moment, then Floyd said, "You're right. It's hard. It's a hard time for you. But you're already on probation and using drugs won't help. There are consequences for—"

"Like what?"

"Like losing privileges, freedom—"

"You're not my fuckin' father."

My throat tightened at the mention of our father, and I wondered if Rick would be acting this way around Dad.

"No, I'm not. But while you're staying in my house, you will live by my rules. You're not to use any drugs or alcohol in my house. Is that understood?"

Silence again.

"Rick?" Mom said.

"Whatever."

Sandy wasn't that calm. That evening, we couldn't avoid over-hearing her ranting through their bedroom door. "I don't care. I want him out of my house. Tomorrow."

Floyd mumbled something.

"I still don't care. He took my sleeping pills. What else will he take? I don't want someone like that around Nicole. I want him out. He goes or we go."

Mom insisted, despite Floyd's objections, that we move into a motel. The motel room we rented reeked of mildew, stale smoke and flowery room deodorizer. Rick disappeared that first evening for an hour, saying he was going for a walk but returned glassy-eyed and laughing at everything. When Mom confronted him, he exploded.

"You can't make me stop smokin' pot, just try. Just try and stop me. How are you gonna do that, huh?" He took a few steps toward the door, and Mom grabbed his arm. He tried to twist away, but she held fast.

"If you go out that door, don't bother coming back."

He jerked his arm away from her and, at the same time, swung his other hand toward her, smacking her in the face. I slumped in the corner of the motel room and put my hands over my mouth. The phone was on the other side of the bed, and I considered reaching over for it to call Floyd but decided it would be best if Rick didn't notice me.

Mom's hand trembled as she raised her finger and pointed at him. "If you *ever* lay another hand on me—*ever*—you will go straight to juvenile detention. And as soon as we contact the probation office, this will be reported to him."

Rick slammed the door, and Mom locked it behind him. She rifled through his suitcase and found a baggie with what looked like two loosely rolled cigarettes, tapered at both ends and without filters. So that's what a joint looks like, I thought. She crushed them into the toilet and flushed it.

We stayed in that damp motel for three weeks, until Mom bought a two-bedroom condominium near my uncle's house. My new bedroom was much smaller than the one I had in Florida, but it was on the second story and looked out over a small patio and backyard, with an expansive cornfield beyond that. The other bedroom was across the hall from mine, and that was Mom's, making the upstairs a haven for us. There was a finished den in the basement that Floyd helped Mom convert into Rick's room, hanging curtains across the open stairway to give him privacy. Rick liked the seclusion down there, two floors below Mom's room, and as soon as his turntable was set up, it was blaring his favorite Lynyrd Skynyrd album. Apparently, his room wasn't far enough away from Mom's, because she was soon hollering down the stairwell every day for him to turn down the volume. Having never been in a basement before—they didn't have those in Florida—I found it spooky. Adjacent to Rick's bedroom was an unfinished storage room with bare concrete block walls, no wood paneling like that in Rick's room, and a small cobwebby window near the ceiling that let in a dusty shaft of light. That's where the washer and dryer were. I needed all my courage to slink down the steps, as stealthily as I could to avoid being noticed and taunted by Rick, and enter the dank, shadowy laundry room. As soon as I pushed the start button on the washing machine, I bolted up the stairs, two at a time, hugging the wall furthest from Rick's curtain-wall. I only did my laundry when Mom was home.

After we moved to Ohio, Dad's calls dwindled, as did his child support. Sporadically, he sent Mom an envelope stuffed with cash, a scribbled note for her to give Rick and me a big hug. Over and over, I read his cards and notes, wondering why he didn't want to see me or talk to me anymore. I kept every note he sent me, slipping each carefully into an empty Roman Meal bread bag. I tucked the bag, along with the scrapbook of photos and articles from Dad's police days, under all the stuffed toys he had bought me over the years. I kept the toys clustered on my closet shelf because it was childish to have them on my bed still. Each stuffed animal had a memory of Dad associated with it. My favorite one was an enormous frog with a goofy, grinning red mouth, long legs jointed into a diamond shape and floppy, webbed feet. Dad had won it for me at a carnival shooting game that I had dragged him to, pleading for him to win me that giant toy. All he had to do was knock over all three jugs by shooting the bull's-eye targets attached to the top of each jug. If those toy guns had been pistols, I could've hit the targets myself. But they were toy rifles like Dad shot when he was on sniper duty (Dad said we didn't need to tell that to the poor carnie who ran the game). Three shots, three bull's-eye targets hit right in the middle and the carnie lifted the frog down for me. I had hugged it to my face and chest while Dad laughed, pointing out the frog was about as big as me.

The stuffed frog was now propped on my shelf so that it beamed, happy to see me, every time I opened my closet door.

When Mom and Rick argued, I retreated to my room with my new kitten, Muffin. I locked my door and played with her, enjoying her purrs and carefree pouncing on anything that moved. When their fighting became intense, I pictured Dad whisking me away or, better yet, whisking Rick away.

Nothing ever came from Rick being on probation, not that I could tell anyway. He grew his hair long and tied a rolled-up bandana around his forehead to keep the hair out of his face. The whites of his eyes were often red and his pupils huge.

Mom tried to carve out some time for me—a time when all of her energy hadn't been drained away by Rick or work. We bought a book on macramé and made several hanging plant holders, filling our condo with ferns and spider plants. That made it more like our old home. On paydays, she and I ate at a local restaurant —our favorite was a cramped Chinese restaurant where we ordered at the counter then munched the spicy food off plastic plates. On those rare occasions, we talked and giggled until I felt normal again.

8

ONE HUNDRED EIGHTY DEGREES

I started junior high school without knowing anyone. Immediately, I noticed that kids in Ohio wore different clothes and shoes than kids in Florida: plaid flannel shirts and tight jeans and tan suede shoes with wavy, rubbery soles. Mom purchased some flannel shirts for me, as the weather was much cooler there, but I only had tennis shoes and knew she couldn't afford Earth Shoes. Some of the girls wore make-up already, but Mom still wouldn't let me wear any. "Too young," she said. Whenever I could, I snuck a compact out of her medicine cabinet, took it to school, hunkered on a toilet and, peeking in the round mirror, stroked the flesh-colored powder on my face. I relished its fresh, cakey scent and the way it made my eyes prettier, concealing the shadows under them.

The first few weeks of school, no one talked to me, and I was too shy to start a conversation. I pretended to look for something in my locker, so I wouldn't arrive at my next class with any time to kill. Lunchtimes were the worst. On my way to the lunch line I dawdled, afraid I would be the first to sit alone at a table meant to seat eight. I preferred to scooch into an empty spot at the end of a table where others were already seated. Aware of the chatter and laughter all around me, I picked at my food to avoid any stares from other kids. Sometimes I hid in the bathroom during lunch, heading into a stall when someone came in, as if I had just walked in there too. Eventually, I started eating my sandwich outside, wandering around until the lunch period ended. Out there, without the sea of strange faces and the pressure to make conversation, I was free. Outside, I could relax without worrying what everyone thought about me.

Within a couple of months, I was finally befriended by a group of students like me. We weren't jocks, cheerleaders, popular kids or brainiacs. We were misfits. Until that point, I had always taken pride in getting straight As, but I kept this under wraps with my new friends, anything to avoid being labeled as one of the nerds who looked and acted even more socially awkward than I felt. The nerds were the students who talked about concepts no one was interested in, like engineering or space travel or the Cold War with Russia, and some wore thick eyeglasses or old-people clothing. One poor guy actually carried a calculator in his shirt pocket. Who even wore shirts with pockets anymore? Those kids were made fun of until they looked wretched and trapped, which always made me pity them. Helpless, I walked away from that kind of mocking, unable to stop it but unwilling to watch or participate. When teachers asked difficult questions in class, I cringed to hear the super-smart kids eagerly responding. I would never draw attention to myself like that, even though I often knew the answers.

The summer after seventh grade, I visited Dad in Orlando. He suggested I fly there instead of Miami so we could visit Disney World, which we did for half a day. I kept expecting we would go to Disney World a second day, but he and Laura dressed up in business suits—I had not seen him wear a suit since we used to go to church together—and went away for a few hours. Something was up with them for sure, but when I asked where they were going, they glanced at each other and said they had some business to take care of in town. That must be some serious business, I thought, wearing suits three days in a row. On top of this evasive behavior, they asked if I would watch Julie, who was only four years old. I didn't have much choice in the matter, stuck there in a hotel in Orlando, obviously invited there to babysit my spoiled half-sister.

While Julie was napping, I got bored watching TV and snooped through Dad and Laura's things, looking for some evidence of their whereabouts. My most exciting discovery was an open pack of cigarettes in Dad's shaving bag. I slid one out. Excitement tingled in my belly. I took a cigarette out to the balcony, so Julie wouldn't see me if she woke up, as I was sure the little brat would blab to Dad what I was doing. The smoke drifted into my face and stung my eyes, but I pulled it into my mouth anyway and tried to blow it out sexily. On the second puff, the smoke went into my lungs, and I spluttered it out in a coughing fit. *Well, that wasn't very sultry.* After my coughing subsided, I inhaled a smaller amount, but again my body forcefully expelled it. My throat was raw, my lungs burned and my mouth now tasted the way Dad's ashtray stunk, so I just let the cigarette hang from my mouth the way Rick and his friends did. Looking at my reflection in the sliding glass door, I tried holding the cigarette different ways and eventually tossed it from the balcony.

While I was swishing my mouth out with Dad's mouthwash, I heard them come into the hotel room. When Julie woke up, we all decided to go swimming. On the way down to the pool, Laura asked to walk with me while Julie ran ahead, Dad chasing after her.

"There's something I need to talk to you about, sweetheart," she said.

I was getting pretty sick and tired of her calling me that. "What?"

"Well, I'm not sure how to say this. I saw you on the balcony when your daddy and me pulled in the parking lot. And, well . . . how can I put this? Ladies don't let cigarettes dangle from their mouths. It's not very ladylike."

I kept walking and stared at the ground. When she didn't say anything more, I glanced at her out of the corner of my eye.

She looked over at me. "It's just not flattering. You hold it in your fingers or set it in an ashtray when you need to use your hands for something else. Okay?"

Stunned, I simply nodded. No lecture about how bad smoking was for me, how I could get hooked, how I was too young, only a lesson on how to smoke like a lady? Mom would have had a shit fit.

Later, I braced myself for the talk from Dad, but he never mentioned my smoking. Maybe Laura was the only one who saw me on the balcony, but I wished I had smoked right there in the room so Dad would have known too. That would have given him something to say to me.

Dad and I hardly talked about anything that week. He asked me the usual boring questions about school and Ohio and friends —questions that acquaintances would ask—to which I shrugged and muttered things were fine.

Before I boarded the plane, Dad stuffed a roll of cash into the pocket of my flannel shirt. "Give that to your mom, okay?" He gave me a long hug before holding me at arm's length and staring at me for several seconds.

"What?" Here we were, once again, saying good-bye without having connected, without me getting his attention or his love. I was angry and disappointed and sad.

"I sure love you a bunch. That's all."

"Me too," I mumbled, blinking a few times to stop the tears from building up. I hated the way saying good-bye to him turned me into a little girl again, my emotions all over the place: yearning for his approval, crushed when I couldn't obtain it, baffled as to why he didn't love me anymore. As I turned to walk down the ramp to the plane, he handed me a note.

Once the plane was in the air, I opened his note, and just the sight of his handwriting produced in me the same anguish I had felt after he had abandoned us years before. Remembering how I had clung to every shred of him, to every card he ever sent, the old, familiar feeling of loss and clamoring for his attention washed over me. I stared out the window for a few minutes, facing away from the passenger next to me, then discreetly swiped a few tears away before reading the note.

Dear Lynn, I love you very much. I have enjoyed these past two weeks more than you will ever know. Perhaps we didn't get to spend a whole lot of time together and do some things that I wanted, but I sure enjoyed our time together. You continue to be as sweet and pretty as you are and remember that I love you. Always, Dad

Baffled, I re-read the letter, searching for connections between our visit and his words, trying to recall when he seemed to enjoy my company. Any sadness I had was replaced with confusion followed by indignation. The note was a bunch of bullshit, and I planned to crumple it or tear it into tiny shreds, but after reading it a few more times, I slid it into my pocket next to the cash.

Back at home, I gave Mom the money. She rifled through it and saw that it was all fifty- and hundred-dollar bills, then marched into the kitchen. I heard her spinning the dial on the phone. As I moved toward the stairway, she said, "What were you thinking giving Lynn that much cash to carry. How *dare* you! Someone could have hurt her. Tried to steal—" She was silent in the kitchen, and I paused half-way up the stairway. "Of course, we need it, you haven't paid child support for months. But that was really stupid." A much longer silence followed. "How long will that take?" She clucked her tongue in disgust. "I don't know what's happening to you, but I don't want any more of your dirty money. Just keep it." She smacked the phone into its cradle.

I slinked the rest of the way up the steps and, after locking my bedroom door, stashed Dad's note in the bread bag with the rest of his letters under my stuffed frog. I also slid the pack of his cigarettes that I had stolen under there, next to my Dad-scrapbook. The frog grinned at me mischievously, and I smiled back.

*E*ighth grade was better than seventh because I had a fascinating biology class, an English teacher who encouraged me to engage in class discussions because she said I had a lot to offer the other students and, most importantly, I made two new friends: Angela and Mike. Angela had moved from Chicago and seemed as lost as me attending a new junior high school where everyone else already had friends. Her mom drank booze every night, probably to escape Angela's dad, who was raging mean. Angela wasn't cute, she was beautiful, like someone you would see in a European painting from a couple hundred years ago, with rosy skin, creamy in contrast to her unruly black hair. The moment I brought her into our house, Rick began flirting with her, and she was clearly drawn to him. Instant chemistry. That evening, I asked Rick to leave her alone, telling him that she was my friend. He extended his arms, hands palm up, all innocent-like. "Hey, can I help it if I'm irresistible?" They were going steady within two weeks.

My other new friend, Mike, never seemed romantically interested in me, and I wasn't attracted to him in that way either. This allowed me a spontaneity I rarely experienced with a boy. He had horrible acne, but as I got to know him, he was so warm and funny and thoughtful that I didn't even notice his swollen, pus-filled pimples.

Mike invited me to hang out during a lunch break with him and his friend Christy, who was outspoken to the point of bordering on insensitive and a bit loud for my preference, someone around whom I struggled to get a word in edgewise. One advantage of her crass manner, though, was that she couldn't care less what anyone else did or said or how they acted, including me. Students could leave the building during lunch break if they were back before the next class bell. Most of the students tossed footballs out in the field or shot hoops on the court, but my friends preferred the shelter of the ravine that bordered the far end of the football field. Mike, Christy and I trudged through the bushes and maple trees down to the bottom of the ravine.

We stretched our legs out on the mossy bank next to the trickle of a stream that meandered around slick rocks and logs. Christy pulled a joint out of her purse. "You guys wanna get high?"

The joint crackled as she toked on it until the tip glowed. She passed it to Mike. Rick had been smoking pot for a couple of years by that time, and I preferred him buzzed on pot rather than drunk; pot made him more mellow, whereas alcohol made him aggressive and loud. Smoking pot didn't seem like that big of a deal, so when Mike passed the joint to me, I put it to my mouth and took a small puff. Instantly, my lungs expelled the smoke.

Looking at them sheepishly, I said, "That happens when I smoke cigarettes too."

"You'll get used to it," Christy said.

When the joint came around again, I took a longer draw and held the smoke for several seconds before I sputtered it out. The third time, the small amount of the joint remaining was warm and moist. I inhaled as much as I could, and as I held it in my lungs, a wave of peace traveled from my head out to my limbs, my body melting into it. As I blew the smoke out in a graceful plume (finally!), I looked up at the sunlight filtering through the golden-colored maple leaves. For the first time in years, I believed that everything—me, my life, my family—would be all right. Above us, impossibly white clouds floated across a bright blue sky. In Miami, the sky was usually hazy with humidity, or the clouds were heavy and gray with rain. "Those clouds look like giant cotton balls," I said, flopping onto my back.

Mike looked up, back at me and chuckled.

Christy lay back and looked at the sky. "Wow, they do."

Mike sat on a boulder nearby and looked at the two of us sprawled on the ground. He nudged our feet with the tip of his shoe and said, "You guys are stoned."

I lifted my head to look at him. "You're the one sitting there like a statue on a rock." This made us all bust out laughing. At that moment, laughing with my friends, my worries sailed away, up with those clouds. The autumn air seemed charged with something that felt like hope.

After that first joint, I understood why Rick was always smoking pot and drinking. Seeking that same joyous reverie that I experienced from my first joint, I tried other drugs and alcohol. I liked everything. Getting tipsy from a few beers, a shared joint or a pill always lightened my mood. And the more often I got high, the more I craved that state of mind. When I wasn't at least tipsy, I was right back to being overly conscious of myself and all my flaws. And the feeling I'd had since Dad had ditched us, that vague sense that something bad was about to happen, had blossomed into a sense of impending doom when I was straight. Nothing could suppress that panicky, physical sensation that I was all alone in the world as well as drugs and alcohol could. Getting drunk was a hundred times more effective than playing word games with Floyd or going out for Chinese food with Mom or concocting some scenario in which Dad came back into my life. Any mood-altering substance made my world expansive and satisfying, like something good was about to happen, like I was just about to be happy any second.

Whenever we could, my friends and I either snuck alcohol from a parent's cupboard (not mine, as Mom didn't drink) or asked someone to buy beer for us. Eighteen was the legal age for buying three-two beer—the stuff with only 3.2% alcohol. You had to drink an awful lot of three-two beer to get a buzz, which made you pee a lot, but it was better than nothing. There were also a few drive-thru places that would sell the stronger beer and the premixed cocktails in a bottle, like screwdrivers, to minors who looked old enough. The good stuff, hard liquor, was only sold in state-regulated liquor stores to those twenty-one and older (or who appeared to be so or had a fake ID), making it more difficult to get your hands on than drugs.

Rick had a friend named Mark who, though he was only sixteen, could often pass for eighteen and buy beer. Sometimes he even managed to score a bottle of whiskey or mad dog 20/20 wine, which garnered him some prestige and standing. But Mark's greatest notoriety was for beating the shit out of guys. He was fierce and tall with sinewy arms, scarred knuckles and a fascination with guns. Everyone was afraid of him. But Mark had a soft spot for me, buying me alcohol and selling me drugs at a lower price than he charged everyone else.

Brian, another friend of Rick's, was also sweet to me, and I soon had a crush on him. Brian was soft-spoken and mellow, especially compared to Rick and most of the guys who ran with them. He wasn't shy, he just wasn't very talkative and seemed content to be in a room with several other people and not say much.

One evening, I went downstairs to do a load of laundry, which by then I was doing when Mom *wasn't* home, in hopes Rick would be partying down there and invite me to join. Rick's curtain-wall was pulled open, and he and Brian were sitting on the floor cross-legged with Rick's prized possession, an Apogee bong, between them. The bong had two wide plastic tubes in the shape of a letter V on its side, and in the opening of the V was a wooden handle, like one on a handsaw. Rick always warned people before they used the bong what "apogee" meant—the highest point—and bragged they were going to be higher than they'd ever been. Brian motioned me into the room, but I paused on the stairs and waited for Rick's response.

Rick rolled his eyes.

"Come on, man," Brian said, "be nice to your little sister. She's cool."

"Oh, whatever," he said.

I knelt on the floor at the edge of their huddle: their knees jutting towards each other, a bag of weed, the bong, an ashtray, a pack of cigarettes and a lighter. Rick stuffed a pinch of marijuana into the metal bowl of the bong, pushing it down with his thumb. The process reminded me of packing Dad's pipe when I was young, only the pot had an oily, skunkish odor.

Brian tucked his hair behind his ears and picked up the bong. "Make sure you cover this hole with your thumb," he said, angling the bong toward me so I could see a hole where a tube ended at the back edge of the wooden handle. He blew all the air out of his lungs then pressed his mouth against the open end of the top tube. The tube at the bottom of the bong was partially full of brownish water. Rick held the lighter flame above the bowl, and as Brian inhaled, the flame was sucked toward the bowl. The weed glowed red, the water in the bottom of the bong gurgled and smoke swirled into the top of the bong. When Brian moved his thumb off the hole, the smoke whooshed out of the bong and into his lungs. Rick took the bong from him, sucked out a wisp of remnant smoke and grinned as Brian held the smoke in his lungs.

After fifteen or twenty seconds, he exhaled forcefully and said, "Holy shit! That was a good one."

Several minutes later, they reversed roles and Rick smoked a bowl. Then he said, "You ready for your turn, li'l sis?"

I wished he would stop calling me little, especially in front of his friends. "What if I can't suck all the smoke in?"

They both grinned. "Don't worry. If there's any left in there, we'll take it," Brian said.

Their eyes were bloodshot and droopy, lazy grins spread across their faces. I wanted that feeling too, that feeling of not having a care in the world. "Okay. I'm ready."

"Just give her half a bowl so she doesn't get too much to start with," Brian suggested. To me, he said, "It can be intense, and if you suck in too much, you'll just start coughing and won't get a buzz. So just inhale as much as you think you can hold without coughing." His protective attention made something inside me melt, and I gave him what I hoped was a sexy look.

As Rick was packing my half-bowl, he started in with the bragging. "You know what apogee means—"

"Yeah, yeah. I know. The highest point. Come on. I'm ready for my hit."

Using the bong was easier than I expected. After a couple of half-bowls, I was able to inhale nearly all the smoke from a full bowl.

Brian raised his eyebrows at that. "Damn, you're a party animal."

I blushed with pride.

This buzz was way more intense than smoking a joint, or this pot had way more THC in it than most. After my fourth hit, I sailed right out of my body, like part of me was drifting around the room. Being disembodied was weird, but I was enjoying the sensation, until Rick cranked up the stereo. The blaring music snapped me back into my body, back into my head, noticing the minutiae of everything I said and did. Everything was exaggerated: my thoughts, my movements, my words. My eyes felt like they were bulging out of my head. Rick's laugh was menacing. Brian's smile was now molesting. A buzzing filled my ears, and I couldn't tell if it was coming from inside my brain or from the stereo or from somewhere in the house. My skin grew clammy.

"You okay?" Brian asked.

Afraid my words would come out so meekly as to be inaudible, I only nodded.

"Ah shit, Lynnie, you're not gonna lose it, are you? You better not cuz Mom'll be home in a few hours." He strummed his hands in front of him, playing an imaginary guitar to the music. Brian continued to watch me.

Random thoughts popped in my mind to make sense of why he was watching me. *Do I look funny? Maybe he likes me. Can he tell how stoned I am?* I had to get out of that room.

Without a word, I stood, and, so as not to take a misstep, walked deliberately out of the room. I focused on each step, lifting my left foot then my right, faster now, left, right, left, right.

"You better not get us busted," Rick called up the stairwell after me.

In my bed, I crawled under the covers and tried not to think about anything. I focused on my breathing. At first this was comforting, grounding. Just breathe, I told myself. You're okay.

Everything's okay. I paid attention to every part of my breathing: the sound of my respiration, the rise and fall of my chest, the moisture of my breath against the sheets. The more I focused on my breathing, the more fixated I became. There wasn't enough oxygen under the sheets, so I frantically threw them off my face. I feared breathing was too complicated a function for my body to continue. *I should go tell Rick, or better yet Brian, that I might be forgetting how to breathe. Walk down to his room and ask if I could stop breathing from all the bong hits.* But I couldn't leave the cocoon of my bed. Later, I heard Brian and Rick thumping up the basement steps. The front door opened and closed. Silence. Unmoving, I lay in my bed listening for any other noise, both relieved they were gone and devastated that I was now alone in the house. As my awareness zoomed in and out, from my very own breath to sounds outside the house that I imagined were the spinning of the planet, I lost track of time. Either a few minutes or an hour later, I heard the door open again then the sounds of Mom home from work: her keys clattering on the table, water flowing from the kitchen faucet, the vitamin cabinet opening. The sounds of her moving about in the kitchen comforted me, or the bong hits were fading, so that, mercifully, I fell asleep.

After that episode, I became much wiser about my drug use. No more marijuana from bongs, even if sweet Brian invited me. The highest point was too high for me.

Brian was the first of Rick's friends to show interest in me. His attention jolted me at first, because I didn't think I was attractive. I was thin but getting curves, finally. I prided myself on my long, golden-blonde hair and had been told all my life that I had beautiful eyes. Later, someone would call them bedroom eyes. But I didn't think I had the allure of some girls, the ones who drew men's attention, the ones like North Carolina Sara who had some kind of power over men. Angela taught me how to pluck my eyebrows into thin arches and how to apply make-up. At the roller-skating rink or at the mall, I practiced flirting. Alcohol and drugs allowed me to flaunt myself with less and less self-consciousness. The more titillating my behavior with men, the more familiar I became with their roaming gaze. It caused a fluttering in my groin and made me feel so alive, so wanted. I also became aware that the more men noticed me, the more vicious glares I received from other girls.

The next time I used with Rick and Brian, we drank rum and Cokes while Mom was at work. Late that evening, Rick went to get some more cigarettes, and Brian said he was staying put because he was too drunk to walk to the store. We sat on the sofa, and I was struggling to find something to say when Brian leaned over and gave me a quick kiss. He pulled away from my lips before I had a chance to kiss him back, as if he wasn't sure I wanted to be kissed. I did. But as I was figuring how to encourage him to try again, Rick barged through the front door.

He took one look at Brian and me sitting close together and groaned. "Aw, that's sick. That's my little sister."

Brian jumped up. "So what, man. I like her. Really. It's cool."

"No, it's not. Keep your hands off her. C'mon, let's get out of here. My mom's gonna be home in an hour anyway."

Brian looked back at me, shrugged and said, "I better go. Sorry." At least they left the bottle there on the table with an inch or so of rum remaining in it. I continued to drink, daydreaming about Brian, about us kissing again, about going steady and fooling around with him. Joy bubbled up inside me every time I thought about him. We had run out of Coke, so I sipped the rum from the bottle, marveling that it no longer burned my throat. I drained the last of it while slouched on the stairway that led up to my room and Mom's, to our little haven.

I regained consciousness being shaken and hearing Mom's voice. "Lynn! Wake up, wake up! Lynn! Are you okay?"

Why is she so frantic? I blinked several times, trying to focus on her face. There were two of her, two faces blending into one, then blurring into two again. She slumped down to the floor next to me, releasing a rush of air. The hallway light streamed into the darkened room, and I scanned my surroundings. I was sprawled on my back in the middle of Mom's bedroom floor. The inside of my mouth was pasty, and my shirt was caked with puke.

Mom put her hands on her knees and stared at me. "You're drunk."

"Am not."

"Get the hell out of my room. Now."

I stumbled into my bedroom and collapsed on my bed.

The next morning, my brain throbbed against my skull whenever I moved. Gingerly, I walked downstairs. The vinyl flooring was cool under my feet as I stood at the sink and sipped a glass of water. I was so dehydrated, I wanted to chug it, but my stomach churned with each swallow. When I heard Mom's footsteps, I steeled myself for the tirade.

What I wasn't prepared for was seeing the anguish on Mom's face. She was close to forty but still looked like she was in her late twenties. Rick would get so pissed when his friends would tell him our mom was hot. But that morning, she looked like she had aged ten years overnight. Her face was drawn and defeated. "I can*not* believe you started drinking alcohol too. Haven't you seen enough of the problems this has caused your brother? And now you're starting? I was afraid you were having a seizure when I saw you laying there, gurgling—"

"I'm sorry. I didn't drink that much. I guess, because I'm so small, it was too much."

"You could have asphyxiated. Do you know that? You were on your back gurgling in your own vomit. Who knows what would've happened if I hadn't come home? You might not be standing here. You might be dead."

I knew all about asphyxiation. She had explained to us years ago that if a person was on their back and throwing up, you had to roll their head to the side so they wouldn't choke on vomit. Between her and Dad, we grew up knowing how to save a life and how to take one. But that didn't seem the right thing to say at the time, that of course I knew all about choking, so I just stared at the repeating patterns in the floor tiles: golden-colored, scrolled floral patterns. Our floor in Miami was real terrazzo, little rocks and flecks of stone set in concrete and polished flat and smooth. So much prettier than this fake linoleum.

"What exactly is going on?" she asked.

"Nothing. I was just . . . experimenting." I looked up and lifted my hands in the air, palms up. "I didn't even drink that much. It won't happen again."

She studied my face. I could tell she wanted to believe me. Knowing firsthand what she had been through with Rick for the past few years, I understood she was desperate to believe me. I didn't want to put her through the same grief as had my brother. She didn't deserve that. I promised myself right then and there that I wouldn't do that to her. But I also knew I wasn't going to stop using. No way was I letting the bleakness of being straight take over my life again. I was finally happy, and I was staying that way.

"Well, you're grounded. Indefinitely. No going out except for school. No TV. No calling anyone. Nothing."

I nodded, knowing full well that keeping me in the house wouldn't stop me from getting high.

9

THE BOTTOMS

I met Jimmy at the Ohio State Fair the summer before high school. He was cute in a puppy-dog kind of way, with eyes that revealed whatever he was feeling—eager, surprised, curious, confused—and a crooked smile that cocked up higher on one side. He was also seventeen so could easily buy alcohol, and he liked to party. Despite all kinds of hardships, like having been raised in the worst part of Columbus by his grandparents, his parents' whereabouts unknown, Jimmy was happy-go-lucky. There were so many things he should have been worried about: being a high school dropout, having no decent job prospects, having brownish stains between his teeth that, at first, I assumed were pieces of food but quickly figured out were cavities. But worrying was not in Jimmy's makeup. He was unflappably happy, which was infectious.

We talked on the phone for a few weeks before I got up the nerve to sneak him over when Mom was at work. He was so excited to see me after weeks of just talking on the phone that he bounced around like a Labrador retriever bringing me a stick. He told me I was his sunshine, and I believed him. I called him Hillbilly because of his West Virginia accent. During that first visit to my house, he tried to lure me up to my bedroom, but I explained that my brother might be home any minute. We spent another couple of weeks sneaking around, which basically involved him bringing a twelve-pack of beer to my house and me trying to keep his hands out of my pants while we drank it. When Mom finally found out about Jimmy from Rick, to my surprise, she suggested he come over for dinner.

When Jimmy arrived that Saturday, I was grateful he had washed his hair, so it didn't have the stench of deep-fried, fair food—stale oil and fried dough and burnt sugar. He boasted to Mom about working at all the county and state fairs around the region, and how he was making a killing. As he described this plan to follow the carnivals around the Midwest and East Coast, he became increasingly loud and talkative. If Jimmy had a tail, it would have been wagging around our dining room table, knocking shit over.

Mom smiled and listened politely. When he paused long enough to take a bite of food, she said, "What will you do in the winter?" The eagerness drained from his face as he looked at her blankly. A confused Labrador. Mom had taken his stick. "For work?" she clarified.

He was stumped by her question, but after several seconds, his face lit up. "Well, this is my first summer working carnivals. Pretty sure I'll make enough to get me through the winter, then I'll look for more out-of-state fairs next year." He beamed at her then at me.

Mom nodded, but I knew what her polite smile meant. She'd been a single, working mom for several years; she took work and good jobs seriously. I cringed inside, because even though I had never had a job, I was certain a person couldn't live on a carnival worker's pay.

While Jimmy and I were watching TV after dinner, Rick came home and, to my disappointment, sat down and chatted with us. He was checking Jimmy out.

When Jimmy left, and Mom went to shower, Rick said, "What the hell are you doing with a carnie?"

I shrugged. "He's nice."

"I don't like him. I'm tellin' Mom you need to stay away from him. He's a creep, and he's way too old for you."

"Oh, you should talk! It's the same age difference between you and Angela!"

"That's different."

"And you guys are having sex already," I hissed. "And she's the same age as me. So, what's the difference?"

"The difference is this guy's an asshole. He better stay away from you, or I'm gonna kick his ass."

After Jimmy's debut with my family, I continued to talk to him on the phone, meet him at the mall or have him over when Mom wasn't home. By that point, he was saying he loved me and was more persistent about getting his hands up my shirt or down my pants. I drew the line at taking off my pants, as I knew once that happened, I would no longer be in control. And while I relished being irresistible to him, I didn't desire him in the same way, or with the same intensity, that he seemed to want me. Like all girls my age, I wanted to have a boyfriend, especially one who could drive and score beer. But I wasn't in love with him.

A few weeks after school started, Angela showed up at our house all upset, mascara smeared under her eyes, looking for Rick. She told me her family was moving back to Chicago. This news felt like a punch in the gut.

She began crying again. "I can't leave. I love you guys." She kept trying to wipe the mascara from under her eyes, smearing it even worse.

I went to the bathroom and came back with some damp toilet paper for her to clean her face. "Thanks. I bet my face is a mess." She ran the tissue under her eyes a few times. "What should I do?"

We went to the back porch to have a smoke and talk about her options. "I think I'm gonna run away. It's my only choice. Just for a couple of weeks." She took a draw from her cigarette, and when she exhaled, a slight breeze blew the smoke back in her face. She waved it away. "After Mom and Dad move away without me, maybe they'll let me just stay. I could stay with you guys. Think your mom will let me?"

There was no way in hell that was going to happen. "I doubt it." Taking a drag from my cigarette, I contemplated how running away would give me freedom to do what I wanted, to drink as much as or whenever I wanted. No more sneaking around Mom, trying not to get caught. That sounded fun, and so did partying and hanging out with Angela, something we hardly did anymore without Rick. "Why don't we run away together?"

"Really? You'd do that for me? That would be *so* fun. Where would we go?"

Mom didn't know where Jimmy lived, and I was pretty sure she didn't know his last name. His place could be a good hideout for us. "I could see if Jimmy could take us in. I've never been to his house. Well, his grandparents' house. It's somewhere downtown. I'm guessing it's not in the nicest part of town. Know what I mean?"

"Shit, I don't care. Anywhere is better than moving to Chicago with my dad. And after a couple of weeks, I hope they'll let me stay here." She gave me a big hug then stood back, a smile and relief now on her face. "I can't believe you're doing this for me. Are you sure?"

"Well, Mom will hardly let me see Jimmy anyway, so it's for me too. I'll talk to him and see if he'll go for it. If he does, then we'll have to come up with some kind of a plan. I don't want to get him in any trouble."

Jimmy loved the idea. For the next week we planned our strategy. He would borrow his cousin's car to pick us up on the night we snuck out. We were to meet on the corner of the street two blocks from Angela's house at ten p.m. the coming Wednesday night. As that night approached, I vacillated between being excited about my pending freedom, mainly to get wasted, and having a nagging anxiety about getting caught.

That Wednesday evening, I stuffed into a bag my make-up,

two pair of panties, shorts, tube tops and, as an afterthought, the diamond and emerald earrings Dad had given me. I lay in bed, fully dressed under the covers, and listened while Mom brushed her teeth then clicked the light off on her nightstand.

Thirty minutes later, I crept down the steps, careful to avoid the one that creaked, glided the patio door open and closed and sprinted through the back lawns to the street.

As I neared the rendezvous location, I slowed to a trot. The sight of a car parked at the corner halted me. The realization hit me like a slap in the face that I had, on some level, hoped Jimmy wouldn't be there; that I could go back home and crawl into my bed. I had already rehearsed telling Angela I was sorry the plan didn't work out. But there he was. Jimmy hopped out of the passenger door and said, "Hey, Sunshine."

"Shhh," I hissed, surveying the nearby houses for any on-lookers.

"Oops," he said, covering his mouth. He pointed at the open car door.

I slinked into the back seat, and Jimmy climbed in next to me. A ruggedly handsome man sitting in the driver's seat looked over his shoulder and raised a few fingers in acknowledgement of me. His long, wavy hair was shiny clean, and I wished Jimmy took care of his hair that well. With that long hair and a strong straight nose, he reminded me of the drawing of Jesus, minus the beard, that was in my childhood bible.

I smiled at him. "You must be Jimmy's cousin."

"Yep. Eddie. Thought there were gonna be two of ya?" He smiled back—a mouth full of healthy, white teeth. *This is his cousin? I sure got the short end of the stick.*

"I'm Lynn. Yeah, my friend Angela should be here soon." I craned my neck around to peer in the direction of her house. No sign of her. We all sipped beers in silence for a few minutes before I saw the shadow of someone running toward us. If she hadn't shown up, I was planning to apologize for the inconvenience and slip out of the car. But there she was.

She slid into the front passenger seat, out of breath. "Did you see anyone following me?"

"Nah," Eddie said, "you're okay." He smiled at her, and a bolt of jealousy shot through me. I wished I could be in the front seat with him instead of in the back with Jimmy; wished he were smiling at me like that instead of at Angela. Besides, she already had a boyfriend—my brother. "Ready?" Eddie asked. "We gotta get before some cop comes by."

One last time, I considered jumping out of the car, envisioned my empty bed on which Muffin was probably waiting for me, but he made a U-turn and drove away. I looked at our condo, dark with all the lights off, as he sped by it.

"Want a beer?" Eddie asked Angela, glancing at her.

Angela looked over her shoulder at me then smiled back at him. "Sure."

Jimmy tossed a couple of beers up front, grabbed me around the waist and pulled me on top of him. He was groping and poking at me everywhere: his tongue too far in my mouth, his hands all over my ass, the growing hardness in his pants stabbing against my thigh.

"Man," Eddie said, "do that shit when you two get home."

Jimmy laughed and I scooted off him and back onto the seat. He pulled my hand over and rubbed it against his erection. His eyelids fluttered and then closed. Intrigued by the arousal I was able to produce in him, I rubbed him a few more times and watched his face glaze over with a sort of frenzy. There was something impersonal about his desire though, and I wondered if he wouldn't react the same way if *any* girl was rubbing his crotch. I pulled my hand away to pluck another beer from one of the two six-packs. Jimmy opened his eyes and had a pleading look all over his face. It wasn't for the beer in my hand, but I passed it to him anyway.

Jimmy and Eddie lived with their grandparents in the part of downtown Columbus called "The Bottoms." The area was called that because a river ran through there, but it was the bottom in other ways too. It didn't get any worse or dangerous in Columbus than that area. They didn't want to sneak us into the house until after their grandma finished watching *The Johnny Carson Show*, so we settled into a broken-down Impala that was in their backyard right off the alley. The windshield of the car was cracked, and the interior was coated with a layer of dust. Where the dashboard was split, the vinyl curled up, revealing yellowed crumbly foam underneath. We all talked and drank for a while, Eddie leaving at one point and returning with two more six-packs of Drewrys beer, for which Angela and I paid. Drewrys was the cheapest beer around, and I hated its watery flavor, but we only had twenty dollars between us and wanted to stretch it out.

When Angela said she had to pee, Eddie offered to sneak her into the house and see if their grandma was asleep now.

As soon as Angela closed the car door behind her, Jimmy was all over me, his tongue in my mouth, his hands all over my body. He pulled me down next to him in the back seat. Through my drunkenness, through his groping and heavy breathing, came snippets of awareness that this wasn't who I wanted to lose my virginity to, or how, in the back of a musty, wrecked vehicle. My next thought was, what the hell? Everyone else is having sex already. He yanked my zipper down and tugged my shorts and underwear off. I could hear him struggling to push his pants down, banging his head on the roof in the process. *What a clutz! Could he be any less romantic?* It was all happening so fast, and my thinking was so fuzzy, that I couldn't figure out if I wanted to extract myself from the situation, from the car, from Jimmy. He pulled me underneath him, my bare skin tugging against the cracked vinyl seat. In a second, he was between my legs, poking his cock against me. My body resisted, and I braced myself for the pain. He grunted and pushed harder until something in me gave way, and he slid inside of me. I felt only a slight stinging and wasn't sure if it was because the first time doesn't always hurt, as I had heard, or if the booze had numbed me the same way it could make a sore throat disappear. The car was full of his moaning and the seat springs squeaking underneath me. Within a few minutes, he climaxed and collapsed on top of me. His armpit was right next to my face. His deodorant had stopped working hours before.

Glad that it hadn't hurt, I was astonished I had finally had sex, done this thing everyone was always talking about. But I was perplexed too. For years, I had wondered what held couples together and had heard and read that it was love, but love was weak and fleeting and seemed to me a mere word. The glue that held a couple together had to be something more visceral—I figured it was sex, desire, lust, this force that pulled a man's attention away from all else. But now that I'd had it, I was even more baffled. It had to be something more than what I had just experienced.

Jimmy ran his hand over my hair. "Love you, Sunshine."

I waited for his words to make me feel something, anything: warmth toward him, a bond between us, a spark of happiness. Nothing. I was glad it was too dark to see his face or for him to see mine. Nudging him over, I flopped out from under him and groped around the floor. I found my shorts and pulled them on as a wetness spread between my thighs.

"D'ya love me too?"

I lit a cigarette, and, in its glow, I saw he was looking at me expectantly. He clearly needed Sunshine, but I wasn't so sure I needed a Hillbilly. I took a lingering pull from my cigarette, blew out a long trail of smoke and mumbled, "Yeah."

"Lemme have one of those." I handed the pack to him. He lit one and said, "Let's go to New York. Before your mama comes lookin' for you. I got a friend there. You can get a job modeling."

"What're you talking about? It's not that easy." I had researched modeling careers at the suggestion of a couple of friends, though I doubted I had the looks for it. The brochures I received described the industry as very competitive and requiring training. I had been skeptical that something as simple as being photographed required training, and I hadn't had money for any training anyway. And I knew Mom didn't have any extra money, so I dropped the idea.

"It'll be easy for you, cuz you're so damn gorgeous."

I envisioned being discovered by a modeling agency in New York—maybe with the right make-up, heels, a professional hair-do—I could get my photo in a magazine or a billboard.

"And I'll find a carnival to work at."

That dropped me back into reality, the image of my boyfriend deep-frying corn dogs at a fair. I wasn't on a model runway in New York, not even close; I was in the back of a broken-down car in The Bottoms. "How're we gonna get to New York in the middle of the night?"

"Hitch. Do it all the time. C'mon." Laughing, he tumbled out of the car, peed in some bushes then hoisted his pants up by the zipper. When he reached his hand in the backseat for me, I tried to think of where else I could go because hitchhiking to New York at that hour didn't seem like such a great idea. I thought about calling Mom or Rick or even Rick's friend, Mark, who by then was my regular drug dealer. For some strange reason, I even thought about calling Dad, but before I could ask to use his grandparent's phone, if they even had one, Jimmy tugged me out of the car.

I grabbed the last few beers to take with us.

In a daze, I followed him out to Broad Street to hitch a ride to New York. I could tell it was after two a.m., because all the bars were closed. I suspected no one would stop for two teenagers that late at night. To my disappointment, he flagged down a car within minutes. A guy in his early twenties, with a scruffy beard and mustache, wearing a ball cap, rolled down his passenger window. Jimmy leaned forward, hands on his knees, to talk to him. The man offered to take us at least to the New York state line if we had the gas money. Standing back up, Jimmy whispered, "All I got is eight dollars. You got anything?"

I dug out of my pocket the six dollars I had left and gave it to him.

Jimmy spread the cash out in his hands. "Here's what we got."

I quickly calculated how far that would take us, assuming the man's Datsun got about twenty-five miles to the gallon. Not far.

"Well, that'll get you to about Pennsylvania."

Jimmy looked at me. Helpless Labrador.

"I don't want to get stuck in the middle of Pennsylvania in the middle of the night," I said. New York, modeling, the possibilities were slipping away again.

Jimmy stuck his head back in the car. "How 'bout I send you some money"—the man started shaking his head—"from New York once we get there?"

"No can do, man. Sorry. Good luck to you guys."

"What a minute." I glanced at the man while I rummaged through my bag until my fingers grasped the small, velvety jewelry box. Extending it toward the driver, I lifted the lid. "I paid a hundred fifty for these several years ago. They're probably worth more than that now."

"They real?" the guy asked, reaching for the box.

I pulled the box just out of his reach but tipped it so he could see them clearly. "They're real. Diamonds and emeralds."

"Okay. I'll take you to New York city for the earrings and the cash."

New York, modeling, the world at my fingertips slipped back into my sights, and I was transported again to a better place, a better future. Jimmy beamed at me as he opened the back door and climbed in. I scooted in next to him, and the guy reached his hand back, palm up. A memory of Dad standing at the jewelry counter smiling at me caused a pang of loss to flash into my alcohol-saturated brain. I pushed the image out of my mind, envisioned New York skyscrapers and slid the box into the driver's hand.

The driver chain-smoked, didn't talk much and fidgeted—tapping the steering wheel, flicking ashes out the window, rubbing his beard, checking the rearview mirror—as he drove us closer to the Pennsylvania border. His twitchiness set me on edge, especially as my buzz wore off. Jimmy passed out next to me, slumped against the car door, and I was starting to doze when I sensed the car slowing down. I opened my eyes to see the man glancing back at me in the rearview mirror.

"I need to make a pit stop," he said. He eased his car off the highway into a roadside rest area. It was deserted.

Jimmy didn't stir when the man stepped out of the vehicle. My bladder was bursting, but I waited until he was in the men's restroom before I hustled out of the car to the women's room. When I came out, the guy was sitting on the curb, between his car and the restrooms, smoking. He shook a cigarette partway out of his pack and extended it toward me. "Want one?" He seemed less nervous out there, and I speculated he had been fidgeting in the car to keep himself awake. Taking one from his pack, I glanced at the man's car and could barely make out the shape of Jimmy, still unmoving, out cold. Exhausted, I lit the cigarette and sank down onto the curb a few feet away from the driver, closer to his car. We sat on the curb and smoked in silence. After a minute, he flicked his butt into the parking lot and placed one hand onto the curb between us. I expected him to push himself up off the curb, but instead he leaned over, ran his other hand over my breast and kissed me, forcefully, his saliva smearing all over my mouth. Fear shot through me, and my body stiffened. Wide-awake now, all my senses amplified, my body prickled with fear.

"Don't." I tried to push him away. His mouth still pressed against mine, he resisted. Sliding his hand under my shirt, his dry, chapped skin scraped against my breast, and he pressed his body against me, pushing me onto the grass. Turning my face away from his, I yelled, "Stop it!" I shoved and kicked at him and somehow was able to twist out from under him.

My body went into autopilot, every part of me zinging with energy. I stumbled to my feet, lurched to the car and yanked open the back door. "Get up, get up!" I shook Jimmy's shoulder violently. The man scooted into the driver's seat, as Jimmy looked around the car, blinking.

"You two can get out here," the man said.

I pulled Jimmy out of the car. Trying to catch my breath, I explained what had happened as the man peeled out of the parking lot.

Jimmy flipped a bird toward the vehicle's taillights and wrapped an arm around me. "You okay, Sunshine?"

My heart was still racing, my limbs blazing with adrenaline. I shook my head, in answer to him and to clear my head.

"Well, let's go thumb down another ride."

I stared at him for several seconds. "Are you fucking crazy?"

He gave me a blank look. Labrador retriever blank. He all but tilted his head sideways. "What?"

"I just about got raped. I'm not hitching any more rides." It was a muggy night, but as my fear subsided, my body felt like it was shutting down. I began to tremble.

"How else we gonna get to New York?"

"New York? What the hell are you talking about? We're not going to New York. We have no money, it's four in the morning and the man we hitched a ride from just tried to rape me." By then, my knees were so wobbly they felt like they would buckle out from under me, so I paced back and forth in the empty parking lot trying to get my blood flowing. I rubbed my hands over my upper arms to stop my shivering. "Shit. This is all fucked-up."

Jimmy stood there dumbly, bleary-eyed, watching me pace.

"Okay. Okay. Let's just hitch a ride back, but you have to stay awake this time, no matter what. And I'm only getting in a car that has a woman in it, or a man and a woman. That's it. A car stops with just a man, or just men, we wave them past."

When we arrived back at his grandparents' house, Eddie and Angela were sitting at the kitchen table, talking to each other in low voices while Jimmy's grandma grilled Velveeta sandwiches. My empty stomach growled at the aroma of cheese sizzling in the pan. We ate off paper plates balanced on our laps and watched some soap opera. While we were eating—I was on my second grilled cheese sandwich—their grandpa had a coughing fit.

Jimmy, Eddie and their grandma didn't even look away from the TV. I set my sandwich on my plate and watched him out of my peripheral vision as he hacked away, wondering if this scrawny old man would choke to death right there in front of us. Jimmy's grandma saw me looking at her husband and waved her hand toward him. "Don't pay him no mind. He's got that black lung. Coughs like that all day long." Jimmy's grandpa finally expelled a dark wad of mucus into an old coffee can on the floor by his recliner. Angela and I glanced at each other, and she crinkled her nose.

The old man coughed once more while clearing the rest of the mucus from his throat, wiped his chin with the back of his hand and grumbled, "From that goddamn coal mine. Worked in 'em thirty years and this's all I got to show for it." He resumed munching his sandwich, though a few minutes passed before I could return to eating mine.

They fed us dinner too. SpaghettiOs from cans, luckily, the ones with the little meatballs and not the gritty little franks. Then Angela and I pretended to leave, thanking their grandparents for feeding us and telling them how good it was to meet them.

Back in the luxurious Impala, I fell asleep as soon as I curled up in the back seat. I awoke sometime later to the sound of the door squeaking open and Jimmy and Eddie beckoning us back inside the house. I guess *Johnny Carson* was over.

I could barely hold my eyes open as I followed Jimmy to his room where, to my disappointment, there was only one twin bed. "Can you just crash on the floor?" I asked.

A goofy grin spread across his face. "No way."

Great, I thought. Just great.

We squeezed into his bed, and he immediately started fondling me. "Hey, I'm on my period now," I lied.

"So?" He groped under my shirt.

"That's gross." I pulled his hand off my breast and pushed it away. "And I've had like two hours of sleep in the past two days. I gotta crash."

"C'mon. I love you." I shoved his hand away a couple of times before he gave up and rolled over.

As exhausted as I was, I kept waking up, either from the distant drone of traffic from the freeway, or Jimmy turning over, or a horn honking, or brakes screeching or someone yelling in the alleyway. My second night of so-called freedom, and already I wanted to go back home.

10

DESPERATE MEASURES

*E*arly the next day, we snuck out before their grandparents stirred. Jimmy and Eddie said they had a job with a friend. Angela said she wanted to snooze in the Impala. She looked beat, with the hint of shadows under her eyes and a hickey on her neck.

I went to buy a pack of cigarettes, avoiding the busier streets where a cop might cruise by. As I walked down an alley, I heard the purr of an engine behind me. It grew louder, and the crunch of gravel under its tires indicated the car was slowing as it neared me. I edged over to the side of the street to let it pass. A sleek white Cadillac with two men inside crept to a stop alongside me. Immediately, I scanned the houses and driveways around me for an escape route, remembering how Dad always took in everything that was happening around him. The passenger rolled down his window, and sweet, sagey pot smoke wafted out. He wore a chunky gold ring on his pinky and a rope of gold chain around his neck. "Hey there, baby. You wanna get high?"

I wanted nothing more than to get obliterated, but I knew they were pimps, and I'd had about enough of being treated like a piece of ass for the past few days. I bolted between two houses, then around the fenced backyard of another house and stumbled into the adjacent alley. I ran as fast as I could, listening over the sound of my breathing for the Cadillac's engine. I ran until my lungs burned with pain. Pausing, I leaned over, hands on knees, and gasped for air while checking both ends of the alley for the car. After catching my breath, I trotted back to the safety of the Impala.

Late that afternoon, Jimmy and Eddie came back with thirty dollars cash, and we went to a hole-in-the-wall market and bought cigarettes, bologna, Wonder Bread, Velveeta, milk, cereal and a case of Drewrys beer. We went back to the house and snarfed down fried bologna sandwiches in front of the TV. I expected Jimmy's grandma to drill Angela and me about where we were from, or what we were doing there two afternoons in a row, but she seemed too old and tired and fed up with those "boys of hers" to care what they were up to. Before we headed out to the Impala to drink our case of beer, I made a third sandwich to hold me over until the bowl of cereal I hoped to eat in the morning. I missed our well-stocked pantry at home.

Angela and I sat in that broken-down car for a few hours each morning then wandered the streets. After my encounter with the pimps, we avoided the deserted alleys now in addition to the busier streets. No cops, no pimps—the safe zone in The Bottoms was getting smaller and smaller. I was certain Mom had reported me missing by then. The cops, at least, had a description of Angela and me. Mom may even have called Dad. Maybe he was trying to help her find me, telling her what to do or what to tell the cops to do. I wondered if he had rescued runaways when he was a cop. The streets we did roam were lined with large, run-down houses with porches piled with broken bikes, shredded furniture, faded and cracked Big Wheel trikes, rusted refrigerators. These homes must have been stately at some point but now were dilapidated and dreary. They looked exactly how I was beginning to feel. All I wanted was to take a shower and blow-dry my hair instead of washing my hair and armpits in Jimmy's downstairs bathroom sink because the only shower was upstairs next to his grandparents' bedroom.

For two more nights, Angela and I snuck in and out of the house. Each evening, I guzzled beer, hungry for it to obliterate the mess that was all around me and the guilt I was beginning to feel about how worried sick Mom must be. For those few hours I was tipsy, I could uphold some illusion we were having an adventure and I was free to do as I pleased. But every morning I woke up sober, and there was the stark truth: I was running from pimps and rapists and sponging Velveeta and bologna sandwiches from an ancient, worn-down grandma and an old man with black lung.

On the fifth morning, Angela and I sat in the Impala staring out of the smudged, cracked windshield. We were at a dead-end. Angela would have to move away, there was no avoiding that. From the sadness on her face, she knew this too.

The person who kept popping into my mind as being able to help us was my drug dealer, Mark. He had run away from home a few times, had recently gotten out of the juvenile detention center, and somehow his mother still let him live at home. He had been sent to juvey as the result of a sting operation that undercover agents had been running at a local gun shop that was rumored to be selling to minors. Mark had been one of those minors. A week before he was busted, he had shown up in the grit pit—the parking lot behind the school by the dumpster where students who smoked (the "grits") were allowed to do so —and motioned for some guys to come over to his car. Mark popped open the trunk and bragged about an Uzi he had in there. He had spent a few weeks in juvenile detention for that offense, and the gun shop had been shut down permanently— no wonder, after selling Uzis to a sixteen-year-old. My father never even had a gun like that when he had been on the police force.

Mark's experience getting out of trouble was the kind Angela and I needed. I stubbed out my cigarette in the overflowing ashtray. "I need to go back home."

Angela nodded, and tears began to slide down her cheeks. "My father's gonna kill me."

"Maybe my mom can talk to him. She might be able to explain that you just didn't want to leave."

She nodded again and stared at her hands resting in her lap. A few tears dripped from her face. She looked defeated.

"I was thinking about calling Mark."

She looked over at me, a puzzled expression on her face. "Mark? Why him? What can he do for us?"

"Well, I can see what he knows about what my mom's been doing and saying. I'm sure he's talked to Rick"—she looked out the side window at the mention of my brother's name—"so he'll know something. He might have heard what your folks are doing too. That could help us decide what to do. And he's run away before, a few times, and his mom let him come back home, so he could give us some advice. We're down to desperate measures here."

A few blocks away, we found a payphone, and I dialed Mark's number, glad when he, and not his mother, answered the phone.

"Hey, Mark. It's Lynn."

"Hey. Where the hell are you?"

"Uh, at a friend's house. Have you talked to Rick lately?"

"Couple days ago. Said you and Angela ran away. He figures you two are with some carnies."

"Has he said anything about my mom? Is she really pissed?"

"Oh, she's freakin' out, I'm sure."

The very thing I promised I wouldn't do to her: give her more grief. Like Dad and Rick hadn't given her enough. I imagined her tossing and turning all night, praying, calling everyone she could think of who might know my whereabouts, just like that Saturday morning long ago when Dad had disappeared. A hard knot of guilt formed in my stomach.

Angela tapped on her chest and whispered, "What about my parents?"

"What about Angela's parents? Heard anything about them?"

"Nah. I know you both've been reported missing."

I looked at Angela and shrugged.

She mouthed, "What?"

I covered the mouthpiece with my hand. "He doesn't know anything about your parents, just that we've both been reported missing."

Angela bit her bottom lip, pinching it under her top front teeth so hard it looked like her lip might spurt blood any second.

"I'm sure they just want you guys home," Mark said.

The phone hummed in silence for a few seconds. "I'll never be allowed out of the house again. I don't know what to do."

"Well, why don't you tell me where you are first. *Are* you with some carnie or what?"

"We're west of downtown."

"How far west?"

"The Bottoms."

"Aaahh." He groaned with disapproval or concern; I couldn't tell which. "You okay?"

It was concern. How sweet. "We've been at Jimmy's place. But he's at work right now." More phone silence.

"Want me to call your mom? At least I can tell her you called and you're alive."

"Would you? That would be awesome. And tell her we're okay. And that I want to come back home . . . if she'll let me."

"She'll let you. No doubt about that. She definitely won't let you *out* of the house again for a while." He chuckled. "What's the address, and I'll ask her to come and get you?"

"I don't want Mom making a big scene in front of his grand-parents. They're really old. Or trip out on Jimmy if she—"

"You don't have to worry about your mom tripping out on Jimmy. *I'm* gonna beat the shit out of him. That asshole."

"Listen, none of this was his idea. He was just letting us stay with him."

"I don't give a shit. I'm gonna kick his sorry fuckin' ass."

Across the street from the payphone was a pizza parlor. "Just pick us up at the pizza place where I am now. On Broad Street." I read him the address. "White building, black bars over the windows. Has a barbed-wire fence around the parking lot."

"Great. Sounds like a real nice place. Stay inside and wait. Don't wander around anymore. You're like fresh meat out there. Some pimp's gonna try to snatch you up."

"How'd you know that would happen? Well, they didn't snatch me up, but they tried."

"What the fuck? You alright?"

"I'm fine. I ran like a bat out of hell. I'll tell you about it when I see you."

"Okay. Just stay right where you are. Don't go back out on the streets. I'll call your mom and tell her you're okay and you want to come home. I'm sure she's gonna drop everything and come down there. We should be there in, like, an hour or two. You okay for another couple hours?"

Silently, I released the air in my lungs and with it the tension of the last several days. "We'll be fine. We'll wait right here. And thanks. I owe you. Big time."

Angela and I hardly spoke as we wound our way back to the Impala and gathered our stuff. Then we sat in the pizza shop sharing a soda, all we could afford, not even a cigarette to share. The smells of baking pizza crust and pepperoni made my mouth water.

An hour later, Mom's car pulled up in front of the shop. As soon as she stepped out of the car, I was overwhelmed with guilt. She looked exhausted, and her brow was all pinched up with worry. Rick followed her toward the front door, while Mark leaned against the car and lit a smoke.

Without saying a word, Mom walked up and hugged me. That broke down all my defenses, and everything I had been feeling rose to the surface: guilt and regret and hunger and terror. I mumbled into her neck. "I'm sorry. Thanks for coming to get me. I'm so sorry."

She held me at arm's length then, with her hands on my shoulders, quickly scanning me, as a nurse or a mother or both. "Don't you *ever* do this again." With a huge sigh, she glanced at Angela then looked back at me. "I'm not sure if I'm more relieved or furious. What if something happened to you? Something terrible could have . . . " She threw her hands up in the air. "Are you okay?"

I hesitated, thinking of all that had occurred, but she had worried enough already. "Nothing happened to me. I'm fine."

"Me too," Angela said, nodding and looking over at Rick, who stood with his back against the wall just inside the pizza parlor door, his hands shoved in his pockets, glaring at her.

When they made eye contact, Rick pushed himself off the wall and took a few steps toward us. "I told you that son of a bitch was no good. It's a good thing he didn't show his face."

Mom held her hand in the air, palm out, and looked at him. "Cool it. Let me do the talking here." Rick dropped back against the wall and crossed his arms over his chest, scowling. Mom turned back to face me. "What the hell were you thinking? Look at where you are. You could have been hurt or killed or—"

"I know. It was stupid. A stupid thing, and I'm truly sorry."

"Well, you got lucky, young lady. And you're right, this was a real dumb move. Why did you do it? What is going on?"

"We did it so Angela wouldn't have to move." With those words, Rick's face crumpled into what looked to me like heartbreak, and he shoved the door open and stomped back toward the car. "Her dad is pretty mean, and she didn't want to move to Chicago." I glanced at Angela, and she nodded in agreement. "She wants to stay here with us, but I didn't think you'd let her do that. So, we ran away. Jimmy just gave us a place to stay so we weren't on the streets. I know it was stupid. The whole idea. I'm sorry, I know you were freaked out."

The young man behind the counter asked if we planned to order a pizza.

"No. We're leaving." Mom shuffled us toward the door. As we exited the pizza place, Mark was still leaning against the car with one ankle crossed over the other, smoking a cigarette and scanning the parking lot around him. That image of him—cool, laid-back and alert all at the same time—was so familiar to me, a déjà vu I couldn't place.

"It's all my fault," Angela said, as we followed her to the car. "Lynn was trying to help so I didn't have to leave . . . to move to Chicago. You have to believe me. It wasn't her fault. It wasn't her idea."

As we neared the car, Mark locked eyes with me and smiled. In that look, I saw that he would have done anything to get me back home. He kept his gaze on me as I scooted into the car, as if he would never take his eyes off me. I sure could have used a man like that over the past week, I thought.

Driving out of The Bottoms, the city zooming behind us, the tension drained from my body, leaving me so completely relaxed my body felt floppy. When Mom accelerated onto the freeway, she said, "You will have lots of consequences for this. And you are not to see that boy anymore. Ever. Do you hear me?"

"Yes."

"Never again."

"I won't."

Mark glanced over and flashed me that smile again. His nearness made me feel safe for the first time in days. Maybe for the first time in years.

11

CONNECTED

*T*he next time I saw Mark at school, he sat down next to me in the cafeteria. "You're not gonna see that dickwad anymore, are you?"

I shook my head.

"You better not. And if I ever see him, I will smash his face."

"Don't worry, you won't see him."

"So, what'd your mom do?"

"I'm grounded. For a month. No phone. Can't leave the house except for school."

"Not too bad. Could've been worse. I'll stop by later this week before she gets off work. Get you a little buzz, something that won't get you busted."

After that first visit, Mark dropped by every week looking for Rick, but if Rick wasn't there, he hung around and chatted with me and even with Mom if she was home. Despite Mark's reputation for being hostile, he was so cool around adults. This fascinated me as he wasn't cocky, he just had this smooth, confident demeanor when talking with parents. If Mom and Rick weren't around, he shared a joint with me. For Christmas, he gave me a bottle of Black Velvet, telling me it was much smoother than most whiskey, so he figured I'd like it, warning me to be smart with it, not to go stumbling around drunk in front of Mom. I couldn't get enough of his attention and was flattered that he showed me, and only me, his soft side—figuratively speaking, because there was nothing physically soft about him. When I had seen him wearing only Army combat boots and cutoff jeans, I was impressed by his six-pack, those blocky abdominal muscles, and his tanned, chiseled pecs and biceps.

When Rick noticed Mark coming over more, he warned me to be careful.

"Why? He's sweet and kind of . . . watches over me."

"*Right.* He just wants to get in your pants."

"No, he doesn't. We're friends, and he just doesn't want me to get in any more trouble."

"*Suuure.* Well, let me tell you this. He's fuckin' crazy. We were skippin' class the other day, and on the way to our house, he punched *every* street sign between the school and here. Every single one. Punched 'em *hard.* Shit, by the time we got here, his hands were all bloody." He shook his head. "Don't tell him I said this, but he's nuts."

Shortly after Christmas break, Mark came by after school acting nervous and saying he needed to talk to me about something important. "Let's go outside and have a smoke," he said.

I shrugged on my coat and followed him out back, hoping he had finally worked up the nerve to ask me to be his girlfriend. While he lit a cigarette, I zipped my coat up to my chin. He handed me the cigarette then lit a second one for himself.

"What's up?" I asked, smiling at him. I shoved my left hand deep in my coat pocket.

He stared at the ground. "Was partying with Rick the other day, and he told me something I think you should know about."

Probably some bullshit story from Rick, I thought. At this rate, Mark'll never become my boyfriend. He took a long draw from his cigarette, staring at the ground, then another draw, eyes still on the ground. I was freezing my ass off. "Well? What was it? What bullshit did he tell you this time?" I switched my cigarette to my left hand, shoved my right hand in my pocket and began jiggling my legs to generate some heat in my body.

"It's about your dad. Said I shouldn't tell you, but, hell, he's your father too. Figured you should know."

There was only the sound of my corduroy pant legs swishing against each other, phish, phish, phish. I could imagine no scenarios where Rick would talk to Mark about Dad. *I* hadn't even talked to Mark about Dad, except maybe when I told him Dad taught me to shoot guns when I was a kid. "This doesn't make any sense. Why would Rick talk to you about our dad? He hasn't even talked to Dad in—"

"He's in prison. Down in Florida."

The corduroy swishing stopped. My cigarette was propped there in my fingers, halted partway to my mouth, the plume of warm smoke dense in the cold air. "What?"

He nodded and took another hard draw from his cigarette, which was almost gone because he was toking on it so hard. "He tried to call your dad a couple months ago, on his eighteenth birthday, but your dad wasn't there. Talked to your . . . guess it's your step-mom . . . and she told him 'your dad was in prison."

"What? For what? When?" I shook my head, refusing this information. My dad was a cop, had been a cop—even though he wasn't on the police force anymore, that was his fundamental identity. Still. Dad was a cop. He would always be a cop. How does a former cop go to prison?

"Got arrested with a bunch of pot. A *lot*. Like, I don't know, thousands of pounds. Guess he's gonna be in there for a few years."

I saw Mark's mouth continue to move, but his words were muffled by a ringing in my ears. My body started shivering, though I no longer felt the cold. He flicked his butt into the field behind the condo, plucked mine from my fingers and did the same with it, then hooked my elbow and took me back inside.

When Mom came home from work that evening, I pounded

down the steps and confronted her. "Why didn't you tell me Dad was in prison?"

She paused to look at me for a moment before continuing into the kitchen. "Shit," she mumbled under her breath.

I followed her. "Is it true?"

She dropped her purse on the kitchen table with a thunk and turned to face me. "Your father said he would tell you. He was supposed to call you and Rick or write to you. I should've known he wouldn't follow through. I was waiting for him. He should be the one to explain what hap—"

"What did he do?" I had no reason to doubt Mark, but I had to hear the truth from her.

"Drugs. I always suspected he was up to no good. Especially after he left the force and stopped showing up for weekend visits. But I didn't know for sure until a DEA agent called. It was marijuana. He was transporting marijuana. In a truck."

My brain was reeling to make sense of it all. He had been a cop and a good one. *How could this happen?* "Mark said it was a huge amount of pot."

"Definitely. His attorney called me before the appeal to see if I would serve as a character witness by sending a letter describing how he was when we were married, what kind of father he was, how seriously he took his job as a policeman. Stuff like that. I asked the attorney about the arrest, and he explained that your dad had been caught with over ten thousand pounds of pot. Ten *thousand* pounds." She chuckled and shook her head. "I said to the attorney, 'Is that a lot?' He laughed out loud and said, 'Lady, that's a cargo truck full.'"

"How long will he be there?"

"I guess that's why the attorney was asking for a letter, in case the appeal was denied—it was a long shot, the appeal—then he could use the letter to support a request for leniency or a reduced sentence or something like that. Because of his history of being a policeman, the attorney thought it might help."

"Did you send one?"

She nodded. "I described what a good father he was when you kids were little, how he went to church and was a dedicated policeman and how after a few years of undercover narcotics work he changed. He became a different person."

"How long will he be there?"

"Eight years. But your father says he'll get out in four. I don't know why. They're letting him serve two sentences at the same time, something like that. And he plans to get out early for good behavior."

"When did all this happen?"

"Well, I guess his initial trial was when you were in Orlando, what was that, a year and a half ago?" It was sixteen months ago but close enough. "So, he must have . . . it must have been going on for a while, the drug smuggling. That explains a lot. He was found guilty during that trial but appealed it this summer. His appeal was denied, so he went to prison right after that, maybe in July or August, I'm not sure. I haven't spoken to him. I suppose they send you to prison right after an appeal is denied, but I'm not really sure how it all works." Mom placed her hand on my arm.

I twisted away from her and charged back upstairs, my vision growing blurry from tears.

In my room, I pulled down my bread bag of cards and notes, certain I had kept my airplane ticket stub from my trip to Orlando. Sitting cross-legged on the floor, I riffled through the memorabilia until I came upon the note Dad had given me before I boarded the plane that day. Holding my breath, I carefully unfolded the note. There it was, the ticket stub with the date printed on it: August 11, 1979. Remembering from Dad's days as a cop that a trial was sometimes held months after an arrest, I counted back from August 1979. We had moved out of Miami more than a year prior to that, so he would have been busted sometime after we moved to Ohio, which meant he was probably smuggling when we still lived in Miami. I reran every visit I had with him in the past few years, every conversation, mining for any indication he'd been smuggling. As I sifted through these memories, details clicked into place like magnets snapping together: all his varied jobs, the shopping sprees, the wads of cash, the no-show Saturdays. With each image, a knowing settled over me and came to rest deep inside me. He must have had to use drugs as an undercover agent to convince dealers he was one of them. I could see him acting eager, pacing while he rolled up a dollar bill, snorting a line of cocaine and saying, "Yeah, man, how much of this shit can you sell me?" Maybe he had started to enjoy that slow numbing sensation in his nose and the bitter taste of the coke draining down the back of his throat. Then he had begun to crave the bliss of that cocaine spreading through him. In the end, he had sought that feeling at any cost; was willing to trade everything for the drugs. Everything.

After getting the prison name and address from Mom, I sat down to write a letter to Dad explaining all about my drug and alcohol use and how I knew what he was going through, but he was still my dad. Somehow, sharing that with him didn't seem proper. And I wasn't sure I *did* know what he was going through. The small quantities of drugs I used paled in comparison to a truckload of marijuana. Cloistered in my room, I composed a letter in my neatest handwriting telling him about school (omitting that I seldom went), our dog, Scooby-Doo (we still had her, and did he remember her?) and Mark (a nice guy I liked). Shuffling through stacks of recent photos, I included the nicest ones of myself and mailed the letter.

I became consumed with Dad's journey with drugs. I conjured a series of deals that could've transferred my father's marijuana from Miami all the way up to Ohio, into Mark's hands and right into mine. Maybe I had gotten some of my own dad's pot. Maybe he had touched the very weed I had smoked. Though I didn't talk to anyone, not even the people I partied with, about my imaginations. I didn't even talk with Rick for fear he would ridicule me. This precious connection to my father filled me with a strange sense of joy. I had turned out more like him than I ever expected.

12

RAMBLE ON

$\mathcal{I}$t was late winter, when the days are short and dreary and I hadn't seen the sun in weeks, when Denise called to see if I wanted to go to the mall with her and her boyfriend, Jeff. She and I weren't that close, just hung in the same circle of grits at school, but she needed another girl to go out with her and Jeff, so they weren't alone (most of our parents required that). Those two had been inseparable since the beginning of eighth grade and even looked like each other. She never seemed concerned about her appearance—she rarely styled her hair and wore large, outdated glasses that magnified her eyes—and I attributed this to the fact that Jeff adored her. I envied her for that love.

Going out with a mushy couple could be awkward, but one of them could have some pot or booze for the evening. Mom dropped me off at the mall and agreed to pick me up in four hours, at ten. Denise, Jeff and I huddled together to see how much money we each had—enough to buy a case of cheap beer. I called Mark from a payphone to ask if he would buy the beer for us. If we would share our beer, he would bring a couple of joints and drive us around town.

Ten minutes later, he picked us up in his rusty Dodge Challenger, stereo booming. We drove around a sprawling new housing development behind the mall, drinking beer, listening to music and shivering because the car heater didn't work. "Hey, fast engine, great stereo, shitty heater. I've got my priorities," Mark said. I admired that about him, he wasn't apologetic or embarrassed about anything. After thirty minutes, our first joint and four or five beers, I was brimming with happiness. These three people were the best friends I ever had. My life was full of promise.

When Denise and I needed to pee, Mark parked alongside a stand of pine trees behind a model home. Denise and I stumbled through the dark woods to the far side, furthest from the house, and tried to stifle our giggles while we unzipped our pants.

"Do you think they can see us?" I asked, squatting.

"Nah. It's too dark. Ahhhh. I had to pee so bad."

As we negotiated our way back through the trees, I saw Jeff and Mark slinking along the back of the model home. "What the hell are they doing up there?"

"Let's go see."

We crept up to the back of the house as Mark pushed against the handle of the sliding glass door. He shook his head.

Jeff pointed at the narrow basement window near the ground then nudged it with his foot. It was unlocked. "Hey, let's go in here."

Denise and I looked at each other, and she said, "I'm not crawling in there. I'll get all dirty."

"You girls go get the beer from the car, and we'll crawl in the window and go open the back door for you," Mark said. Such chivalry!

My teeth were chattering when we returned with the beer. As soon as we entered the furnished model home, the warmth enveloped us. Jeff and Mark explored the house while Denise and I sat at a glass-and-chrome dining room table chugging a can of beer to use as an ashtray. The guys returned after several minutes carrying various items they'd found: a small radio, a roll of paper towels, a flashlight and a construction helmet.

"What're you gonna do with that helmet, a little YMCA dance for us?" I asked, smiling at Mark. *That* I was ready to see! With a cigarette dangling from his mouth, he perched the helmet on his head, turned sideways and gave me an inviting, sexy grin while gyrating his hips and ending with a slight thrust of his hips. *That* I was not ready for! A little pulse of lightning shot through me and landed right between my legs.

As the evening wore on, we became louder, talking and laughing. Periodically, one of us, usually Mark, remembered where we were and said, "Shush!" or "Keep it down guys."

Eventually, Denise smiled and tugged Jeff into one of the bedrooms. Mark and I sat next to each other sipping beers, trying to ignore the murmurs and giggles coming from the other room. He sat so close I could feel the heat from his thigh against mine. Compared to Jimmy's constant pawing at me, Mark's reserve or shyness was a relief. Right when I was hoping he might turn and kiss me, a yelp erupted from the other room.

"Shit. Shit. Put it out," she said.

"I got it. I got it," Jeff said. Suddenly light streamed out from under the bedroom door. "No, turn it off!" The light flicked off.

Mark rapped on the bedroom door. "Hey, you guys cool it down in there before you get us all busted."

She yanked open the door. "Do you want the fucking house to burn up?" She got that way when she drank, kind of hotheaded.

"Chill—the fuck—down," Mark whispered. "And lower your fuckin' voices."

"We dropped a lit cigarette on the bedspread," she hissed.

"I don't give a flying fuck what you did. You need to quit screaming and keep the damn lights off."

"It's okay now," Jeff said. "I poured some beer on it. It's out."

We all agreed it was time to leave. As we were getting our coats on, red and blue lights swirled through the living room window. We stampeded out the back door into the woods. Denise and I were the last out.

As I neared the edge of the woods, the trees thinned out and I picked up my pace, careening through the bushes under the trees. Up ahead, a cone of pale light shone down from a streetlamp. I planned to avoid it, running instead through the unlit lawns of the other model homes, seeking a good hiding spot like a shed or under a porch. My lungs strained for more air. Someone's feet pounded on the ground behind me—Denise, I hoped, until someone snagged the back of my jacket and jerked me to a halt.

I was spun around to face a uniformed officer. He was breathing heavily, so I suspected he was too old and overweight to be running that hard and probably pissed that I made him do it. He hooked my elbow and pulled me back to where two police cruisers were parked, one in the driveway of the model home, one alongside the sidewalk, both with their red and blue lights rotating. Another cop was putting a handcuff on Denise's right hand. My cop nudged me next to her, and the other officer slapped the other ring onto my left arm. It slid right off my wrist. Denise and I looked down at the empty cuff dangling from her wrist. The officer grabbed the empty end, slapped it back on my wrist and clicked the cuff to its tightest setting. As I watched the officer do this, I remembered how Dad had let me play with his handcuffs when I was young. They had always slid off my skinny wrists, and Dad would say, "Well, guess I can't arrest you today." Curious if the cuff would stay on this time, I bent my elbow back, and the cuff slipped off again. Observing this, Denise's shoulders shook as she suppressed her giggles, which made me start giggling. The cop grabbed my arm and shoved me in the back of the cruiser.

While he interrogated me about my name, who else was with me and how we got in the house, two other cops pushed Jeff and Mark into the other cruiser. With his hands cuffed behind his back, Mark had to lean forward. He slowly rolled his head to the side and looked at me. His face was awash in the rotating police lights, most visible when the blue lights flashed. He appeared to be blinking on and off, bright blue face, barely visible red face, blue, red, face, no face, on, off. The image was mesmerizing and becoming a little eerie until he gave me that sexy, sideways-glancing smile. I smiled back and waved. Of course, he couldn't wave back.

We were booked and fingerprinted at the police station and taken to the juvenile detention center in a paddy wagon. My buzz was long gone by then. Being straight was bad enough, but having a buzz wear off on your way to juvey was like having a nightmare you couldn't wake up from, no matter how hard you tried.

Denise and I, along with a few other girls, had to shower in a long stall with stainless steel walls and several shower heads on each side. After showering, we had to lean forward with our heads toward a woman who doused our wet hair with anti-lice powder. Another guard handed us each a gray jumpsuit. Mine was so baggy I had to roll up the pant legs three times so they wouldn't drag on the floor.

A guard escorted me to a cell. *Wasn't I supposed to get a phone call? I have to call Mom and get out of this place.* Another girl, not Denise, was already lying in one of the two beds. She didn't acknowledge me, which was fine by me. She looked like a grown woman, a rough one, and I preferred she just go right on ignoring me.

There was a low murmur of voices from further down the hall. Perching on the edge of the empty bed, I stared through the bars. I wondered what Dad's prison cell looked like and if he had a cell mate. He had yet to reply to my letter, so I couldn't picture what life was like for him. Thinking about how Dad was rejecting me still, even from prison, made anger flare up in me. What excuse could he possibly have for not writing to me now? Too busy working? Too busy writing to his other daughter? Part of me suspected he was too embarrassed to write back. He had always taken such pride in being a police officer, being in prison must have been a huge blow to his ego. It must have shaken him to his core. I certainly related to that. This new solidarity with Dad, both of us now incarcerated, tempered my flash of anger and disappointment.

A guard unlocked my cell door. "Your turn to make a call."

As I followed the guard, I watched her large hips shift back and forth in a uniform she'd clearly outgrown. We walked down a long hall between rows of cells painted the same grayish-green color. Everything was painted that color: bars, walls, even the floor. At the end of that corridor, we entered a room with faded plastic chairs, long wooden tables covered with scratches and graffiti, a few worn couches, a television and a phone on the wall. At the far end of the room was a metal roll-down door spanning from the ceiling to a stainless-steel counter.

"Your call gonna be long distance?"

I shook my head.

She pointed at the phone. "Go on then."

I dialed home and pressed the phone to my ear, turning my back slightly to the guard. When I heard Mom's voice, the tension in my body melted away. Though I dreaded the look that would be on her face when she picked me up. I explained where I was, and there was a hush over the line. "Mom?"

"I've already talked to the police. They called when they booked you at the police station."

"Oh. Can you, are you allowed to . . . to come get me now?"

"I'm allowed to. I could have picked you up at the police station. There isn't even any bail to pay since it's your first offense."

"Are you going to?"

"No. I am *not* picking you up. I'm tired of your behavior. Sick and tired of it. Maybe spending some time in the detention center will give you a chance to think about what you're doing with your life. This is what happens when you drink and party and break into somebody else's property."

I turned my back to the guard. "Please, Mom. We didn't break in. There was an open window and—"

"No. No more excuses. I've heard it all before. I'm not picking you up. You can rot in there for all I care."

The line went dead.

Stunned, I held the phone to my ear for a few seconds longer. My eyes stung, but I refused to cry. Not here. Hoping and praying the movies weren't accurate when the prisoners got only one call, I replaced the phone in the receiver trying to think of who else to call.

"Alright then. Let's go, girl. Back to your cell." The guard ushered me out of the phone room and my cell door clanked shut behind me.

A different guard walked down the corridor in the morning. "Here's the deal, gals. Long as y'all behave, you can hang in the dining hall after breakfast." She swept her arm in the direction of the room with the TV and the phone. "First bit of funny business and y'all go back to your cells." She swept her arm in the direction of our cells. Taking her sweet time, she sauntered down the row, opening each cell as a line of bedraggled girls filed towards the dining hall. I scanned the line and didn't see Denise anywhere. Her parents must have picked her up during the night. Fear rose in my chest with the awareness that I was now completely alone.

In the dining hall, the metal door at the end of the room was rolled up now and trays of food—bowls of stiff oatmeal, a small plastic cup of mixed fruit and a carton of milk—were lined up on the stainless-steel counter. Despite having no appetite, I took a tray and sat down across from a large, pasty-skinned girl with straggly hair. She scowled at me. When someone sat next to me, I scooted over to give her some more room and so as not to be sitting directly across from the scowling girl. All I could force down was the mushy, syrupy fruit cocktail.

Later that morning, as I was staring at *General Hospital* on the TV, the pasty girl walked past and mumbled, "Scrawny bitch." I glanced in the direction of the guard sitting at a desk at the other end of the dining hall, her face glued to a smaller TV. Standing, I moved toward the restroom, which was closer to the guard, when the girl chucked one of her shoes at me. Luckily, the shoes they gave us with our jumpsuits were lightweight, canvas slip-ons. It missed my face and bounced off my shoulder. Mindful of how tiny I was relative to her, and to most of the girls there, I acted unfazed by the shoe and headed to a stack of long outdated magazines on a card table by the indifferent guard. It didn't seem wise to risk getting cornered in the restroom. These girls weren't from the suburbs; they were from the city, from areas like The Bottoms or, worse, had been living on the streets. Some of these girls might not have escaped the pimps. For the rest of the day, as best as I could, I hovered near the edge of the TV room, keeping my distance from the others but trying to stay within view of the guards.

Two days after I was arrested, Uncle Floyd showed up at the detention center. When he walked into the visitors' room, he wrapped those strong arms of his around me. I wanted to collapse into his arms and suppose I did, emotionally. He patted my back and let me cry for a minute. "Your mom asked me to come and talk to you." Hearing that she hadn't given up on me, not yet anyway, filled me with a mix of relief and remorse. Floyd sat down and patted the table across from him. "Come on. Sit down and tell me what happened. I can help you, but I need to hear it all. The truth. It's important you tell me everything that happened." His face was serious and full of concern.

The metal folding chair was icy through my jumpsuit. This was my best chance of getting any help. After all, he worked with kids like me in his job. And I assumed he had already heard everything from Mom. I told him the entire story, in detail. "That was it. When the cops showed up, we booked out the back door. That was probably stupid, but it was like . . . instinct, to just get out of there and try not to get caught."

He leaned forward on the table, which wobbled under his muscular bulk, and explained that an arraignment would be held in two days and described what would happen there. "And this part is very important"—he locked eyes with me—"when the judge asks you how you plead to the charges, you need to plead *not guilty.*" He palmed his hands on the table twice, in time with the words. Not. Guilty.

"But we *did* break into that house."

"I know. But if you plead guilty at the arraignment, they may decide to keep you in the detention center until your hearing, and that could be weeks or even a month." The shoe-chucking girl came to mind. "Do you understand? Not guilty." Two hands splayed emphatically on the table again.

Sitting before a judge two days later, I pled not guilty to the charge of breaking and entering. The judge released me to Mom's supervision.

At our hearing a month later, Denise, Jeff, Mark and I were all charged with breaking and entering. Because it was a first offense for Denise, Jeff and me, they reduced the charge to trespassing, and we each received three months of probation. With a prior record, Mark was sentenced to four weeks in the juvenile detention center. His face revealed no emotion as the judge sentenced him. He seemed unperturbed. And he probably didn't have to worry about any guys in there chucking shoes at *him*.

Several weeks later, I was in the grit pit having a smoke with my usual group when Christy glanced over my shoulder then did a double take. I turned to see what she was looking at, and a jolt of excitement shot through me to see Mark's car come to a stop by the dumpster. He opened the door and Led Zeppelin's "Ramble On" blared out. The way he locked eyes with me, I knew he was there to see me. And he had probably picked that song for me too.

As I walked toward his car, a big grin spread across his face. Normally he looked angry, but he had a great smile that loosened his sharp jaw line and softened the crease between his brows so that his entire face lit up. He looked good.

"Hey, you're a free man again. When'd you get out?"

He leaned against the car, ankles and arms crossed, again with that aloofness I found so attractive; it had a pull on me. *He* had a pull on me.

"Just got out this morning." Just out, and he's here already looking for me. The song he was playing was definitely intentional. A message for me. "Hoped you'd be out here during lunch. You want a ride home after school?"

"Sure. That'd be great. But Rick can't see you at my house." I scanned the grit pit looking for Rick. "I'll get in trouble if he tells my mom. I'm not allowed to hang out with you anymore. Shit, I can't hang out with anyone right now. Not while I'm on probation."

"I figured. I'll just take you home but won't stay. You can fill me in on what's been goin' down while I was in juvey. See you here at three."

I watched him circle his car back out of the parking lot before I headed back toward my friends. They stopped talking and watched me approach. My face grew hot under their expectant stares. Denise cocked one eyebrow, inquisitively.

"What'd he want?" Christy asked.

I shrugged but couldn't stop a smile from tugging at the corners of my mouth. "Not much. Just wondered if I wanted a ride home from school."

Jeff started teasing. "Uh-*huuhhh*. Just wants to give you a ride home. Sure, that's all he wants."

Denise elbowed him in mock indignation. He pushed her elbow away, and they both broke into giggles like an old, married couple.

Mike shook his head, frowning. "Just be careful, will ya? He's a little . . . I don't know . . . "

"Intense? I know. But he's really sweet to me."

Mark started taking me home from school a couple times a

week, and while I did like his attention, I remained self-conscious about everyone in the grit pit watching me get into his car. Everybody was afraid of him, especially after he had been arrested with that Uzi the year before, which had done nothing to diminish his obsession with guns. Mark knew a lot about guns, and he certainly took good care of them (he had been impressed that I knew about Hoppe's No. 9 oil). But what gave me a gnawing uneasiness was that he didn't treat guns with the same respect that Dad had taught me to have for them. Mark's pride and joy was a shotgun he had sawed off to fit inside his leather jacket, snug alongside his arm, without the barrel sticking out the end of his sleeve. He had brought the shotgun to a party one time, dropped it out of his sleeve and slung it out in front of him. Everyone around him cursed and told him to put that goddamned thing away, while he countered that they were all a bunch of wusses and told them to relax because it wasn't loaded. The thing was, no one could relax with Mark slinging a shotgun around, loaded or not. I had persuaded him to put it back in his trunk that night. It was as if no one—his dad had died of a heart attack when Mark was ten —ever taught him basic gun etiquette. In the back of my mind, I believed I could teach him the proper respect for guns, the same respect my father had instilled in me. I would be wrong about that.

Mark often shared a joint and a six-pack with me on the way home from school (and stopped charging me). Just enough for me to feel buzzed but not so much that Mom could tell when she came home a few hours later. Having a slight buzz made my evenings more pleasant. Usually.

Late one afternoon after Mark dropped me off, I was at the kitchen table eating peanut-butter-and-jelly toast when Rick walked in. He took one look at my plate and said, "What are you eatin'? Is that blood on your toast? Or guts? Or what?"

I rolled my eyes. "It's strawberry jelly."

He looked at me, back at my toast, then cackled. His pupils

were so dilated hardly any blue showed around them. They were scary dark.

"What the hell are you on?"

"What am I on? What makes you think I'm on anything?" He snickered. "Man, I got some *good* acid today. Kick-ass shit. Best acid I ever dropped." Moving over to the kitchen counter, he slid the biggest butcher knife out of the block and poked the tip of it into the chopping board, repeatedly. Thunk, thunk, thunk.

Something inside me lit up, like radar or an antenna picking up every signal in the room. I stooped, hoping it wasn't obvious that I was leaving the table, and inched my way around the table furthest from him. When he saw my motion, he turned to face me and tilted his head sideways, watching me. Even though he was looking right at me, he wasn't seeing me, he was somewhere else altogether. As soon as he stepped in my direction, I moved closer to the kitchen entryway. He paused at the garbage can and began whacking it with the butcher knife so hard he was grunting. That was my chance. I bolted upstairs.

He shouted after me. "Ha! I see you. I'm gonna get you." I heard him bounding up the steps as I slammed my bedroom door, locked it and sat with my back to the closet wall, legs outstretched, feet jammed against the bottom of my door.

The doorknob jiggled, and he laughed. "Awww, come on out. I'm not gonna hurt you."

"Leave me alone."

"You pussy. I'm not gonna hurt you." He rapped on the door. "Open up."

"No! Go away and fucking leave me alone."

The doorknob jiggled again. "Whatcha gonna do, tell Mom?"

Sweat broke out under my arms. "Leave me alone, or I'm calling Mark." I had told Mark all about the craziness of our household, and he had been unfazed. Having someone I could talk to about what was really happening in our house was such a relief. And in this instance, Mark probably *was* the only person who could help me.

The doorknob stopped moving. "Go ahead and call your fuckin' boyfriend. See if I give a shit."

After I heard him loping back down the stairs, I scurried on my hands and knees to the phone and dragged it back closer to my door. The phone cord wouldn't stretch all the way, but I was able to get back into my position with my feet pressed against the door, my back against the wall. I leaned forward and clumsily dialed Mark's number.

"Mark. It's me. Things are crazy over here. Rick's trippin' on acid, and he's losing it."

He let out a disgusted grunt. "That asshole. What's he doing this time?"

"Chopping our garbage can up with a butcher knife. Chasing me around the house with it."

"I'll be right over."

"No, no. Wait. Don't hang up. Please stay on the phone with me in case he comes back. If he knows I'm on the phone with you, that'll stop him. I could even give the phone to him. You could talk to him."

"I don't like this. I don't want you there alone with him while he's that out of it."

"But if you're on your way over, and he gets in—"

"I can be there in five minutes."

"That's too long. It's better if he hears us talking. If he knows you're on the phone . . . I don't know. It'll cool him off."

"Where are you? Where is he?"

"In my bedroom. I'm in my bedroom with the door locked and —" The front door slammed. "Wait, I think he just left. I heard the front door shut. Hang on."

"Don't go out—"

I dropped the phone and tore through Mom's room to peek out her window. Rick was walking down the sidewalk.

Back in my room, I locked the door and slid a bottle of Black Velvet out from under my dusty stuffed animals, patting my Cheshire-Cat-grinning frog on the head. I picked the phone up and sat again with my back against the closet wall. Instead of jamming my feet against the door though, I drew my knees up to my chest, cozy in that nook but ready to hold the door shut if necessary. "It's okay, he's gone." I tipped the bottle back and took a long swig. My throat burned.

"Good. He gets so nuts on acid. Don't know why he keeps takin' it."

"No shit! I'm pretty sure he won't come back now. He's way too wasted to risk being around Mom like that, and she gets home soon." I took another swallow and shuddered from the strong alcohol in my mouth and down to my stomach. And this was supposed to be the smooth stuff! But the whiskey warmed me from the inside out and gave me that light, floaty, sparkly sensation I craved. "I'm drinking some of the Black Velvet you gave me. You're so sweet to keep buying it for me."

"Just don't get busted with it. If you do, don't tell your mom I gave it to you."

I looked at the clock and was calculating how much time there was before Mom came home. As I was getting up the nerve to invite him back over, Mark spoke up.

"Well, call me if he comes back and gets crazy. I'll see you at school tomorrow."

I hung up and took another long swallow of whiskey. My body relaxed and began breezing away—from my house, from my brother, from my reality. After another few drinks, the whiskey was, at last, velvet. And so was I. My brain had stopped whirring with hypervigilance for any sound of Rick, and I mused about Mark becoming my boyfriend. Rick would think twice about harassing me again, of that I was certain. I would have a steady supply of booze and drugs, and Mark was hot. He also had a singular focus on me, which made me feel secure. A man who needed you wouldn't leave you. Mark would never leave me. Even years later, when I would beg him to let me go, he wouldn't.

13

LOSING MY VIRGINITY, AGAIN

That summer, I partied whenever Mom was at work and tried to limit my consumption when she was due home soon. Sometimes, I overshot my goal and still reeked of alcohol or had slurred speech when she showed up. Rick had stopped even trying to hide his habit, staggering around in front of her, smashed, almost daring her to try to stop him. She gave us consequences, grounded us, restricted Rick's car use, but she couldn't control us when she was at work all day. She even had a college student come over and study at our house for a couple of hours each afternoon, requiring us to tell him where we were going, with whom and what time we would be back. While that did stop us from having anyone over at our house to party, Rick still walked out whenever he wanted to, and I simply lied to the guy. That lasted about two weeks before Mom realized paying a chaperone was a waste of her money and his time. Mom was seeing a counselor and attending a parenting group, but our house was still full of screaming, door slamming and wall kicking.

On a particularly bad day, I watched Mom absolutely lose it with Rick. She was yelling into the house from the back patio. "I told you no more drugs or alcohol in this house. I warned you."

I checked my stash—untouched—then peered out my

bedroom window to see what she had found. In one hand, she held his Apogee bong and, in the other, a hammer. *Holy fuck, he's gonna flip out.*

Rick lurched out the sliding glass door. "Give it to me! Now!"

Mom kneeled with the bong in front of her. "This is gone."

He moved toward her with his fist raised. "You bitch. Don't—you—dare."

She stood back up with the hammer raised over her shoulder. "Don't *you* dare."

Shit, shit, shit. I glanced at the phone and thought about calling the police but didn't have the number or a phone book in my room. There was always Mark, but I didn't want to step away for fear Rick would punch her. Or she might hurt him. She *was* holding a hammer. Not that I could have stopped either of them, but if I yelled down to them that I was calling the police, they might both cool down.

To my great relief, Rick stumbled back a few steps. She knelt again and struck the bong with all her fury. Shards of plastic and wood splintered across the patio.

"Go fuck yourself," he screamed, going back inside then slamming the front door behind him.

Rick rarely came home after that bong smashing, spending more and more of his time with a woman named Vanessa who was a few years older than him and who had a newborn baby. Though she still lived with her parents, they were never home. It was just Vanessa, her brother, her sister (who had a toddler) and that little baby in their home. Without any parents around, their place was a notorious party house, so Rick was typically there. That suited me fine because Mark was at my house after school most days by then.

I kept expecting and waiting for Mark to at least kiss me, but he never even tried. When he didn't think I was paying attention, he checked me out, so I knew he was interested. I found myself longing to be touched by him and changed into my tightest shorts and tube tops after school hoping he would be unable to resist me.

Not until I brought out my bikini was I able to break through his restraint.

I was lounging in the sun when Mark arrived with a frosty twelve-pack of Heineken beer, which I had never tried. After a few beers, I was buzzed and ready to seduce Mark if he didn't make a move soon. Back inside, I put on The Cars album and that "Good Times Roll" beat pumped *me* full of good times. Jubilant and carefree, I started rocking my hips to the beat then let my towel fall to the floor so I could snap my fingers above my head. I twirled around. Mark's eyes flitted over my body then glanced away. Amazing willpower! I was going to have to club him over the fucking head! Dancing my way over to him, I said, "So, what do you want to do?" I sidled up next to him on the sofa.

Finally, he put his hand on my thigh. "Hey, let me ask you a question. I've been wondering something for a while. I want you to tell me the truth, though. Seriously. Do you still talk to that carnie?"

"What? You mean Jimmy? I haven't seen him for months."

"Does he still call you? You guys talk on the phone, shit like that?"

I shook my head.

"Did you have sex with him? When you ran away?"

I cringed at the memory of losing my virginity in a broken-down car in an alley to a carnie I hadn't even loved who climbed out of the car and pissed in the bushes after we were done. If I could, I would have undone that whole shitty-ass week in The Bottoms.

"You did, didn't you?"

Nobody else knew but Jimmy—I never even told Angela. I didn't want it to be true. I looked directly at Mark. "No. I didn't."

"You had a hickey on your neck when we picked you up at that pizza parlor."

"He wanted to. He tried to, but I wouldn't. I told him I was on my period. Besides, why does it matter to you?" Those Heinekens had given me a cocky confidence.

The edges of his mouth turned up slightly. "Just wanted to know."

"Why? Why do you care anyways?"

He shook his head and looked down at his hand still resting on my thigh.

I dropped my mouth open in mock surprise. "You're *jealous*."

"Nah. Just hate the idea of him touching you."

I leaned my face close to his ear and neck and lowered my voice. "What about the idea of *you* touching me?"

He turned only his face toward me, his hand unmoving on my leg. "Oh, I like that idea. I like that idea a lot." His self-control made me want him even more. I nuzzled his neck and tasted his salty skin there until something in him broke loose. He turned his upper body toward me, kissing me, finally. Parting my lips with his, his tongue explored my mouth without prodding, just inquisitive, beckoning. A current of heat shot from between my legs through my entire body. We were still sitting side by side, sort of, with our chests and shoulders twisted toward each other. As if he couldn't tolerate the space between us any longer, he pulled me onto his lap.

Straddling him, I untied my bikini top and let it fall between us. "Kinda small, I know."

He cupped my breasts with his hands. "Well, you know what they say. More than a handful's a waste." That was so sweet and gentlemanly of him. I was hooked. He slid his hands down and around my hips. "Damn, you're so tiny, I can almost wrap my hands all the way around your waist." Okay, that was it. I was in love with this man. His gaze roamed over my body and back to my face. He seemed so full of awe that I could have stopped right there, basking in his adoration and the foreverness of his attachment to me. In his face, I saw love.

His breathing grew heavier, and his look changed to one of desperation and need. His voice was hoarse. "Wanna go upstairs?"

I smiled. "Thought you'd never ask."

He released a guttural sound, almost a growl, while sliding his hands under my bottom, scooping me up and standing all in one fluid movement. Either he was so strong or so aroused that I weighed nothing to him. I wrapped my legs and arms around him and let him carry me to my bedroom.

At the edge of my bed, he knelt and set me down. Through our kissing, he muttered, "Are you sure—you want—to do this?"

I slid my bikini bottom off and stretched out on my side, my hip in the air, head propped on my hand. He stood, kicked off his shoes and stripped out of his clothes. When he stretched over the top of me, he hesitated until I guided him into me. For the first few minutes, he moved inside me slowly. I couldn't get close enough to him, so I wrapped my legs around his hips and pulled him deeper inside me. That must have given him the message that what he was doing was *very* okay, and he moved in and out with increasing urgency until he moaned and shuddered. My body felt suspended in mid-air, in time, in outer space, like at the very top of a rollercoaster when it pauses just before crashing down the other side. Then something inside me exploded, and my pussy went into wild spasms. Then, too soon, I was plummeting back to my room, back to my bed, back underneath Mark. It was safe and warm there and I never wanted to leave. Maybe *this* was what held couples together.

My body was spent, and I let my legs buckle and splay out on the bed around us. He stayed perched above me with his fore-arms on the bed, so he didn't crush me—he probably weighed twice as much as me. His breath was warm against the side of my cheek.

After a few minutes, he pushed himself up enough to kiss me. Only a little tongue this time, a gentle, unhurried kiss. His lips were full, soft and perfectly moist, not slobbery at all. He pulled his face away and his brow was furrowed, his lips not frowning but no longer smiling either.

"What?" I thought he was about to ask if that was my first time. Maybe he could tell that it wasn't, that I wasn't a virgin.

"You're not gonna go out with anyone else now, are you? You know, other guys?"

"What? How could you even ask that after what we just did?"

"Hey, some women do."

"Well, *I* don't. Of course, I'm not gonna see any other guys now." A big smile pushed all the worry off his face. "What about you? Are you?"

"Nah. I'm not gonna see any other guys either."

We both laughed, and I tried to push him off me in jest, but there was no budging him; he was unmovable, like a rock. "Serious," I said. "You better not see anybody else."

He looked at me for a long moment, then shook his head. "Trust me, I won't. There's no one else. I don't want anyone else. Ever."

I looked over at the clock. "Shit, you better get out of here before my mom gets home."

He kissed me again, jumped out of bed and, after pulling on his pants, gave me one last peck. I smiled at the sound of him galloping down the steps with those long lanky legs of his.

<hr />

*T*hat fall, Mark talked his mom into letting him drop out of school. He was allowed to continue living in her house as long as he had a full-time job and paid rent. Within a week, he found a job at a local store, stocking shelves at night. He liked those hours because he could still pick me up from school. We got together whenever we could, two to three times a week, and used whatever drugs he could buy. Drugs were easier to conceal from Mom, because I wouldn't stink of alcohol and, with some of them, wouldn't have slurred speech either. Though I still tried to avoid her whenever I was loaded.

He arrived one afternoon, eager to show me something. With his index finger pressed on a small paper packet, folded up like a miniature envelope, he slid it slowly across the table to me. I opened it carefully and peeked inside to see two tiny, purple, barrel-shaped dots.

"It's called purple microdot. Acid. You've been wanting to try it, so here it is."

I jumped into his arms, and he caught me, lifting me to him. Burying his face in my neck, he inhaled there, breathing me in and muttering that he loved me. Wiggling my way back down to the floor but still wrapped in his arms, I leaned back so I could see his face. "I love you *so* much. You know I've always wanted to try LSD. They're so tiny, though. Don't we need more than this?"

"Nooo. This is supposed to be some good shit, and you don't need much. If you take too much, you can have a pretty bad trip. That sucks. But it won't happen. You're gonna love it."

"Okay, so how do we take it? Swallow it? Oh, wait a minute. My mom'll be home around five. Should we wait until we've got more time?"

"Leave her a note. Tell her you went to a movie and to Arby's with some friends or some bullshit like that."

I calculated how many hours I could be gone; around six. "You think the acid will wear off by nine, so Mom won't know I'm tripping if we come back then?"

"You should be good by then. I think you'd be able to be around her without her knowing. As long as you don't have a bad trip. But, even then, you'll still come down enough by nine."

Mark placed one of the dots under his tongue and slid the other one under mine. I wrapped my mouth around his finger.

He watched my lips intently, letting out what seemed like an involuntary, *Mmmm*. I sucked his finger further into my mouth. His reaction aroused me, and I felt myself swelling and becoming wet.

"I have something else you can suck on. Maybe while you're sittin' on my face."

Half an hour later, the LSD had kicked in and everything was intensified. I could see the love there between us, vibrating between our naked bodies, between our legs and our chests and our lips. I had never been so deeply in love with Mark as I was right then.

Later, as we drove around deserted country roads, the entire world was amplified: the tires vibrating on the road, the vast, green cornfields, the music. I turned down the radio volume. "Shit. This is intense. It's almost too much."

Mark glanced at me then back to the road. "What's too much?"

"Everything. The music is so loud, and has so many words, so many instruments. I can see it coming out of the speakers." His hands appeared to be clutching the steering wheel. "Do you know how to drive? I mean, can you figure it out? Right now? So many things you have to do, steer and brake, shift gears, stay on the road and in the right lane."

He chuckled, and his laughter seemed to roll around inside the car, which made *me* start laughing. We were eventually cracking up so hard he had to pull the car over, coming to a stop on a dirt road.

Catching my breath between laughs, I said, "Why are—we —laughing?"

"I don't know, but it sure was hysterical." This prompted another bout of laughter.

As that round subsided, I wiped my eyes, and Mark cracked open a beer. He took a big swig and handed it to me. I took a few glugs and felt the liquid travelling all the way down my esophagus, thought I heard it sloshing to a stop in my belly. It was cold and clean with no taste whatsoever. I held the beer can out in front of me and stared at it. "This has absolutely no flavor."

"It's the acid. Not sure why, but it takes away your taste. Don't drink too many, though. You won't feel the effect, but you'll still get shit-faced. Then when you come down and I take you home, you'll be stumbling all over your house, drunk, reeking like booze."

"Why are we drinking it at all then?"

He shrugged. "Keeps you a little mellow, so you don't get too freaked out from the acid. Don't want you to have a bad trip or anything."

I took another sip, a small one, pondering still if it was only ice-cold water. We were parked on a short spur-road that was more like a long driveway leading partway into a soybean field. There wasn't a barn in sight so it must have been where the farmer entered the field with equipment. Soybean plants stretched out in every direction as far as I could see, the bushy green rows like waves on a beach. I closed my eyes and recalled ocean waves washing over my feet and foaming around my waist. Dad was there next to me. In between waves, the sunlight danced under the water and around our feet. Another wave surged, the spray salty on my lips and stinging my eyes. The sand hissed and fizzed as the water frothed around us again. Then came our favorite part, the tug of the sand being sucked out from under our feet as the wave pulled back to sea.

"You okay over there?" Mark asked.

The crashing surf disappeared. Dad disappeared. Again. I opened my eyes. "Just remembering the beach in Miami." I surveyed the landscape around me: only an ocean of soybean plants and Mark. No white sand. No salt spray. No Dad. Would saying good-bye to my father ever stop causing a stab of pain in my gut? "I have to pee."

"Go on. No one's gonna drive by out here in the middle of nowhere."

The car door squeaked open, and I wandered down one of the rows.

"That's one of the things I love about you, you're not prissy. Love a girl who's not afraid to piss outside."

"You just like seeing me with my pants down."

"That too."

Squatting between two rows of soybeans, I became mesmerized by the heart-shaped leaves of the plants. I stroked a leaf then plucked it off to examine it up close. A fine fuzz ran along the stem and underside of the leaf that tickled when I rubbed the leaf between my fingertips.

Mark leaned forward and peeked at me through the open door. "What are you doin', takin' a shit over there?"

"No. Check this out." I bounced a couple of times before pulling my pants back up.

Twirling the leaf by its stem, I offered it to him. "Feel it. It's fuzzy."

He rubbed the leaf between his fingers, inspecting the top and bottom surfaces. "Cool."

"You know, plants make the whole world go around. Seriously. Think about it. Most animals have to eat plants, or they die. We have to eat animals, or we die."

"What about vegetarians?" he asked.

This launched us into a rambling, convoluted conversation at the end of which we declared we had discovered the secret of life. We basked in our magnificent discovery, scanning the sea of soybean plants surrounding us—the foundation somehow of our very existence—the two of us in the tiny car like a boat bobbing on the waves.

As the sun set that evening, we gawked at the shifting colors that painted the sky: glowing orange turned to dusty pink then faded to a feathering of purple. With the darkness came an awareness that the LSD was wearing off. Everything began to appear dimensionless, and I wondered if I too had lost all dimension, if I had become merely a cut-out of a person, a drawing or a photograph. Like the one I had recently sent to Dad with a letter that he still hadn't responded to. Thoughts of Dad stirred up childhood fears and sadness. God damn it, I needed to get my father out of my head. "When do I have to be home?"

Mark looked at the clock in his dashboard. "Shit. Right now. We gotta go."

As we drove out of the soybean fields and began to see more and more farmhouses, the world illuminated in our headlights began to look stark. As we drove into residential neighborhoods, my heightened senses became overwhelmed by all the houses and cars and lights and people and trees. Everything was now harsh and sharp around the edges instead of vividly crystal clear. The music from the radio was abrasive and jarring. I snapped it off.

Up ahead was a lighted Dairy Queen sign. The sight of it made my stomach growl. "I am starving. Let's get a burger."

In the bright lights spilling from the glass door, my pupils constricted painfully. People sitting at the tables inside seemed to be staring at me. As we neared the door, another couple exited and with them came the aroma of greasy fries and burgers, onions and syrupy sweet ice cream. Gnashing my teeth together, I couldn't go through the door.

Mark looked back at me. "What?"

"Can you order one for me? Bring it back to the car?"

He paused. "Are you grinding?"

I hadn't the faintest idea what that meant, but it sounded exactly like what seemed to be happening, the world and everything around me was grinding to a halt, grinding against my every sense. "I don't know . . . I guess, if that's what happens when you come down off acid. It's like everything is grating against my nerves. I definitely can't go in there. How long does grinding last?"

"Maybe an hour or so. Just go back to the car and wait for me. And don't go anywhere else."

I scooched down low in the car with my eyes closed, shutting out everything around me. When Mark climbed in with a bag of food, my mouth watered as soon as I caught a whiff of the onion rings. "Onion rings. You remembered."

"Course I did."

I unwrapped the burger. Ketchup had oozed out from under the bun. Lifting the bun, I peeked at the meat. It looked like a pulverized scab topped with fluorescent green pickles.

"Don't look at it, just eat it. You'll feel better. It will help you come down some before I take you home. You can't go home like this, that's for sure. Your mom'll know you're wasted."

I gagged down half the burger. Each bite was flavorless and turned into a masticated, chewy mass of what, I didn't even want to fathom, before I forced myself to swallow. The onion rings were a little better until an onion slipped out of the crunchy coating and slithered down my chin like a worm. "Ew! Ew! Ew!" I flicked it off my chin onto the floor.

"Cool it! Just eat. Stop thinking about the food and just eat it," Mark ordered.

I broke a few onion rings in half, slid the onions out and ate the hollowed-out crunchy batter until the roof of my mouth felt scraped raw.

Mark parked around the block from our condo. "Take the Dairy Queen bag, proof we did go eat. Just say hi to your mom, tell her you gotta get to bed. Call me when you get to your room."

I ran my fingers through my hair and pushed it behind my ears. "How do I look?"

"Hot. Like always."

"You know what I mean. Do I look wired?"

"You look fine. You'll be fine. Love you." He leaned over and kissed me, our tongues touching. His mouth locked me on to something in the world that was real and soft and warm. My body didn't want to move away, didn't want to go back to the flat, meaningless world waiting outside the car.

He pulled away enough for our lips to part. "Wish you didn't have to go." His voice was gruff with arousal. I kissed him again, and he cupped a hand over my breast. With our mouths pressed together, his warm breath on my lips, he said, "You're gonna get in trouble if you don't get inside."

I backed out of the car, the jagged world crashing all around me. All I wanted to do was slink upstairs to my room but knew that would make Mom suspicious. She would follow me and question me, and I couldn't handle being interrogated.

In the kitchen, Mom sat at the table with a stack of bills and her checkbook. "How was the movie?"

"Good. Want some Dairy Queen? I couldn't finish my burger. Ate too much popcorn." I extended the bag to her.

"No, I already ate. What'd you see?"

I stared at her blankly.

"At the movies?"

Desperately, I tried to recall a new release. My armpits stung as I started to perspire. "Christy wanted to see *Mad Max*, that Mel Gibson movie. Too violent for me. So, we saw *Partners*. It's a comedy about two undercover cops. Kinda reminded me of Dad and Carl." I hadn't thought of Carl in years. Suddenly, the memory of my father was like a vapor all around me—Dad clowning around with Carl, Dad laughing, Dad happy. My mind, no my soul, felt stripped wide open and exposed. There was the gaping hole my father had left in it. Afraid Mom might be able to see right into my soul, I had to get the hell out of that kitchen before I lost my shit. I took a glass from the cupboard, filled it with water then plopped in some ice.

"Sounds good," Mom said and began shuffling through the bills.

Stay cool. Just go upstairs and call Mark. You're okay, you're okay. Taking a sip of water, I realized how thirsty I was and gulped down the rest of the water. Purposely, I made eye contact with Mom and hoped she couldn't see how utterly obliterated I was. "Well, I gotta a little homework to finish before I hit the sack."

"Okay. See you in the morning."

As I climbed the steps, she called after me, "Sweet dreams."

I didn't have any dreams, sweet or otherwise, because I barely slept. I talked with Mark on the phone until one o'clock in the morning, then chain-smoked out my window until three or four a.m., waiting for my body to stop humming with energy and my brain to unwind. The next morning, I headed out as if I were on my way to school. Then, after Mom left for work, I went back home and slept.

LSD was the first drug I had used that kept me up all night (it wouldn't be the last), but I considered that a small price to pay for a mostly fun acid trip out in a soybean ocean. Drugs were like that: some knocked me out too quickly; some kept me up all night; some made me feel crazy or paranoid; and some filled me with pure elation. Just like Goldilocks, I never knew which ones would be just right, but I chased that promise of escape at almost any cost. And I had set the bar pretty low—though it would go much lower: all the substance had to do was change the way I felt and carry me away from myself.

My PCP trip didn't go as well as did the LSD trip. Mark sprinkled angel dust into a joint, and we toked it down on our way to a party at Vanessa's house. When we arrived, a dozen people were there, passing around joints and a bottle of Jim Beam while the stereo blasted. Mark and I scooched onto one of the couches, but before the bottle even made it to us, a guy across the room began to look strange to me, his face seeming to melt into a distorted mess of lips, nose, eyes and brows. I jerked my face in the other direction, toward a couple who looked like they were laughing, but since I couldn't hear them over the music, I wondered if they really were laughing or if their heads were tossed back and their mouths wide open because they were screaming in pain or gasping for air. Then their faces also began to melt, two jiggling pizza faces. I jumped up and hurried out of the house.

Outside, the cool air and the darkness lessened my growing hysteria. The music was muted out there, now only a vibration that I could tolerate. *I'll hang out here, wait for Mark to come. Or I could walk home.* In my peripheral vision, I saw the shadow of a person peek out from the side of the house then duck back behind it.

I jumped behind a bush and crouched there with my butt on my heels and my hands on the ground next to my feet, listening for any sounds from the side of the house. Come on, Mark, hurry up, I thought but knew he wouldn't follow me out until he got his tokes on a joint, his pulls on the Jim Beam.

Finally, the front door opened and closed. "Lynn? You out here?"

"Shhh. I'm down here," I whispered.

Two footstep sounds came closer to my hiding place. "What the fuck are you doin' down there?"

"Someone's watching me. From the side of the house." My heart was thumping wildly. Or was that the pulsing from the stereo?

"Come on. I'm getting you outta here." He pulled me up from behind the bush. As he ushered me to his car, I kept my hands cupped around the sides of my face and stared at the sidewalk to avoid any visual stimulation.

When Mark dropped me off at home several hours later, he said, "No more angel dust for you."

"What? Why? I liked it."

He stared at me. "Are you nuts?"

I stared back. "No. It was fun. Kind of weird, but fun."

He threw his head back against the headrest and laughed. "Lynn, you were fuckin' losing it. Hiding in the bushes, seeing things that weren't there. You aren't doin' any more angel dust. Some people get paranoid as shit on PCP, and you're one of 'em."

"You can't tell me what to do. It's my body."

"No, this"—he ran his hand up my thigh and began rubbing my crotch—"is *my* body."

I pushed his hand away, or at least, he let me push it away. "No, this is *my* body. And I'll do whatever drugs I want to."

We argued for several minutes. I called him controlling and insisted he wasn't in charge of me, and he snickered dismissively, which pissed me off even more.

"I don't care what you say, you're not doin' any more PCP."

That was the first time I felt controlled by Mark's protectiveness. It wouldn't be the last.

14

HORSE TRANQUILIZERS

*A*fter my PCP argument with Mark, I told myself I could party with other people and use whatever drugs I wanted to, whenever I wanted to, but in the back of my mind, I saw that door had been closed—or slammed shut. Mark would go ballistic if I wanted to spend an evening with friends instead of him and doing so wasn't worth the battle that would ensue. This was one of the many freedoms I traded for the promise of regular oblivion that Mark offered. He provided a steady stream of mood-altering chemicals, and those substances were my liberation.

The last time I had gone out with a couple of girlfriends, one of their older brothers went with us, primarily because he had his license and could drive us. When we returned to my condo, as soon I stepped out of the back seat, I saw someone walking towards the car. Even in the dark, I could tell by his stride and height that it was Mark. I said good-bye quickly and shut the door, but before her brother could back his car out, Mark opened the door and yanked him out of the car.

The driver struggled to twist out of Mark's grip. "What the fuck? Who the hell—"

"Stop!" I yelled, as Mark punched the guy in the face.

Mom pushed open our screen door and flipped on the front

porch light. When she saw what was happening, she shouted at me. "Get in the house! Now. And you all"—she gestured toward Mark and the man buckled over next to his car, holding his nose—"get out of here before I call the police."

Mark questioned me for days about that guy. I kept reassuring Mark that I loved *him*, and nothing was going on with my friend's brother, he had only given us a ride. After a week of his interrogation, I told Mark to get off my back, or I *was* going to ask that guy out. That shut him up.

School was the only place I could still use with other people without Mark's interference. The other grits and I used anything we could get our hands on—pot, prescription pills from parents' medicine cabinets, anything being sold in the grit pit. One of our favorites were these big, green gel capsules stamped with the words "Placidyl 750." Christy and I bought the Placidyls from a guy one morning before school. We didn't even know what they were, but he said they were tranquilizers sure to get us blitzed. And they were cheap. Twenty minutes after taking them, after we were already sitting in our first period class, the Placidyls kicked in. I could barely hold my eyelids open. Glancing at Christy, I could see she was in the same condition. When the bell rang, we leaned into each other to keep from stumbling too badly and stared at the ground all the way to the grit pit. Our speech was so slurred we didn't dare go to our next class and planned to wander around the neighborhood for a few hours. Walking was far too challenging, so we went to the ravine by the middle school and spent the rest of the morning slumped against some boulders drifting in and out of consciousness. That afternoon, we slinked back to the side of the school, trying to keep out of sight while Christy waited to catch the bus home, and I waited for Mark.

That evening, I lugged Mom's *Physician's Desk Reference* off the bookshelf and read that Placidyls were sedatives prescribed primarily as sleeping pills, and 750 milligrams were the highest dose made. The next time we got our hands on these "horse tranquilizers," as we called them, we skipped *all* of our classes for the day.

By then, the principal, Mr. Justus, was calling Mom in for parent-teacher conferences every couple of months. I usually took my time getting to the office so Mom wasn't also sitting there in the front room, scowling or grumbling at me; better to roll into the office a minute or two late and be waved directly back to Mr. Justus' office by the secretary. Crammed around the table with the principal would be the counselor, Mom and a few of my teachers.

At one of these conferences, I was surprised and uplifted to see my art teacher, Mrs. Holt, in that huddle. She was one of my favorite teachers, always telling me that I had strong artistic abilities and encouraging me to try more challenging projects. Because I had a good grade in Art, I was surprised she was there. But that was how she was, interested in her students as people, whole people, not only for what they could do in class.

The principal pointed to the one empty seat at the table. "Come on in." Scooching between the wall and Mom's chair, I took a slow deep breath and braced myself for everyone sitting too close to me and focusing too much attention on me, lecturing me, giving me ultimatums. Mr. Justus kicked things off. "I'm sure you know why we're all here. You skipped several classes this month. And Mrs. Carlos suspects you were high in P.E. last week."

I didn't bother to respond. There was no point in refuting the facts. My experience was that being contrary only further agitated the authorities—cops, principals, teachers, parents, all of them. I found it best to lie low during interrogations. As I stared down at my hands, my hair came loose from behind my ear. I let it hang there, partially hiding my face, giving me some cover. I could hear one of them rustling through papers.

"Surprisingly, your grades aren't too bad," Mr. Justus continued. "You've got a B in Art." I snuck a peek at Mrs. Holt, and she winked at me. "That's great. You've got a C in Biology and a couple of Ds. One F."

An F in French, how fitting. Learning French wasn't that hard, but the teacher was so old and boring, and he droned on and on in a completely monotonous tone in French. So much for a Romance language. I usually skipped his class.

My English teacher, Mr. Moseley, chimed in. "That's one of the problems. Even when she skips classes, Lynn can keep her grades up." That didn't sound like a problem to me. My fingers found a rough spot on the edge of my thumbnail, and I began scraping my tooth against it to smooth it off. "Because she does really well on tests," Mr. Moseley added.

"Same with biology. You do pretty good on the tests. If you studied some, did the assignments, you'd have an A in my class." I peeked up through my hair. My teachers were all nodding, apparently serious about their confidence in my abilities.

The principal caught my eye and gave me the warmest smile. "What do you think? You don't have to study very hard to ace a test, do you?"

I shook my head.

He looked from me to Mom.

"But I want her in her classes too. She needs to be at school," Mom said.

"Oh, so do we," said Mr. Justus. "We all do. In fact, if she misses much more school, I'm obligated to report her to a truant officer."

I looked back down at my lap, the snag now splintering halfway across my fingernail.

"What does that mean? What would a truant officer do to make her go to school?" Mom asked.

"Well, the juvenile court could get involved. She could end up on probation, reporting weekly to a truant officer. Or she could . . . become a ward of the court. Then the courts will decide how to make her go to school. Or where she'll go to school."

"Do you hear that? Is that what you want?" Mom said.

The possibility of going to the juvenile detention center again did frighten me, but I couldn't figure out how to use drugs and alcohol the way I wanted and still go to school. I just need to be more careful, I thought. No more using before school or not so much or—

"Lynn, can you look at me?" Mr. Justus said. "I'd like to see those pretty eyes of yours." I peeked up through my hair again. There was his disarming smile again. That should be a requirement for all principals, a big, welcoming smile. "What do *you* want to do?" he asked.

Lots of ideas popped into my head, none of which I could share with the authorities sitting around that table: about Mark and how I loved him, and he kept me safe, sort of, but everything we did revolved around getting inebriated; about how possessive he was becoming; about how unbearable it was to be straight. And I wondered how long before everyone—my teachers, the principal, the counselor, Mom—gave up on me. Like when I was a kid and that one time I had refused to dive into the ocean from our boat. I had wanted to, but fear kept me on the boat with Dad where I was safest. The moment everyone had stopped coaxing me into the water, had given up on me joining them, I was finally ready to jump in. Of course, there *had* been a shark in the water that day. And my father wasn't keeping me safe anymore. He was long gone.

"Lynn? What do you want to do?"

I shrugged.

"Well, I don't want to call a truant officer, but if things don't change, I have to." He motioned with his hand to the circle of adults sitting around the table. "We all want to help, but you have to tell us what is going on. What you need."

My focus went back to the snag, which I had since torn all the way off with my teeth, leaving the tip of my thumbnail jagged and crooked. Mom blew her nose—not her usual allergy sniffles. I hated when she cried. Her crying reminded me of Dad walking out on us and her roaming the house, lost and despondent, for weeks. I was never letting myself become that weak and needy and helpless.

"Let us know what more we can do. Any of us," Mr. Justus said, in a tone that meant he was talking to Mom. To me, he said, "We all believe in you, Lynn. It's never too late to turn things around. And we're all on your side here. We want to help. You just have to let us know what you need."

The problem was I had no idea what I needed. I only knew that when I was straight, the old panic engulfed me, the sense that something bad would happen any day, and only drugs or alcohol could squelch it. When I was buzzed, the world was right, and I was beautiful and smart and funny. If one was good, a second drink could only make things better. With the third drink, I was effervescent with happiness. After the fourth or fifth drink, all that mattered was keeping the drinks coming to maintain the feeling that everything was almost perfect. That I was almost perfect. How could anyone help me with that problem?

On New Year's Eve, Mom took me to a party at her boyfriend, Bob's, house, because I was grounded for one or another offense and didn't trust leaving me home alone. Bob was boisterous and outspoken, irreverent even by my standards, and had only one leg —a result of the Vietnam war. He wore his wavy hair long enough that it looked almost unkempt, giving him a classic Italian look. Bob drank a lot of booze and often left half-full bottles of wine— "vino," as he called it—at our house. I liked him right away. Bob was a social worker at the psychiatric hospital where Mom worked, so there were a lot of their co-workers at the party. I wasn't expecting a party with a bunch of therapists to be much fun, but when I saw all the booze bottles scattered around the kitchen counter, I was suddenly glad Mom brought me.

Whenever the kitchen was empty, I sauntered in there to get a soda from the fridge, poured some into a coffee cup then filled the cup the rest of the way with booze. Each time I went, I poured more alcohol into my cup from different bottles, so I wouldn't noticeably drain any one of them. Not that anyone was paying attention; everyone was at least tipsy.

Late in the evening, I was smashed. Bob plopped down next to me. "I bet this wasn't your idea of a New Year's Eve party, huh? Sitting around with a bunch of old fogies. Are we boring you to tears?"

I shooed him away with my hand. "I'm havin' a blast."

He grabbed my coffee mug and sniffed it. "Sweet Jesus, child, what are you doing?" He scanned the room, then hollered over the music. "Linda, get over here. Your daughter's drinking my booze."

Her face grew red, she grabbed my arm and pulled me outside. I stumbled as she shoved me into our car. She stomped around to the driver's side, slammed the door and sped away.

"It's New Year's. C'mon. I only had a few."

"Don't even talk to me. I am disgusted with your behavior. Drinking! Right in front of all my co-workers."

"So? Everybody's drinking there!"

"But you're only fourteen!"

As soon as I opened my eyes in the morning, saliva flooded my mouth, and a wave of bile rose up from my stomach. I raced to the bathroom and hugged the toilet, heaving until my sides hurt. I told myself I was sick from drinking so many different kinds of booze. As I rinsed my mouth out and gargled with water, I overheard Mom murmuring into the phone downstairs. Any minute, I expected her to pound up the stairs, ranting. But she never said anything to me: no yelling, no threats, no demands. Her silence was unnerving.

A few days later, she sat both Rick and me down at the kitchen table for what she called a family meeting. I slumped into a chair and Rick stared out the sliding glass door.

Mom had her hands extended in front of her on the table, fingers laced. "I won't tolerate any more of your drug and alcohol abuse. There will be no more drinking or drugging while you live in my house. I pay the bills. I own the house. You follow my rules or you—"

"Oh yeah? I'd like to see you make me do that," Rick said.

Here we go, I thought. He just doesn't know when to shut up.

"I will. Next week. You're both going to juvenile court. I'm charging you with being unruly. You're both truant at school and breaking my house rules. You two are out of control, and I won't sit by any longer and watch you destroy your lives. I love you too much to do that."

Rick jumped up and knocked his chair over backward. "This is bullshit." He stormed toward the front door, while I sat there staring at her.

She yelled over her shoulder after him. "If you don't show up, the police will issue a warrant for your arrest. And you can't be in this house under the influence anymore. If you're drunk or stoned, don't come home."

The front door slammed, shaking the walls. Her gaze returned to me. "That goes for you too."

15

THE HONOR ROLL

*I*n a brief and to-the-point hearing, a judge sifted through several sheets of paper and informed Rick and me that we were to obey our mother and the court social worker assigned to our case—he gestured toward a thin young man wearing round wire-rimmed glasses (the type everyone was wearing since Lennon had been assassinated)—or we would be removed from our home. The judged peered over his desk at us. "Do you know what it means to be a ward of the court?"

I had absolutely no idea, but I was pretty sure he was going to tell me regardless of my response. I nodded.

Rick stared at the table in front of us, his arms crossed defiantly over his chest. "Yeah, I hear you."

The judge looked back and forth between us as he spoke. "It means that you're now under the control of this court. For the next year, I'm in charge of your well-being. We can do this while you're still living in your mother's home, if you cooperate. If you don't, you'll be taken out of the home and placed in the juvenile detention center. This court is now in charge of your lives. Do you understand?" He scrutinized Rick, who was still boring holes in the table with his eyes. "Young man, look at me."

With his arms still rigidly crossed, he glared up at the judge.

"If you can't live in your home and follow your mother's rules and the rules of the social worker I'm assigning to your case, then you will live in the juvenile detention center. Either way is fine with me. It's your choice. One violation, I don't care how small, and you'll be back here in front of me." He released his eye-lock on Rick and turned back toward me, raising his bushy gray eyebrows in question.

My instinct was to smile at him—not seductively but charmingly—but he was formal and gruff and seemed disinterested in me. I envisioned how Dad would have spoken to the judge during his trial, picturing the way he had always behaved during church—solemn, respectful and quiet. Church was about the only place Dad had ever been quiet. Keeping my face serious, I said, "Yes, sir."

He closed the two folders on his desk. "Okay then. I hope I don't see either of you in my courtroom again." He handed the slim folders to the social worker and gave Mom some instructions on regular contact with the social worker.

Determined to stay out of juvey, I didn't drink or do any drugs and started attending all my classes. Within a month, I brought my grades up to A's, except for a B in History and a C in French.

When I next saw Principal Justus in the lunchroom, my belly fluttered with anticipation, wondering if he was tracking my recent grades. The way he powered toward me, I was certain he had checked my grades. "I'm so proud of you," he said, giving me a high-five. He was so full of belief in me, I couldn't stop the grin from creeping onto my face. Mike, Christy, Denise and Jeff, who were sitting at the table with me, gawked at Mr. Justus. He scanned the table, taking in all their surprised looks. "At this rate," he pointed at me with his thumb, "she's going to be on the honor roll."

The words "honor roll" reverberated through my mind all afternoon. There weren't that many students at the school who were on honor roll each year, and he believed I could be one of them. That idea lodged in my brain like a small seed, tucked away in a dark corner, dormant.

The court-appointed social worker came to our house every few weeks to check on us. I was required to see an addiction counselor named Tom Donaghy. He was a stocky man with broad, beefy shoulders. His voice was gravelly, I assumed from many years of smoking, and he had a thick accent, from New York, I guessed. He told me about his own battle with drugs and alcohol and how he cleaned up and became a drug counselor. Everything I said in his office was confidential, he assured me, so I could tell him anything, but he didn't plan on taking any bullshit from me.

"Okaaay," I said.

"I don't like sarcasm either." He leaned back in his leather chair and trained his eyes on mine. "Why don't you tell me a little about your drinkin'. Your mom says you been getting into trouble for a few years now: truancy, B and E—"

"Trespassing. The breaking and entering charge was reduced."

"Fine. Trespassing. You still got arrested. Seems like drugs or booze are always involved when you get in trouble."

"I haven't used anything in a couple of weeks."

"How's that goin'?"

"So great. Lovin' the straight life."

He chuckled. "You miss it? Maybe wish you could get just a little buzz going?"

Oh, he had no idea. That was virtually *all* I had thought about the past few weeks. I shook my head and wedged my hands under my thighs.

"How long you been using?"

"Couple of years."

"Feel better when you're straight or loaded?"

I hunched my shoulders into a shrug and left them there, folding into myself, trying to shrink away. His questions drilled into me, into my core, like he already knew what I never told anyone. He sat there, waiting for a reply. "I don't know. Loaded, I guess. Doesn't everybody?"

He laughed out loud, a sound as raspy as his speech.

I glanced at him to see if he was laughing at me. Something in the smile spread across his face—that smile looked like it would crack his rough, dry skin—told me otherwise. Underneath his crackly laugh and his crusty exterior was softness and compassion. He knew what I was talking about, something I seldom experienced with an adult. And I was certain he was laughing because he knew that I knew everybody didn't feel better when they were tanked. If that was true, more than just a handful of my peers would be out getting loaded with the rest of us grits.

"No, everybody doesn't feel better high. Most folks like having clear minds. They don't like losing control. Alcoholics, we have different brains. When we start to feel that buzz, we want more of that feeling. That first drink or drug sets off a craving for another and another." He paused, watching me. "Sound familiar?"

I didn't like how he used the word "we" in that description. I glanced away.

"Is your drug and alcohol abuse—"

"You mean use?"

He shrugged. "Whatever. Is it causing any problems?"

"Not now."

"How about a month ago?"

"Maybe. My mom thinks it was."

"How about a year ago?"

I let my eyes roam around his office but could feel that his eyes stayed on me. "Guess it caused a few problems. Things are fine now."

"How come you're a ward of the court then?"

"That was my mom's doing."

"You didn't have any part in that? You're just an innocent victim here?"

Another shrug from me.

Tom got a lot of shrugs from me. Each week, he asked how things were going, and I told him everything was fine. At each appointment, he encouraged me to talk, but I barely spoke. Part of me wanted to blurt everything out, to tell him that when I was straight, I couldn't stand the bleakness of my life and the only time I came close to feeling normal—or what I suspected normal felt like—was when I was at least buzzed. Some part of me wanted to explain I had hooked up with Mark because he adored me and needed me, but his jealousy and possessiveness had become isolating, overwhelming and, at times, frightening. But I couldn't get the words out. None of them. Not to Tom or anyone. We had a few more sessions where I said nothing meaningful, and he sat at his desk and did paperwork.

During our last session, Tom invited my mom into the room. "I tried to get Lynn to talk, but she won't open up or be honest with me. She won't tell me what's goin' on. It's a waste of your money and my time seeing her week after week."

Mom turned to me with a sad, sobering look on her face then back to him. "Is there anything else I can do? Anything else I should try?"

"Make her go to some twelve-step meetings." He took a small booklet from his drawer, flipped through it circling some of the words with a pen and slid it across the desk to her. "Those are some of the meetings with more young people at them. She might meet some other kids in recovery." He tossed his hands up toward the ceiling. "Might help."

He looked at me, empathy showing through that crusty shell of his. "You can come back or call me when you're ready to get honest. With yourself and with me. I'll still be here."

As we left Tom's office, an intense feeling of being all alone in the world welled up in me. I hadn't had a drink or drug in a couple of months by then, the longest time since I had started using a few years earlier, and without any substances, I was unable to block the emotions that continually rose up in me, unbidden and unwelcome. I couldn't shake the sadness that Tom had given up on me, that I had blown my chance. *He was really cool. I should have talked to him.* Once again, I waited too long to jump in the ocean, and everybody was moving on without me.

And I had no clue where the sharks were anymore. I needed a drink, or a toke, or a pill, anything to shut down all these fucking feelings.

The court social-worker and Mom agreed with Tom's recommendation that I attend weekly twelve-step meetings. Twelve-step meetings were, in part, how I convinced Mom to let me hang out with Mark again. He could take me to the meetings, I had argued, I almost had straight As, and I had been behaving perfectly for two months. Mom probably suspected Mark and I were sneaking around seeing each other anyway and agreed he could come over when she was home, and I was allowed to go to his house when his mom was home. He still snuck over right after school sometimes so we could have sex, but I refrained from drinking, even though he was usually pounding down a six-pack right in front of me. That really sucked.

I talked Mark into going into the first recovery meeting with me. The room was packed, mostly with people my mom's age, sitting around tables, a haze of cigarette smoke collecting at the ceiling, drinking coffee from Styrofoam cups and talking about drinking and how to quit. Mark lasted about ten minutes before he leaned over and whispered. "I'm not listenin' to this bullshit. I'll be in the car." After that, he dropped me at the meetings and waited the hour in the parking lot. I never grasped how the meetings, or the twelve steps, were supposed to help a person quit drinking. Since I had zero interest in quitting, I never asked anyone either; I just ducked in as the meetings started and hurried out as they ended.

Over the next few months, I changed my behavior dramatically, going to twelve-step meetings, attending all my classes and pulling my grades up to straight A's. Being on the honor roll gave me a giddy feeling, as if I were about to be tickled. At first, I thought the feeling was vindication—proof that a grit could get straight As. But that giddiness persisted even after Mark dismissed with a wave of his hand my news of being on the honor roll. Later that evening, when Mom told me how proud she was of me, that feeling fizzed up in me again. I recognized then that what I was feeling was pride.

Sometime during the year I was a ward of the court, I started using again. As always, it started with one drink. Before I did my homework or studied or did chores—whatever it was—one drink would make the task easier and more fun. One beer or a few tokes always gave me some motivation, a little boost. If I chugged a drink straight down, one could even give me a slight buzz, lighten my mood, take the edge off any anxiety or self-consciousness. But I was vigilant about using only when certain I wouldn't get caught. I managed to walk the tightrope of using without getting busted for several months; no small achievement. It was like being on the partying honor roll.

For a year, I convinced the social worker that I was doing really well, convinced Mom I was obeying all her rules and remained on the honor roll (the academic one). By the end of tenth-grade, Mom and the social worker agreed to close my case. No more meetings, no more social worker. Free again.

SWEET SIXTEEN

*R*ick, who was now eighteen, had dropped out of high school and was now living with Vanessa and her daughter. The evening before my sixteenth birthday, Mark called and said he, Rick and Vanessa had a surprise for me. That was terrific because Mom had picked up a late shift at the hospital. In front of Rick's house, Mark and I picked our way across the wooden planks that spanned the mudholes and trenches in the driveway. Vanessa's daughter was napping in the bedroom, despite the music blaring from the stereo. We all four sat on the sofa, because there wasn't anywhere else to sit in their living room. The recliner was covered with wrinkled clothes—dirty or clean I couldn't tell—and the coffee table was piled with empty beer cans, ashtrays, rolling papers and a bag of weed. The rest of the room was cluttered with toddler toys and boxes from when Rick had moved in. The lower three feet of the walls had crayon markings scribbled on them.

The three of them sang "Happy Birthday," and Mark handed me a baggy with a dozen or so white pills stamped with "Lemmon 714" on them.

"Cool. Quaaludes. I love these things." I gave him a deep kiss, a promise of what would come later. He slid his hand down around my ass.

"Ah, come on you fuckin' love birds, save that shit for later," Rick said.

Rick passed beers around, and we each swallowed a Quaalude. After about thirty minutes, none of us were feeling any effects. Mark was bitching about the pills not being any good, how he'd gotten ripped off and was gonna kick some ass. As he paced around the living room, his eyes grew darker by the minute. His escalating anger twisted my insides up with anxiety. This could ruin my entire sixteenth birthday.

"Just relax," I said. "Let's take another one. Maybe these are just weaker than the last ones we got. There's plenty in there for us to all take another one."

Thirty minutes and a few beers later, the Quaaludes had kicked in. I was soaring. Giggling, I weaved my way to the bathroom. After peeing, I swayed in front of the toilet while trying to button my jeans. Forcing my droopy eyelids open wider, still the button came in and out of focus. Should've worn sweatpants, I thought. But I wanted to look nice for my party. A stab of sadness followed my next thought: some girls were taken out for fancy dinners by their fathers on their sixteenth birthdays. A flash of panic shot through me as I remembered Floyd was supposed to take me to dinner that evening.

I staggered back to the living room and steadied myself against the wall. "Shit! I was s'pose to meet Floyd for dinner."

Rick snickered. "Call 'im up. See if he wants some ludes."

Vanessa laughed loudly and clapped her hands. "Yeah. He can celebrate with us."

All three of them were slouched together, grinning and laughing, leaning onto each other. Then Rick stood and pointed at me. "Listen. Seriously. You can't go home now. You'll be *sooo* busted. Our uncle knows a stoned kid when he sees one. Trus' me." He flopped his fingers against his chest. "Then he'll tell Mom, and you'll be back in juvey or some tough love shit like that. Know what I'm sayin'?"

I went back to the bathroom, the only place where I could escape their taunting. There was no more soaring; I wanted to curl up on the cold, hard floor. I sat down on the toilet lid and cried. Quaaludes did that, either made me sad and forlorn or happy and horny. I had been hoping for the latter. I'm sure Mark was too. Someone rapped on the door. The last person I wanted to see was Rick, with his smirking, telling me he couldn't believe what a big baby I was still, or teasing me because I was afraid to face Floyd. Another rapping.

"Lemme in." It was Mark.

I unlocked the door and leaned against the counter.

He closed the door behind him. "I'll take you home if you want." Quaaludes made him so mellow and easy-going, which was always a nice change. In fact, they made him an almost ideal boyfriend.

On the way home, I made him pull over just in time for me to throw up. Some sweet sixteen, hanging out the car door and retching into the weeds.

When we pulled into the parking lot, I was stunned to see Floyd's car still sitting there in the driveway. Pretending I didn't see his car, I jogged into the house, figuring the faster I moved, the less obvious would be my staggering gait, and locked the door behind me. Upstairs, I curled up in my bed and pulled the covers over my head.

Sometime later, could have been minutes or hours, I regained a groggy consciousness to find Floyd sitting on the bed gently shaking me. "Are you okay? Lynn! Can you open your eyes and look at me?"

I forced my eyelids open, then let them flutter closed. The taste of vomit was still in my mouth. "Think I'm sick." I tried to articulate the words concisely, but my tongue was thick and slow, which is how my words came out.

"You're high, aren't you?"

I shook my head.

"What did you take? And how much? Can you tell me that?"

"Know what? I'm sixteen tomorrow."

"Tell me what you took."

Oh, what the hell, I'm busted anyway. "Ludes." I held up two fingers.

"Quaaludes?"

I nodded. "Two of 'em. An' some beer. Few beers."

I drifted into sleep again, coming in and out of consciousness, aware at some point of the murmur of voices, Mom's and Floyd's, down in the kitchen.

In the morning, I was resigned to whatever consequence Mom would give me but stayed in my room, not ready to face her and too hungover to even think about eating.

Around noon, Floyd called. "Hey there. How about we try that dinner again tonight?"

I felt a physical pang in my chest, a mix of shame and hope, and the pressure of tears behind my eyes and in my nose. "Really?" I couldn't believe he would give a fuck-up like me a second chance.

"Yes, really. How about six?"

"What should I wear?"

"Something nice. There's a fancy new restaurant I want to take you to."

Mom helped me pick out one of her silky polyester dresses, a silvery gray one, and black high heels to wear. I was giddy with excitement about my second chance at a sweet sixteen dinner, and about getting away with being loaded, though I kept waiting for the hammer to drop. As Mom helped me style my hair with a knot at the nape of my neck, she finally said, "I'm concerned that you're using drugs again."

I glanced at her in the mirror, but she didn't meet my gaze.

Her focus remained on pinning my hair twist in place with bobby pins. "It might be okay for some kids to use or drink, but you have a history. And so does your father. So, you're more likely to have an addictive personality. It's called a predisposition. And you've already had some pretty bad outcomes when you use. That's a sign of alcoholism or drug addiction. You know what I'm saying?"

"I know. I've heard this all before. But it's not fair. Other kids are experiment—"

"You've done plenty of experimenting already. I hope you don't start using drugs and acting out again. You know, your case can easily be reopened with the court."

She shielded my face with her left hand. "Okay, close your eyes." She blasted me with hairspray, then held up a hand mirror for me to see the knot at the back of my neck. "There. How's that look?"

The style was elegant and classy. "I love it. Thanks."

She smiled at me in the mirror. "You look beautiful."

When Floyd picked me up, he actually held out his arm for me and said it was an honor to take such a lovely young lady to dinner. His words sounded a little corny, but I could tell he meant them. I could not fathom what kept him from giving up on me. Maybe because he was like a father to me and that's what fathers did—loved their daughters no matter what. Some fathers. Mine hadn't contactĕd me in so long, I doubted he loved me, cared about me or even thought about me anymore. Where Dad was concerned, I had a blank space I could no longer fill with dreams or illusions or even hope. He had so completely evaporated from my life that I wasn't sure he had ever loved me. Believing in my dad required the kind of faith Grandpa had preached about—you can't see or hear Him, you just had to believe He was always present. That hadn't worked for me either. I had *had* it with invisible fathers!

I hooked my arm through Floyd's and let him escort me to his car. Halfway there, I realized why men gave women their arms on fancy occasions; those wobbly high heels were tricky as hell to walk in.

Over dinner at One Nation, a restaurant at the top of a

skyscraper building overlooking downtown Columbus, we talked about current events and my dreams for my future. When he asked about school, Floyd said, "I'm not sure you know this, but it's not easy at your school—it's one of the more rigorous ones in the area—to be on the honor roll." I wasn't aware of that and felt the flush of blood to my face. "If your grades for the next two years stay as good as they are now, you'll definitely have options for which universities you can attend. There are some great colleges here in Ohio, and if you stay in state, tuition will be much lower."

An image formed in my mind of me on a university campus, independent and confident, bopping around to classes and getting straight As.

"There's only one thing that can keep you out of college."

"What's that?"

"You."

You don't know Mark, I thought.

That conversation with Floyd gave me a sliver of hope that I could do something with my life. But the drugs and alcohol still called to me incessantly. They had a chokehold on me. I remained on the honor roll and continued to be cautious about when I used, while Mark's drug and alcohol use escalated. We argued about this, especially when we were drunk—big blowouts in which I cajoled him to slow down on the drinking, because I was trying to keep my shit together, so I didn't end up back in juvey, and he yelled at me to get off his back.

More and more, I drank alone in my room at night because it was more peaceful than drinking with Mark after school. Holed up in my room, I was less likely to get busted by Mom. And having my driver's license allowed me to be less reliant on Mark.

I took a babysitting job for a mother who worked nights at a local nursing home. The job got me out of the house and away from Mark, at least one evening a week. The lady's husband worked out of town every Wednesday, so they needed someone to sleep there with their child. When I arrived, the mother wore a robe over her scrubs, tucked her fourteen-month-old daughter into bed, slipped off her robe and drove the mile or so to work. If the baby woke, I was to call the mom, who would rush home to comfort her daughter and put her back to sleep. The whole process seemed complicated, but all I knew about children I had learned in a child development class.

That first night babysitting, I poked around in their cupboards, thrilled to find the cabinet above the stove stocked with alcohol, so I drank as much as I could out of several different bottles so none of the volumes looked lower. The next week, I drank out of different bottles, and the week after that went through the bottles again but added a little water to each one. When I decided to leave the bottles alone, I rummaged through their medicine cabinet and was ecstatic to find a full bottle of Darvon, pink and white painkillers I knew would get me plastered, especially with a shot or two of booze. The bottle was dated several months prior, so they probably wouldn't notice a few capsules missing. After finding those, I hardly needed to drink any of their alcohol.

There was not a peep from the toddler for two months. The first time I heard a whimpering from her room, I was jolted into the reality that I wasn't alone in that house. My next thought was that I was way too stoned on Darvons to call her mother, as I had been instructed to do. I paced back and forth in the living room, murmuring, "Please, please, go back to sleep." Her whimpers escalated into cries, and then her crib started rattling. I recalled my child development class and was certain a fourteen-month-old could stand and climb. Afraid she would climb out of her crib, I crept up the steps and peeked into her room. In the glow of the nightlight, I saw her standing in her crib, her face red and her cheeks glistening with tears.

"Hey there," I said, soothingly, hoping she didn't detect my panic. She took a quivering inhalation and stared at me. Smiling, I inched closer to her crib. "It's late sweetie, what are you doing up?" She smiled back at me, causing an unexpected warmth to spread through my chest. I patted her crib mattress, and to my great relief, she flopped down onto it and began sucking her thumb. *Thank you, thank you, thank you.* Releasing a silent, long breath, I covered her with a blanket and gently rubbed her back and watched her eyelids droop once, twice then stay closed.

I tiptoed downstairs and outside for a smoke. Running possible scenarios through my mind, I reassured myself a fourteen-month-old couldn't talk much yet, so she couldn't tell her mom what happened, but the image of her tiny body so soft and warm and delicate in that crib made my chest ache. As I waited for my pulse to return to normal, I listened through the open door behind me for any more sounds from upstairs. I crushed my cigarette out in the grass and took the butt inside to flush the evidence.

Once the toilet tank finished refilling, the entire house was quiet except for the hum of the refrigerator motor. I stared at the cabinet, knowing a couple of shots would relax me, but in that silence, I could not ignore the truth that was all around me. I was way too wasted to be responsible for a helpless baby.

In the morning, I told the mother I had to quit because I was having trouble keeping up with my schoolwork.

WHITE WEDDING

*T*here was no excuse for the stupid, grave mistake I made before my last year of high school. Early that summer, I was in the shower when I noticed my breasts were sore and swollen. I was frantic to remember when I last had a period but couldn't recall. Over the years, Mark and I had not been consistent about using birth control, though I was usually aware of when I was ovulating. And while Mark never refused to wear a condom, he never initiated the use of any birth control. Sometimes we were so shit-faced, we didn't take any precautions.

I drove to the grocery store and bought a pregnancy test. While I waited to see if the strip on the test would change colors, I sat on the toilet and begged the universe, and any gods in it, for the test to be negative. When that faint blue line appeared, I wedged my hands between my knees, willing away the result. *No, no, no. Please, no.* Rocking back and forth, I tried to force away this reality. That I had allowed this to happen was unforgiveable. I knew better.

Stuffing the test strip into the box it came in, I jogged outside and chucked it all in the dumpster. Back inside, I went to the bookcase and pulled out the *Physician's Desk Reference*. The word "miscarriage" wasn't listed in the index, only drug names and categories of drugs, no side effects. Next, I read about all the drugs I knew I could get my hands on. None of them listed miscarriage as a side effect. Some listed cardiac arrest, respiratory depression or death associated with overdose. Those words gave me pause. While I wanted a way out of my pregnancy, I didn't want to die. I scanned several more pages, reading about the side effects of drugs I had at least heard of and might be able to get my hands on. Nothing that would end the pregnancy.

When I broke the news to Mark that evening at his house, he was stunned. We both sat there in silence for a few minutes before he strode out to the front porch for a smoke. He tapped a cigarette partway out of his pack and offered it to me. I stared at the cigarette but didn't take it. He shook the pack at me.

"I shouldn't."

Blank look on his face.

I pointed at my abdomen. "I can't smoke anymore."

He slid the cigarette back into the pack. As I watched him take one long draw after another, I became more and more annoyed with his lack of concern for my—our—situation. He pinched his cigarette so forcefully and inhaled so deeply that the butt was collapsing, probably hot and damp and brown with tar and nicotine, by the time he flicked it into the yard. "Guess we're gettin' married."

A spike of fear shot through me as I envisioned my world closing in around me, becoming smaller and tighter as the years passed. That would mean no college for me, no bopping around on a university campus, no more straight As, no career in the sciences or the arts. Having a baby with Mark would bind me to him for life.

"I can't get married, I just turned seventeen. I have another year before I graduate from high school."

"So? We're gonna get married eventually anyways."

"Well, for one, Mom probably won't let me." This, I knew to be true. She had given up trying to keep me from seeing Mark, but I was certain she didn't think he was good for me. Her refusal to allow me to marry would allow me to stall for at least a year. "And you can't support a family on your job. You can't even afford your own apartment."

He frowned. "I'll get a better job. And you could drop out and get one too."

I looked down. My throat tightened so that I didn't think I would be able to say the words. "I want to go to college."

"Hah," he sniped. "That's it, isn't it? You'd rather go to college than marry me." He went back into the house, letting the screen door slam behind him.

You got that right.

The next several days were full of anguish as Mark refused to discuss our options or even acknowledge how upset I was. All he had to say was, "What's the big fuckin' deal? Let's get married and have this baby."

Knowing how damaging alcohol could be to a fetus, I refused to drink or take any drugs, despite Mark badgering me to have one drink or smoke a joint with him. I wanted nothing more than to get drunk, to escape into oblivion, but if I decided to give the baby up for adoption and it ended up with fetal alcohol syndrome, no one would take it. So, I was stuck feeling every-thing: confusion, anger, fear—lots of fear—disgust with myself, remorse. Many times, I contemplated telling Mom, but I wasn't sure what her opinions were on adoption or abortion. We had never talked about either, and I didn't want to disappoint her. She believed I was doing so well. I *had* been doing so well. Our home was peaceful with Rick gone and me concealing most of my using.

In the shower each day, I pushed on my uterus, praying for a miscarriage. Mark still wanted to party and have sex every time we were together. When I explained I had morning sickness, and not just in the morning, and tried to nudge him away, he didn't relent. His idea of a compromise was just having oral sex, or maybe since I was pregnant, he wondered if I wanted to try anal. Sex, in any form, was the last thing I wanted, but placating him with quickies or blowjobs—rarely could I talk him into a simple handjob—was easier than dealing with an eruption of his anger.

Two weeks after my positive pregnancy test, we were eating at Long John Silver's when Mark opened a small box containing an engagement ring. With a big smile spread across his face, the smile that I had loved so much when we first became a couple, he said, "I love you. Let's get married." It wasn't really a question.

As he slid the ring on my finger, everything in my body shrieked, *No!* But how could I turn him down without triggering his fury?

On the way home, Mark suggested we take a drive, which meant he wanted to go park somewhere and have me sit on his lap, because that's basically the easiest way a six-foot-tall man can comfortably fuck in the backseat of a car. Not exactly how I had visualized a romantic proposal of marriage.

Whenever I was at home, I took the ring off, and each time I saw Mark, I slid it back on. I kept this up for a few days until he came over when Mom was home. Trapped, I had to wear the ring but tried to keep my left hand out of Mom's sight.

After he left, Mom said, "What's that on your finger?"

I faked a smile, but it felt more sheepish than proud. "Mark gave it to me. He wants to, you know . . . get married . . . sometime."

She nodded. "Soon?"

"I want to go to college," I blurted.

"Well, you can go to college first. There's no hurry. To get married, I mean. Is there?"

"No. Not for me." My words hung there between us for a moment. *This is my chance. I should tell her now.* I could tell she was choosing her response.

"It's your life, you know. You don't have to do anything you don't want to."

The next afternoon, I looked up a pregnancy counseling center in the yellow pages and called to discuss my options. While I answered questions about when my last period had been, how old I was and whether my parents knew, Mark sulked at the picnic table on our back patio and chain smoked. When I hung up, I dropped my forehead into the palms of my hands, elbows on the table. I heard the sliding glass door open then close behind me.

"Well?" he said.

Leaning back in my chair, I scanned his face to assess his mood. I took a deep breath and exhaled it all at once, but the tension in my shoulders and neck would not release its clutch on me. All I wanted was to crawl in bed and crash. "We can give the baby up for adop—"

"No. No way." He shook his head, his lips pressed together in a hard line. I knew that if I birthed his baby, he would never let me give it away.

"Or we can have an abortion," I said.

Hypnotically, he stared at his pack of smokes, which he was slowly spinning on the table, round and round. "How much? For an abortion?"

"Two hundred dollars."

He shook his head again, slightly this time, his lips still in a tight line.

"We have to wait two more weeks, though. I have to be at least eight weeks pregnant before I can have the ... procedure." That seemed like a cruelty, to have to allow the embryo to continue growing in order to terminate the pregnancy, but that was the clinic's policy.

He nodded. "That's good, cuz I need a couple weeks to save up two hundred bucks."

I made an appointment for two weeks away. While I counted the days, full of dread and all the while wishing I would miscarry so I didn't have to terminate the pregnancy, I must have apologized to that baby a hundred times. Up until that point, I had never spoken to it or even thought of it as a baby. I had been reminding myself the embryo was only one-fourth of an inch long, hardly a person at all yet. But after deciding to terminate my pregnancy, the cold, hard reality became impossible to ignore. I told myself I could have children later when I was ready. In that scenario, the father was never Mark. Every night, I cried myself to sleep wondering if I was making the right decision. Sometimes, I wept silently; other nights, I cried hiccupy sobs, muffling them with my pillow so Mom wouldn't hear me.

Mark drove me to the clinic for our appointment. As I opened the car door, he sat there with the engine running. "What?" I asked, not wanting another argument, not there, not then. It would be hard enough for me to walk through those clinic doors.

He lifted his hip off the car seat and slid his wallet out of his back pocket. "I'm gonna go across the street and grab some lunch." He ticked his head in the direction of the Pizza Hut and slid some cash out of his wallet. "I wanna try one of those new personal pan pizzas."

"You're gonna eat a fucking pizza while I'm having an abortion? This is your baby too, you know." He kept his eyes on the cash then jiggled the wad. Snatching the money from his hand, I climbed out of the car without looking back.

As he drove past me, he said, "Be back after lunch. I'll wait here in the parking lot."

I didn't respond or even look back at him before entering the clinic. As I waited for the elevator door to open, I visualized turning and running out of the building. I imagined walking across the street to Pizza Hut and joining Mark for lunch; imagined joining him for the rest of my life. A cold fear cinched around my chest.

The elevator door slid open with a whisper, and I stepped through it.

In the recovery room, I vowed to that embryo I would do something with my life to make up for what I had done. I promised the baby who would never be that someday, somehow, someway I would help children. While I lay there, two other women were rolled in after their procedures. I curled up on my side, partly to relieve my cramping abdomen and partly to tune out their conversation as they began to babble about how relieved they were that it was over. For one of them, it was her second abortion! Having berated myself for weeks about how stupid I was to let this happen to me, I couldn't comprehend how or why someone would let this happen twice. The other woman said she felt free now that she was no longer pregnant. *Free? What the hell is wrong with these women?* Perplexed by her description, I searched my heart for any sense of freedom, but all that came remotely close was that I bought myself some time to postpone marrying Mark. In no way had I freed myself from his bondage. The engagement ring he had offered as a solution to our unplanned pregnancy now served as a glittery stranglehold. And I was certain I would never be free from the memory of my baby who would never be.

For months after the abortion, I moved through the motions of life as if underwater, plodding through the day, the world around me dull and deadened. I had no appetite and lived on peanut butter and jelly or grilled cheese sandwiches. Usually a big breakfast eater, the mere thought of eggs now caused me to gag. I told myself the nausea was residual morning sickness, but when it continued for a few weeks, I understood it was eating a chicken fetus I couldn't tolerate. Each morning, I lay in bed trying to think of a reason to get up. Some days, I lay in bed until an hour before Mom came home, then showered quickly, ate a sandwich and acted like I had been up all day. Sleep was all that provided escape from my reality. It was a better escape, even, than getting intoxicated, which was the only other activity I cared about.

Returning to school that fall filled my days and provided a welcome distraction from my grief and depression. Principal Justus and a few of my teachers amped up the pressure on me to apply to colleges. Flipping through brochures from various universities stirred a hungry curiosity in me. There was an entire world of subjects I could learn about and careers I could pursue. I broached the subject again with Mark by encouraging him to think about taking the GED and going to college. To my surprise, he told me about a gunsmith school in Colorado that he had looked into. If he went to a trade school, he might tolerate me going to a university. But that hope withered when he resumed his accusations that all I wanted to do was find other guys at college. The more we talked about college, the more agitated he became and the more suffocated I felt. College seemed to be my only way out of the shithole I was now in. And there was that promise I had made in the clinic recovery room a few months earlier.

Mark picked me up for lunch one afternoon from the grit pit. One glance at his face and I knew he was seething, probably because he noticed a couple of men standing in the group I was talking with. To avoid a scene, I hurried to his car and hopped in before he could get out. I never feared Mark would beat me up but knew he would thrash any man who he suspected was hitting on me. He peeled out of the parking lot, and my body bristled as I realized he was drunk.

As Mark sped down the road, Billy Idol's voice screamed in time with the hammering of "White Wedding," my eardrums pulsating along with the beat. I turned the radio down. "Slow the fuck down!" He glanced at me, jacked the radio back up and stomped on the gas pedal. "What the hell's wrong with you?" I yelled over the music. He stared ahead, fingers gripping the steering wheel. The straight part of the road was coming to an end. I pushed the radio off. "That's it. Slow down or let me out." No response. "Now! Let me out of this fucking car. Now!" I slammed my fist against the car door. "I'm not gonna get killed in this car because you're raging drunk."

He let off the gas some and turned into a sprawling park with roads winding through a dense maple forest. Mark was still driving way too fast, hugging the winding, hilly road.

"Pull over and talk to me. Please, Mark. Just pull the fuck over."

Finally, he pulled into a picnic area, took a big swig off the beer can that was shoved between his legs and lit a cigarette. I took the beer from his hand and drained it while he scrutinized me. Leaning over, I kissed him, but he refused to kiss me back.

"Was that one of your boyfriends you were talking to? That why you don't want to get married yet?"

"Not this shit again. You've gotta be kidding me. I'm so sick of your jealousy." I *was* attracted to Ronnie, one of the seniors I had been talking with when Mark had pulled up. But a guy had to be pretty brave to get close to me and a lunatic to flirt with me. That, or he had to not know Mark. None of these scenarios applied to Ronnie, but Mark couldn't tolerate me even talking to other guys anymore.

"Who was he?"

"Who? Who was *who*?"

"The guy you were flirting with."

I shook my head. "I have no idea who you're talking about. I was standing with a group of people, we were all talking, smoking. I wasn't flirting with anyone. I can't even talk to a man without you accusing me of flirting."

Mark flicked his butt out the window—he knew I hated when he did that, but this was one day I wasn't going to argue with him about littering—and popped open another beer.

"Can I have one?" I knew better than to try to convince him to lay off the drinking once he had started, but the more I drank, the less there was for him. He handed the beer to me, and I drank as much as I could before he took back the can.

"We've been together for years now. I don't even look at other men. What do I have to do to get you to chill out about this?" I sidled up next to him, but he remained rigid, unreachable.

He guzzled the rest of the beer and slammed the car into gear. The tires squealed around a corner and hit a patch of snowy slush, and the back tires skidded out from behind the car, jerking us into a spin. Everything moved in slow motion: the road to the left of us, the road out in front perpendicular to the car, the road to my right, a clump of trees in front of us and coming closer, then only one tree trunk.

I braced my hands against the dash and jammed my feet against the floor under the glove box as the car slammed into the tree with a THWACK! The impact snapped us forward, my forehead hitting the dash and Mark's nose cracking against the steering wheel.

He jumped out of the car, cupping his hands around his nose as blood began dripping between his fingers. "Goddamn it! Mother fucker!"

Steam was hissing and billowing from under the buckled hood. I stayed in the car and fingered the bump swelling on my forehead, calculating how long it would take me to walk back to school.

After pacing alongside the car for a few minutes, Mark jimmied the hood open, clinked around under it, then jammed the hood back down. Yanking the car door open, he climbed in but wouldn't look at me.

"I have to get back to school. Can you get me back there, or should I start walking?"

He turned the key and, amazingly, that smashed engine turned over. He drove back to school at the speed limit, stopping at a gas station to put water in the radiator. While I waited, I rotated the rearview mirror to examine the bump on my forehead. It was already bruising.

Everyone in the grit pit, including Ronnie, looked at us when he pulled into the lot. Mark stopped the car but didn't put it in park. I followed his gaze and saw him staring at Ronnie. The last thing I needed was for Mark to pick a fight. "You need to get your shit together," I said, slamming the door behind me.

*W*ithout telling Mark, I applied for admission to Ohio Wesleyan University, a small private liberal arts college driving distance from our condo. Mom thought this was a great idea and calculated she could afford the tuition, more easily if I received a scholarship. Otherwise, she could only afford Ohio State University. OSU was the second-largest university in the country, which sounded very intimidating. Since Art had always been my favorite subject, I applied for a scholarship from the Wesleyan Art Department. When I received a letter from one of the art faculty inviting me to meet and show him my portfolio—whatever that was—I was thrilled.

I asked Ms. Holt to help me prepare a portfolio. As she spread my drawings on a table, she was practically bouncing. "This is so exciting. Let's see." Sifting through them, she set a few aside. "These show your work in three different media. That would be good. Hmm. I think one more, four isn't too many." Patting her finger against her pursed lips, she surveyed my other pieces. She tapped another drawing. "This one. Your self-portrait. It's one of your best pieces and shows your skill, because charcoals are such an unforgiving medium."

"Isn't that a little, you know, um . . . self-centered, to include a self-portrait?"

"It's actually pretty brave. It shows you can look at it as art instead of as a portrait of yourself. Lots of artists, really famous ones, did self-portraits. Promise me you'll take it."

She had such a big grin, so full of pride for me, I couldn't resist her suggestion. "Okay, I'll take it." She stared at me with her hands on her hips. "I will. Promise."

In the professor's office, I fumbled to remove the portfolio from my backpack and hoped I didn't look as clumsy and unprofessional as I felt. He examined each piece while I described the media I had used to create them: a landscape in watercolor, an abstract in acrylic, and a still-life in oil. He commented on each, praising my work and also suggesting ways I could have improved them. I held my breath as he slid the still-life over, exposing the last piece, my self-portrait.

He studied it, glanced at me then back at the charcoal. "That's a powerful piece, very moody. This is an impressive portfolio. I'd like to have you attend here, and we offer a handful of scholarships each year. Not very large ones, but they do help with the tuition. Let me see what I can find for you." He smiled and stood to shake my hand. "We'll send you a letter with an official offer. Likely by the end of the month."

I practically floated to my car.

Wesleyan's offer of a $500-per-term scholarship arrived the same week as did a letter from Dad. At the mere sight of Dad's handwriting, that emptiness long associated with my father was flooded with emotion. I was elated he finally wrote, then a wave of anger crashed over me. This was the first correspondence I had received from him since he went to prison. Faster now came fury that he hadn't known, or cared to find out, how I was doing. He had no inkling what life had been like for me.

I ripped open the envelope.

Until then, I wasn't aware of how I had buttressed myself against this moment, how I had constructed a fortress around my heart. With the stroke of his pen, all my defenses crumbled.

He was getting out of prison and wanted to come for my graduation. Another emotion came then, a bubble of giddiness starting in my belly and expanding until pure joy radiated throughout my body.

My life was finally taking a turn for the better. I was going to college, and Dad was getting out of prison.

18

GRADUATING

a month after Dad was paroled from prison, he drove up from Miami for my graduation ceremony. On his way, he picked up my grandparents in North Carolina. It would just be the three of them he informed me, since Laura had divorced him earlier that year. Dad called when he arrived in town. "Lynn, is that you?"

My hand was sweaty against the phone. "Hey, Dad. How are you?"

"I'm good. Boy, you sure do sound like your mom."

I was shocked he even remembered what Mom sounded like. They hadn't talked in years. Of course, neither had we. "Yeah, people tell me that all the time."

"Well, we're here at Rick's, me and your grandparents. It's late though, so we'll just come over in the morning."

"Are you staying at Rick's while you're here?"

"I will, but not your grandparents. It's a little . . . well, there's no room for them here. I'll get 'em a hotel."

I knew exactly what he meant, that party house was no place for my sixty-five-year-old grandparents. "I could come over to Rick's now to see you."

He explained that by the time he settled Grandma and

Grandpa into a hotel and went back to Rick's, it would be late, so I shouldn't bother driving over there. Besides, he said, I hadn't seen him in five years, what was one more day?

That comment stung. Competition for his attention swelled in my chest. This was *my* graduation. "Okay. I'll just see you in the morning then." This was all too familiar, waiting for Dad to show up again.

The next morning, I found myself watching out front for him, another behavior so etched into my memory, I was transported right back to Miami. I was a little girl again. When I finally heard the doorknob turn, I was spinning with anticipation, excitement and a titch of dread.

"Where's my little sister?" Rick belted out.

The sound of Dad's laugh was glorious, but at the sight of him, my mouth went dry. His eyes were duller than I remembered, with gray shadows underneath, and his cheeks were slightly gaunt. I'm not sure what I was expecting for a forty-two-year-old man who had been in prison for years.

"There's my darlin'," Dad said, embracing me.

I never wanted to let go of him. The intensity of my desire should have been a warning. He had vanished from my life for years, and the moment he waltzed back through my door, I was clamoring for his love. I was defenseless. He tossed me about still, this way and that, and whichever way he was going, so was I.

Grandma's frown was droopier and the crease between Grandpa's brows much deeper than when I had seen them ten years earlier. I moved past Dad and hugged them both. She continued patting my back even as I hugged Grandpa, and I wasn't sure if she was nervous or just happy to see me, so I gave her a second hug.

Mom came down the steps and hugged my grandparents. The three of them stood there, rather formally, while Dad, Rick and I shuffled backwards to give everyone more room. As we opened that space, Mom and Dad came within clear shot of each other.

Dad leaned forward, ever so slightly, almost in a bow, some

sort of deference to Mom. "Linda, you look terrific. How are you?" This was the most formal and subtle I had ever seen him.

Mom flashed him a tight half-smile. "We're good. How about you?"

"Real happy to be here. And so proud of Lynn." He pursed his lips into a contemplative knot and nodded. "You sure did a great job of raising her."

Hah! If you only knew the hell I'd put Mom through.

Mom gestured for everyone to sit, and they did, Grandma with a grunt of relief. We all sat around making chit-chat for a while, then an awkward silence settled over the room.

"Hey. How 'bout I run to the store and get some shrimp? I can make scampi for lunch. It's a new recipe I make at the restaurant," Rick said.

"Great idea," Dad said, standing up. "I'll take you. Who wants to go?"

My grandparents said all they wanted to do was relax, because they were wiped out from the drive. Mom began flipping through the channels to find something they could watch on TV.

Dad pointed at me with his keys. "You coming?"

I stood and tugged down my cut-offs, hoping Grandma and Grandpa didn't notice how short they were, too short for a young Christian lady, which perhaps they thought I still was.

"Come on then." He jiggled his car keys. "Time's a wastin'."

Rick and I looked at each other. There between us, without a word, was the shared astonishment that Dad was back, just like that, bigger than life, acting like he'd never left.

At the grocery store, Dad said he had to find a restroom. He caught up with us as we stood in the checkout line. As we inched up to the register, Dad chatted up the cashier. "How you doin' there? These are my chillens, and my daughter's graduating tomorrow." Blood rushed to my cheeks.

The cashier smiled at all of us. "Well, congratulations."

"And my son's makin' us a gourmet lunch to celebrate." Dad pulled out his wallet. "What do I owe you, ma'am?"

"Twenty-two thirty-seven."

As Dad opened his wallet, Rick and I both took a peek at it. Lots of cash. We glanced at each other. Dad handed the cashier a twenty and a ten and moved towards the door. I grabbed the grocery bag.

"Here's your change, sir." She held out the bills as coins spit out of the change machine.

Over his shoulder, Dad waved her away. "Keep it."

She shook her head with the money still in her outstretched hand. "I can't." She wagged the bills at Dad's back. The next customers in line had moved up to the register, and the exit doors had slid open in front of Dad. Rick and I were poised between the cashier and Dad, who clearly was not coming back for his change. Rick plucked the money from her hand.

Back at the condo, Dad was more talkative than ever. He had always been boisterous, but this was different. He never stopped talking. While Rick and Mom rattled around in the kitchen preparing lunch, the rest of us sat in the living room. The TV was a welcome distraction for me, but Dad couldn't stay seated for more than ten minutes before he was up to change the channel, outside for a cigarette, into the bathroom or out to his truck.

Then he started in about being hungry. "Man, I am *starvin'*. When's that scampi gonna be done, Rick?"

"Starting the rice now," Rick hollered from the kitchen. "About half an hour."

"Can't wait that long. I'm starvin' out here!"

"Where are your manners?" Grandma swatted Dad's arm.

Dad flinched in mock pain, rubbing his arm and faking a painful wince. He leaned over toward me and whispered, "Where's your phone book?"

I pointed to the drawer of the corner table and, next thing I knew, he was flipping through the phone book and ordering a pizza.

Grandpa glanced over at Dad. "Isn't Rick making his new

recipe for us, something with shrimp? Why are you ordering a pizza?"

"A large pepperoni pizza," he said into the phone, waving his hand toward Grandpa, who went back to watching TV. Grandma clicked her tongue and shook her head.

Incredulous, I walked into the kitchen and bulged my eyes at Mom, raising my hands in the air, as Dad rattled off our house address. Rick kept his focus on the cutting board, chopping onions and looking furious.

Dad took a few bites out of one slice of pizza, offering pizza to everyone else. We all refused, saying we would wait for Rick's scampi. The entire pizza congealed in the box on the table, one slice partially eaten.

My excitement about seeing Dad was being replaced by disappointment. Another very familiar experience.

After the scampi, Dad said he had to run a quick errand. Then, returning an hour later, he sat down for a few minutes before announcing it was time to take my grandparents back to their hotel. The day was a whirlwind. I suspected he was using cocaine. Having gotten good at hiding my drug use over the past couple of years—I was mostly still on the partying honor roll—I was embarrassed to see Dad so obviously wired. And he was on parole!

The next day, Dad insisted on taking me shopping for a graduation present. As we inched along in rush-hour traffic, I tried to make conversation, chatting about my plans for college and my art scholarship. That sounded better than telling him about my arrest, my increasingly crazy boyfriend and my abortion. He wasn't being truthful either, because when I asked about his job, he said he was starting a car polishing company.

Sure you are.

When we arrived at the shopping mall, he excused himself to the restroom and came out clearing his throat. Cocaine for sure.

"I'll buy you anything you want, doesn't have to be clothes. How about a car? You want a Porsche? Corvette? Just name it. Let's go get you a car."

I recalled a sweet, dusty-rose convertible Mercedes I had seen around town that Mark always said he was going to buy me. (Though for my graduation he gave me a cookbook and an apron —his intentions for me were clear.) "You don't have to buy me a bunch of stuff. Definitely not a car. Mostly, I just want to hang out with you."

"We'll hang out while we shop, but I wanna buy you something special. This is a big deal, you finishing high school. Think you're the only one in our family that did. Except your mom."

Nothing I said would make him back off, like the day he had bought me the emerald and diamond earrings. He was a train barreling down the tracks, and all you could do was jump on or get the hell out of the way. Or get run over. "Well, you're not getting me a car. You already came all the way up here and brought Grandma and—"

"Oh, you have no idea how big a deal that was! Driving with your grandmother for eight hours is no small feat." He let out a laugh from deep in his belly. "I didn't think I was gonna make it."

I chuckled at his joke, but his disrespect for Grandma made me feel sorry for her. She was getting old and frail, and was always such a worrier, and here was her son, a convicted felon still using drugs—though I wasn't sure she knew any of that—making fun of her.

"Anyway, it's just good to see you. The best gift is you coming all the way up here. All I want is for you to, I don't know . . . just . . . be my dad."

"Well, I *am* your dad. Always will be." He rubbed his hands together briskly. "Now let's go shoppin'." He sniffed and cleared his throat again. There was no question why he was always "running to the restroom."

I was gripped by my old inability to reach Dad; his armor was impenetrable. I let him buy me a few inexpensive dresses and a nice camera case for the 35-mm that Mom and Floyd had bought me, then suggested he take me home.

When he dropped me off, I loped up the stairs to my bedroom

and slammed the door. A minute later, Mom tapped on the door before letting herself in. She sat down on the edge of my bed and placed her hand on my back, which got me crying. I hated how her sympathy opened up my floodgates, so I couldn't contain my sadness. She let me cry for a minute before saying, "It's your dad, isn't it? He's as bad as before he went to prison. Maybe worse."

I wiped my face with a t-shirt draped over the foot of my bed. "It's the same old shit. We don't have anything to say to each other, and all he wants to do is buy me stuff."

She nodded slightly. "You know, he loved you kids like crazy when you were little. If one of you got hurt, he couldn't stand to even look at your injury—and he was a cop, so he'd seen plenty of blood and busted up bodies. It was like he had a tender spot where you kids were concerned; he was so protective. He never drank or even smoked cigarettes in front of us. Never. Not until the divorce." She took her hand off my back, and we both sat there, staring at the floor. "Something in him changed, from the drugs, I think. He lost himself. He just doesn't know how to be a father anymore."

She nailed it. He hadn't been a father to me for a decade, and I was mad at myself for fantasizing, once again, that he would or could. Nothing I did captured his attention like when I was a young girl. Back then, he had been mine whenever I needed him, no matter what. Without either of us speaking a word, he always knew what I needed. Now, all we had in common was drug use, and I didn't have the guts to tell him about that. If he knew that I used too, we could at least be real with each other. Maybe then he'd let down this façade with me.

"You know, this isn't about you. It's his problem. He's all messed up."

I looked at a picture of Dad I always kept on my dresser. The photo had been taken at the police department and he wore plain clothes, so it would have been after he became an undercover agent. He was young and striking, his hazel eyes bright and clear.

In the photo, he is laughing naturally, like someone had just said or done something funny.

Mom glanced over her shoulder to see what I was looking at then back at me. "Try not to let him ruin your graduation."

That evening, when I watched Rick and Dad come into a crowded restaurant for my graduation dinner, they scanned the room before coming to our table. They avoided eye contact with all of us as much as possible, joked between themselves and hardly ate a thing. They were definitely using coke. I visualized them sharing this secret and could see how it bonded them to each other, which made me broil with jealousy. There they were, connected to each other again as if Dad hadn't been gone from our lives for the past decade, and there I was on the outside. And I wanted in.

19

NOT WHAT YOU WANT

*A*fter graduating from high school, I took a job at the psychiatric hospital where Mom worked, so I could bank some money for college. Co-workers told me how much I looked like my mom, asked how I liked working there and what I planned to study at college. I acted the bubbly soon-to-be college student, talking about my scholarship to study art and photography but was so hungover I was shaky. No one knew about my drinking, my depression or the fact that I was suffocating in a relationship with a man who probably had an antisocial personality disorder—I had looked up Mark's behavior in the *DSM-III*, a tome of a book that described every kind of crazy there was.

Turned out the hospital was a great place for a drunk fraud like me to work. There were dozens of buildings, most were large, old houses built over seventy-years earlier, scattered across a fifty-acre campus. A creek, bordered on both sides by old-growth maple and oak trees, meandered through the campus. Each building was geared toward the treatment of a specific type of patient: those with eating disorders, adolescents, outpatients, addicts, severely mentally ill. My job was to make three rounds per day to each building, picking up and delivering charts, paperwork and mail. Between rounds, I returned to my office to sort and stamp mail. Most of my time was spent walking around the grounds or alone in the mailroom so limited interaction with other staff unless I went to have a smoke in the break room. When the aftermath of the prior night's drinking was horrible, I closed the blinds in the mailroom, set an alarm and crashed under my desk during lunch.

All summer long, Mark harped on me to work full-time at the hospital so we could afford an apartment together. Unable to stall any longer, I finally told him I had enrolled for college that fall. He punched his fist right through the wall.

His mom marched in from the living room and looked at the hole. "What the hell is going on in here? This is *my* house. Get that wall fixed or you're *out* of here. For good this time. And I mean it."

He jutted his chest close to her face and stared down at her. "Mind your own fuckin' business."

"How dare you! This *is* my business. It's *my* house."

I wedged myself between them. "Mark, stop it!"

Pointing at the kitchen door, she said, "Get—out—of—here."

Mark shoved the screen door open so hard it slammed against the side of the house as he charged down the back steps.

His mom pulled the door shut. "What's gotten into him this time?"

I dropped into a kitchen chair. "College. I'm going to college."

She sat down across from me. "All of this," she swirled her hand around in a circle around us, "because you're going to college?"

I nodded.

She shook her head, looking more exhausted than angry. "I just don't know what to do with him anymore."

"Me neither."

Right after I started college in September, Mark moved into his own apartment. He wanted me to stay over there, but I made excuses: I had to study or his place was too far from the university for my early-morning class. Being in college and working gave me a sense of freedom, as if I were about to soar. Everything about Mark was a tether. The more I pulled away, the more hostile he became. Each day before I walked onto campus, I removed my engagement ring and left it in the cup holder of my car.

I tried to keep up my grades but was so thrilled to be invited to parties, I couldn't resist. The first one was at a fraternity. I went without telling Mark. The next day, he launched into a tirade about my whereabouts, refusing to believe I had been with a few women from one of my classes. The second time I stole away to a party at the same fraternity, the quarterback of the football team came on to me, and he was persuasive. He wasn't a big man but had clearly been an athlete for years, with a trim, muscular build and a great ass. He was good-looking in that clean-cut way, but he didn't drink in a clean-cut way, he drank like me. After rolling around with him on a tattered couch in the back of a crowded room, music blasting from a stereo, he hollered that we should go up to his room where we could hear each other. I was torn. We hadn't been talking, so there was no need to go to his room to "hear" each other. I knew what he wanted. He could have any woman he wanted, and he was interested in *me*. Me, who had only been with a carnie and crazy Mark. I could have this all-American football player though probably not for long, perhaps only for the night. But having him placed me in the same league with the other college women, the beautiful ones who were self-possessed and poised. But then there was Mark, always Mark. I felt guilty making out with the quarterback, but my predominant feeling was fear. Fear of what Mark would do to this poor guy if he found out about him. I stayed out of his room.

Then I met Dave who worked on the grounds crew at the hospital, and my desire to leave Mark became pressing. He was several years older than me, confident, but not cocky like the quarterback, just sure of himself. Dave had played basketball when he was in college and had that lanky swagger that basketball players have, like my father had. When he invited me to come watch him play at a local pick-up game, all I could think of was

Mark finding out. My fear felt like a clamp squeezing around my chest. I told him I had a big test to study for and asked for a raincheck.

Every time I saw Dave at work, I wondered what it would be like to have a mellow boyfriend like him. He seemed so normal, maybe dating him would make *me* normal. It wouldn't erase my arrest, my having been a ward of the court, my abortion, but if I was in a healthy relationship, I could leave all that behind me. I would always remember the baby who was never to be, but maybe I could erase everything else.

At Mark's apartment one Saturday, after we plowed our way through most of a pint of whiskey, I mustered enough courage to tell him I wanted to try being just friends for a while. When I slipped the engagement ring off my finger and set it on the coffee table, his face went rigid.

"Let's just see how it feels," I said. "Maybe things'll work out if we take a little break. Maybe you could check out that gun school in Colorado."

"Four years we been together. I thought we were gettin' married. Thought you loved me. What the fuck is happening? You met someone else, didn't you? I fuckin' knew this was gonna happen."

"No. There's no one else. I just want to cool it for a bit."

"Am I too stupid for you now that you're in college?"

"Of course not. All I'm saying is I want to take a break. College classes demand a lot of my time and attention. So does work."

He took several long drinks of whiskey, and, as his eyes grew glassy and dark, I regretted drinking hard alcohol with him. I knew better. Then he started pacing between the two rooms of his apartment saying, "Four years. Four fuckin' years. Gone. Like it was nothin'."

I sat on his threadbare sofa and smoked a cigarette while he ranted. He sat down next to me, looked over at me for a few seconds, jumped back up and stomped to the bedroom. I was thinking of how to exit the apartment without agitating him further when I heard the pop and shatter of glass in his bedroom.

"Mother fuck!" he yelled. I lurched into the bedroom to see him standing in front of a busted TV screen, his hand in the air with blood streaming down his arm and dripping off his elbow. He pushed past me and locked himself in the bathroom.

Over his cursing, I could hear the water running in the sink. With all the blood I had seen running down his arm, I was afraid he'd cut an artery in his wrist. *Shit! He's gonna let himself bleed to death in there.* "C'mon, Mark. Come out and let me see it. If it's bad, I'm taking you to the ER."

"Fuck off."

I glanced over at the front door of the apartment then at the bathroom door, but before I could decide what to do, he jerked the door open. One look at the rage bulging in his eyes, and I knew instantly I should have left.

Adrenaline, like a current of electricity, shot through my arms and legs. I darted to the front door, but he beat me to it and leaned against it with his left hand. Still, I tugged on the doorknob. His right hand was wrapped in a bloody rag, but he grabbed my arm with it and pulled me into the bedroom.

"This is not what you want, Mark. You know it isn't."

"Shut up. You don't know what the fuck I want." He shoved me on the bed and yanked my pants off. Out of the corner of my eye, I could see his sawed-off shotgun where he kept it every night, propped in the corner of the room near the headboard, easily within his reach. He stood between me and the door, dropped his pants and rubbed himself to an erection with petroleum jelly.

"This isn't what you want," I said, as he spread my legs and climbed on top of me. I looked at the shotgun while he began thrusting himself inside me. Over and over, I repeated that this wasn't what he wanted.

"Oh, yes, it is," he said, pumping hard and fast against me, smashing his pubic bone against mine. With a final plunge, he ejaculated then pushed himself off me.

"You're right. *This* is what I want." He grabbed the shotgun, shoved the butt into my hands and the barrel under his jaw. "This is what I want. Pull it! Pull the fuckin' trigger!"

My body, previously numb, now vibrated with fear. "No! Stop it. Put it down." Then the memory of Dad's voice was there, like a breath in my ears, steady, serious and calm, telling me to never point a gun at anyone unless I planned on shooting them. *If I don't shoot him, he's gonna blow* my *brains out.* There was the memory of Dad's hands now, warm and solid and big around mine, his finger on the trigger right below mine. My eyes flicked down to the trigger of the shotgun, and my body grew hot, my heart pumping so hard that my pulse throbbed against my temples.

"Pull the fuckin' trigger! Put me out of my goddamn misery. Just pull it!"

With the short distance of the sawed-off shotgun between our faces, everything around me disappeared: the walls of the room, the reek of his perspiration, the sound of his breathing, the sour whiskey on his breath. Dad was gone too. All I was aware of now were Mark's eyes glaring at me, pinning me there, in pure madness. Not anger, but true madness.

Then he blinked. As his eyes reopened, in that first flash of seeing them again, I recognized this was not madness. It was fear. The fear of a trapped, wild animal.

"Mark. Listen to me. It's me, Lynn. Please. Put—it—down."

He snatched the gun away from me and thundered out of the apartment.

The room rushed back into focus, and I was now hyperaware of everything: the sound of the front door being opened but not shut, my pants at the foot of the bed, the shards of glass in front of the TV. My body screamed into motion. I pulled on my pants and grabbed my purse, digging for my car keys. The door to his apartment was ajar. I peeked out, checking up and down the walkway. As I ran toward the parking lot, my brain was buzzing, listening and scanning for any sign of him. *He's out here somewhere. I should hide. No, no. Get as far away as possible. Fast.*

As I reached for the door handle of my car, I saw his silhouette at the other end of the parking lot. He was moving toward me, his shotgun swinging by his side. Every nerve in my body prickled as I dropped into the driver's seat, locked my door, turned the keys in the ignition. I looked over my shoulder as I shoved the gear stick into reverse, certain that he would appear right next to my car, or I would hear the shotgun go off. Sweat trickled down my sides. As I backed out of the parking space, I saw him closing in on me. Jamming the car into drive, I floored the gas pedal and watched his dark shape grow more distant in my rearview mirror.

His screaming voice trailed after me, "I hate you, you fuckin' baby killer."

One last stab where he knew it would hurt the most.

When I got home, Mom took one look at me, and said, "What's wrong?"

"I broke up with Mark."

She reached behind me and locked the deadbolt.

I slumped into a chair and released a long sigh. "He lost it. Went berserk. Threatened to kill himself."

Holding up her finger to indicate she would be right back, she went to the kitchen. I heard her wedge the two-by-four into the track between the sliding door and the jamb. She knew him better than I realized.

Sitting down next to me, she said, "Did he hurt you? Are you okay?"

Such a simple question. But how to answer it? I was okay, physically. I was still alive. And after what he had done to me, he would surely stay away from me now. Even if I didn't press any charges—and I wouldn't, because it would be my word against his, and what proof did I have?—this rape would always be hanging over his head. He had crossed the line in his rage this time. Maybe now he would leave me alone. As each day would go by and he wasn't approached by the police, the more incentive he would have to stay away from me. Hopefully forever. The realization sank in through my jangled nerves and racing thoughts that this was my way out.

"Yeah. I'm okay."

For months, I numbed myself with alcohol and steered clear of men. I was as disconnected and lost as the day I had learned my father was never coming home. Over the previous few years, my life had narrowed to just Mark and getting wasted. Now all that remained was getting wasted. But I couldn't drink enough to erase the loneliness and isolation engulfing me. I had long ago dropped all my female friends; I wasn't even sure how to make friends with women anymore. As far as women were concerned, I couldn't navigate the fierce competitiveness I sensed from them or the even stronger sense I had that most women didn't like me. Until I met Jenny.

I arrived late to campus with a hangover and opted not to go to my first class rather than walk in thirty minutes late. In the back of the building on the third floor was a restroom, seldom used by anyone, that had become my regular hangout when I skipped a class, which I did more and more often. There was a small sitting area with two pink Naugahyde-and-chrome chairs, a rickety end-table between them and a clunky, green glass ashtray, all from the 1950s. Right as I sank into one of the chairs, the door whooshed open. In walked a woman with wide brown eyes, long eyelashes and pouty, full lips—cute, without a speck of make-up. She had a head full of loose natural curls; no permanent could give a woman curls that soft and relaxed.

She plopped down in the other chair. "You skipping class too?"

"Yeah. Didn't want to walk in this late."

She lit a cigarette and blew out a puff of smoke. "I know, it's so embarrassing. If I walked into philosophy class this late, my teacher would stop talking and stare at me 'til I found a seat. Just to embarrass me, you know?"

I nodded, intensifying the throbbing in my temples.

"What class are you supposed to be in?"

"Algebra."

"Brutal. Algebra at nine in the morning."

"Tell me about it. I'm flunking it anyways." Gingerly, I leaned over to dig my smokes out of my backpack.

"I'm avoiding math classes for now. For as long as I can. My dad's an engineer, so he wants me to take math, but I suck at it." She watched me for a few seconds. "Hey, you okay?" I'm sure I looked like shit, despite the concealer I stroked under my eyes that morning. "You're moving a little slow over there."

"I've got the worst headache."

She stubbed out her cigarette in the '50's ashtray, pulled a bottle of aspirin from her backpack and gave me two of them. "I carry them 'cause I get super bad cramps when I'm on my period."

I had already taken two Tylenols that morning, but they weren't working, so I took the aspirin from her. As I cupped my hand under the running water and washed down the pills, she rattled on about her classes, told me her name was Jenny and was so disarming I was swept along in the conversation, swept along in the current of bubbly, sparkly water that she was.

We exchanged phone numbers before leaving for our next classes. I had no intention of calling her, but to my surprise, Jenny called me that weekend and invited me to a local bar with some of her friends. After that, I began calling her every weekend to see what her plans were and usually tagged along wherever she went. Jenny was feisty and outspoken, but what fascinated me most was that she was indifferent as to whether a man liked her, approved of her or was even attracted to her. After meeting her dad, I understood exactly why she didn't need the attention of men; she had all she needed. Her father adored her. The easy love that flowed between them roused in me a longing so intense I could have buckled over right there in their posh, cozy living room from the pain of it.

And Jenny's relationships with her mother and younger sister were downright affectionate, hugging hello and good-bye, sitting close to each other, propping their feet on each other's laps. Once, I saw Jenny reach over and brush her sister's hair out of her face, then she left her hand resting there on her sister's shoulder for a couple minutes. It was such an intimate and tender gesture, I had to look away. She had friendships like that, warm and natural, with other women too. The only closeness I had experienced with a female that was even remotely similar was with Diana, but we had been little girls, so that hardly counted.

That winter, Jenny and I decided to rent a place together and found a cheap, two-story apartment a few miles from campus. We scrounged a worn loveseat and chair—matching tweedy brown and orange plaid fabric—a coffee table, a boom box and a small TV with a pretty decent picture. Later, we found a kitchen table and two chairs by the dumpster and dragged them inside. My room contained a waterbed a co-worker had given me and a flimsy plastic bookcase I had found at a thrift store.

No longer needing to hide my alcohol use from Mom, I kept myself saturated, often waking in the morning with a screaming headache and too nauseated to eat until the afternoon. Many mornings, I promised myself I wouldn't drink again, but as soon as a hangover loosened its grip—usually by noon—I would tell myself I simply needed to drink less or more slowly. By dinner, I would convince myself I could have a beer. One beer. I would plan to go to some event on campus, or jogging, or to the gym after dinner. Sometimes I even threw away my smokes. Despite my best intentions, that first drink always led to another and another, and the next thing I knew, I was staggering out of a bar at closing time.

I began seeking the attention of men again, very selectively. First, I set my sights on grounds crew Dave. After the volatility of Mark, he was a reprieve. He was predictable and showed little emotion. I went to a few of his basketball games, we went out for drinks then, eventually, just hung out at his apartment. There, we watched sports on TV, ate dinner, drank a lot of beer and had sex; many evenings, all four occurred right there on his living room sofa. And he kept up with my drinking, so I didn't have to hide how much alcohol I consumed each evening.

Dave and I lasted several months, most of our time together a blur of heavy, uneventful drinking. After that, I went out with a tender-hearted, deep-thinking philosophy major, and later, a psychiatric technician from the hospital. I struggled to feel close to any of these men. Even when I pretended to, I couldn't genuinely connect with them. And I rarely spent the night with any of them —I simply couldn't fall asleep with a man lying in bed next to me. I kept expecting to feel the tug of love or even the domesticity I had with Mark, but all I experienced was a compulsion to make myself irresistible to whatever man was on my radar. Anything to prevent me from feeling worthless. When a man wanted me, the world was mine again, and I was whole. Invariably, I'd walk away from these men, either because a man wanted to know more about me than I was able to share or hiding my drinking and drugging required too much effort.

The more I drank, the more often I had snatches of an evening I couldn't remember. I dreaded awaking with a blank spot about what I had done the night before. There was no way to know if I had done something degrading or dangerous during one of these blackouts unless someone who had been with me told me. I never asked; it was too demoralizing to acknowledge I couldn't remember an evening.

Once, I came out of a blackout in the middle of a street screaming at Alex, with whom I had been drinking shots of tequila all evening. I had met Alex a few weeks earlier in a photography class for which he was the graduate teaching assistant. He wanted to photograph me, saying he had to capture those eyes of mine. I brushed off his idea but had drinks with him a few times. His persistence about photographing my "bedroom eyes" began to border on obsessive, which had set off a tiny alarm in the back of my mind. When my blackout ended with me standing on High Street, I was immediately aware of Alex's hand gripped around my upper arm. My arm hurt where he was holding on to it, and my skin twisted painfully as I writhed to get away from his grip. He was tugging, pulling me somewhere, and I was screaming, "Please! Please! Don't. Don't touch me."

Alex released my arm and held his hands up in front of him in surrender. "Jesus! Calm down. I'm trying to get you out of the street." He looked up and down the road.

Trying to clear my head, I saw that we were standing in the middle of the street, which was deserted. I was dizzy-drunk, my head swimming, and nothing made sense—how we ended up in the street, why I was screaming at him, why I was clammy, why my heart was hammering in my ears. Once on the sidewalk, I wished a car *would* drive by so I wouldn't be out there in the dark alone with him. A diffuse fear spread through my body, energizing me, compelling me to run, but I knew he would chase after me. "I gotta get home. Where's my car?"

"It's at my house but you can't drive like this. You're shit-faced. You can just stay at my place."

I picked up the pace, walking as quickly as I could without running. He kept up but didn't touch me again. As I was settling into my car, he said, "Just stay. Please. You can crash on the couch. Or I can. I just don't think you should drive."

I began backing out of his driveway. It was all I could do to not slam my foot down on the gas pedal. Not until I drove away did my heartrate slow to the point that I was no longer conscious of it pounding in my chest.

Alex and I never went out again. I was never comfortable with him, and I imagine I scared him. At least my drinking did. Hell, my drinking was starting to scare me.

20

A LONG, WHITE LINE

One evening, Rick invited me over to get high. He and Vanessa were already strung out when I arrived. I was grateful her toddler was in bed. Though I had always loved being around little kids, after my abortion, being around them was always a buzz-killer.

Vanessa's tongue roamed incessantly about her lips and mouth, and she chattered without ceasing. On their peeling wood-veneer table was a sandwich-sized Ziploc bag bulging with cocaine. But this wasn't the uniform white powder I had seen before. It was a dense, crusty cocaine, off-white, almost pinkish in color, and the larger chunks were flaky and glinting. Next to an overflowing ashtray was an assortment of paraphernalia: a glass pipe, its bowl darkened with brown residue; a couple of wide soup spoons that were blackened on the bottoms; a few lighters; a small knife; a box of toothpicks; and a box of baking soda. Having once freebased cocaine with a neighbor, I knew what they were doing.

"Want a hit?" Vanessa asked.

"Sure, but I don't have any money."

"Don't worry about it." He pointed at the baggie. "We got plenty."

They rarely had cocaine. None of us did because it was too expensive. They most certainly couldn't afford *that* much. "You're getting this from Dad, aren't you?"

He looked directly at me. "Yep. We're in business together now."

"Business?"

"Uh-huh. I'm distributing for him." He held the flame of his lighter over the bulbous bowl of a glass pipe while Vanessa gently inhaled, the crack vaporizing into the pipe stem.

"How is Dad dealing when he's—"

"He ain't dealin'. He's smuggling. Big time. He's movin' like fifteen, twenty kilos a month."

"How? I thought he was on parole?"

Rick pumped his head up and down. "He is! You wanna know how he does it? He's got *balls*. That, or he's got ice water in his veins."

With a credit card, he chopped at a small pile of cocaine, mixed in a big pinch of baking soda, scooped up some of the mixture with the corner of the credit card and carefully tapped it into a spoon. He held the spoon toward Vanessa. She squeezed water from an eye dropper into the spoon, and we all watched as she swept the flame from a lighter back and forth under the spoon until the liquid simmered. When oily blobs formed on the surface of the liquid, Rick carefully rested the spoon on the coffee table. While the spoon was cooling, he explained how Dad had flown up to Ohio recently with a couple of bags of blow taped to his chest. "Man, he walked right through security at the Miami International airport like that. Then he turned around with a briefcase full of thousands of dollars in cash and walked right back through security at the airport here. He's got a fake ID, so his parole officer won't find out."

Rick swirled the tip of a knife through the globs floating in the spoon until they coalesced into one mass. He lifted the mass that was clinging to the knife out of the liquid. Mesmerized by the process of cooking down the cocaine and the story he had been telling me, I didn't notice Rick holding the pipe out for me until he jiggled it.

"Go for it, li'l sis. Don't suck on it hard like a bong hit though, or toke on it like a joint, just breathe in slow and steady."

"I know."

"What do you mean, you know? You tellin' me you freebased before?"

I nodded.

"No fuckin' way. When? With who?"

I so seldom impressed Rick that I couldn't stop the smile from spreading across my face. "I don't know, like a year ago. With Jack. Remember him? Our neighbor's grandson?"

He held the lighter over the rock of cocaine in the pipe. "I can't believe my little sister freebased before I did. You believe that shit, Nessa?"

The nugget of crack turned into a pungent, slightly medicinal tasting vapor as I slowly pulled it into my lungs and held it as long as I could. Rick and Vanessa leaned back, watching me, grinning. Within seconds, a pure bliss radiated to every part of my body, warm, swelling and building like that moment right before orgasm. Everything in my world fell into place, perfectly, and I imagined my mind would explode if my life got any better. "Whoa, this stuff is amazing."

"Tell me about it," he said.

"Too bad it doesn't last longer," Vanessa said, reaching for the pipe.

"Dad's stuff is uncut. Straight from Colombia."

We sipped on beers and smoked cigarettes, and Rick air-strummed a pretend guitar along with Lynyrd Skynyrd. When the song ended, he jumped up to change the album.

"Stevie Nicks," Vanessa said.

"And not so loud," I added.

"The chicks want to hear some chick music. Alright. Alright." He made a downward pumping motion with his hands, like he was quelling the crowds. He looked so much like Dad making that gesture. A thread of connection stretched between us, stretched from me to Rick to Dad—a long thin white line connecting us all. We were family again. I was glowing with our camaraderie.

"Good shit, ain't it?" he asked.

"I love it. It's the perfect high."

"This stuff is almost pure cocaine. When I cook up a gram, I get point-nine-seven grams freebase. When you cook it up, you can tell how much cut is in it by what's left in the spoon. Best shit you'll find anywhere. It's a drag when you come down, though. Feel even worse than before. Not as bad as grinding off acid, but you want another hit. Bad. And soon."

"Yeah, but we got plenty," Vanessa said.

"We gotta sell that," he said, pointing at the bag. "Can't cook it all up."

After thirty minutes, my burst of elation started to dissipate, leaving in its place a frantic need for more. *I can't be a leech and ask for another hit. Wait, this is my* brother, *I can ask him. No, I should leave, but they might offer me another hit.* Watching each of them smoke another hit made me desperate and painfully aware I was sitting there waiting, watching and not speaking.

I was about to split when Vanessa said, "Give Lynn another hit."

"Want one?" he asked.

"Well, I don't want to sponge off you guys . . . and I don't have any money"

"Go on." He handed the loaded pipe to me again. "Like Nessa said, we got plenty."

My intestines cramped with anticipation. As I smoked that rock, euphoria spread through me again, and with it the warm glow of being attached to my family once more. I was cool enough to be let in on this secret, to be sharing our dad's cocaine. Life could only get better, and at long last, I could see a clear path back to Dad. "How'd all this start with you and Dad? With you selling his stuff up here?"

Rick shrugged. "When he was up for your graduation, I told him I was dealing a little marijuana for extra money. Said he didn't much care for pot, but if I was interested in making some real money, he could set me up. So, we kept talkin'. I pulled together some people and some money, and we got some of his stuff delivered up here."

"He didn't offer me any coke when I saw him."

"Ah Lynnie, he don't even know you do drugs. He thinks you're a goody two-shoes, in college and everything."

"Hah! My grades are so bad I'm about to get kicked out of college. So, Dad doesn't know about my partying? About my being arrested? None of that?"

"Nah. Mom never told Dad any of that. He was in prison. They didn't exactly write to each other, you know."

"I don't care if you tell him about me."

"I ain't telling him. *You* tell him."

***

When Jenny invited me to spend a week at her parent's time-share condominium in Naples, Florida—without her parents—I immediately thought of stopping by to see Dad. She agreed to a quick detour through Miami to visit him, saying it would be fun to meet my father and see where I grew up. Yes, fun. If nothing else, Dad could be fun. He could also be unreliable. Most likely, he wouldn't be home when we got there, or if he was, he would be flying on cocaine, enough that Jenny would notice. Angst about swinging by Miami welled up in me then receded as my reverie of connecting with Dad around cocaine resurfaced. I was being tossed about by Dad, and I hadn't even seen him yet. But this was my chance to let him see the real me. If I shared that part of myself, I was certain we could be close again.

Jenny and I drove the seventeen hours to Miami straight through the night. I had a Kodak film can full of cocaine that Rick had given me, though I told her I bought it from a guy on campus as a special treat for our trip. With Dad on parole, I wasn't about to tell anyone our family secret. When we became drowsy, we snorted a pinch and drove on. The day was growing warm when we reached Jacksonville, so we folded down the top of her convertible. When "Walking on Sunshine" played on the radio, we cranked up the volume and sang along. The balmy air, the coconut trees, the anticipation of seeing Dad and the cocaine made it seem like I *was* walking on that Florida sunshine.

When we arrived in Miami that afternoon, we couldn't find Dad's apartment. Having driven and used coke all night, I couldn't make sense of the directions I had scribbled on a scrap of paper, so I called him from a payphone and was relieved he was actually home.

"Hey, Dad. It's me."

"Thought you were coming to my place?"

"We are, but I can't find it."

"Where are you?"

"At the Seven-Eleven store on Highway One."

"You're close. Wait right there. Be there in five."

When I returned to the car, Jenny was dozing in the passenger seat. I scooted into the driver's seat and checked my reflection in the rearview mirror. My eyes were all pupils, hardly any green. I brushed my hair and popped a stick of gum in my mouth.

Dad pulled up in a brand-new red Mustang and hopped out grinning, arms opened wide. How I wanted to jump into his outstretched arms like I had as a child but instead took a few halting steps toward him. We hugged each other briefly, and I introduced him to Jenny, who had groggily stepped out of the car, eyelids heavy with exhaustion.

"You forget how to get around in Miami?" he asked.

"Dad, I was twelve when we moved out of Miami."

"Oh, right. You weren't drivin' then." He chuckled. "Well, follow me."

When we walked into his apartment, a woman named Suzy

greeted us. She wore a heavenly, rich, musky perfume, of which I kept trying to catch another whiff, and a shimmery gold-colored pantsuit. One glance around his apartment and I knew he was making good money. Car polishing company my ass, I thought. The apartment was fully furnished with lots of chrome and glass and leather. Suzy showed us to a spare bedroom where a dark, wooden four-post bed was made up with a bedspread and several throw pillows of different shapes all in complementary patterns and colors.

Back downstairs, Dad sat in the living room having a smoke. "How long can you two stay?"

Jenny explained we were on our way to Naples, to a time-share. It didn't matter what day we arrived; the condo was ours for the entire week.

"We're just passing through. I wanted to see you and say hi. And wanted you to meet Jenny," I added.

"Why don't you let me send you two on a cruise while you're down here? To the Bahamas."

Suzy became animated. "We went there this winter. Oh, you should go. You'll love it."

Jenny looked from Dad to me.

Here we go again. "No. That's okay. We'll probably head over to Naples tomorrow."

"At least let us take you out to dinner," he said.

"Sure. That'd be fun," I said.

Jenny, looking bleary-eyed, said, "Thanks, but I've *got* to get some sleep."

"Why don't you two go." Suzy shifted her finger back and forth between Dad and me. "Just the two of you. I'm sure you have some catching up to do."

Dad looked at me and raised his eyebrows in question.

"Alright. I'm game. Let me get cleaned up a little first. Maybe take a shower."

"Take her to the Criterion," Suzy said. She looked at me. "Do you have anything nice to wear? It's pretty fancy,"

I shook my head.

She jumped up. "I'm sure I have something. Let's go see." She motioned for me to follow her. "That new dress you bought me, don't you think that will be perfect, John?" she said over her shoulder not waiting for his reply.

I showered and changed into a flimsy dress made of a black crêpe fabric, so soft I had to check the tag: it was silk, not polyester like the dresses Mom bought. Draping from the right shoulder down to a cinch on the left side of the waist was a subtle swath of dark green fabric with a sprinkling of sequins. The dress would have looked stunning with those emerald earrings I had lost years before. As I looked at myself in the full-length mirror, I was certain Suzy filled out that dress better than I did, but I didn't care, the dress was exquisite and looked good on me. As I put on my make-up, I promised myself our evening would be different than our last visit, because I would let Dad know who I really was. He would know I also used drugs and was cool, so he could be honest with me about his life. Perhaps he would even tell me the story about how he got arrested with 12,000 pounds of pot. I had been dying to hear that story for years.

Back in our bedroom, Jenny was sprawled on our bed, in her clothes, sound asleep. To battle the exhaustion, I snorted a couple of pinches then slid the film can underneath the clothes in my suitcase. Partway down the stairs, I went back to our room and stuck the film can in my purse.

When we arrived at the Criterion, Dad tossed the keys to the valet and extended his arm to me. As we walked into the plush, dimly lit restaurant, I noticed a few men look in our direction. Dad seemed proud, as if he were showing me off, but I wondered if it was fatherly pride. When Floyd had escorted me to the car for my sixteenth birthday dinner, *that* was fatherly pride. Or when Bob, who had remained a friend of the family after he and Mom split up years before, introduced me to someone as his goddaughter, *that* was fatherly pride. *How can Dad feel pride for me? He hardly knows me.*

"Dan, my man," Dad said to the bartender.

"John. How are you?" Dan nodded once at me.

"This is my daughter, Lynn."

Dan smiled. "Nice to meet you."

"You too," I said, smiling back as I slid into one of the soft leather bar chairs.

"You want a drink?" Dad asked.

Tequila was my preference, but I wasn't twenty-one and the last thing I wanted was for Dan to card me. I wasn't even sure if I could buy beer in Florida as a nineteen-year-old. "Sure. I'll have a Coors."

Dad waved my request away. "Give us two sambucas." He held two fingers in the air then drummed them on the bar.

I fiddled with the napkin Dan had placed in front of me. "Dad, do you care if I smoke?"

"Go on. You're an adult now."

I tapped a cigarette out of my pack, and Dan had a lighter in front of me before I even put my cigarette to my lips. Classy, I thought.

Dad watched this exchange and said to Dan with a grin, "Hey! What about me? You lightin' mine too?" But he already had his lighter out.

"Nah, not for old crusty men like you!" He turned his attention back to making our drinks.

"I bet that happens a lot," Dad said, shifting his finger back and forth between Dan and me. "Because you have become a beautiful lady. You look so much like your mother. That's a good thing because you sure wouldn't have wanted to turn out lookin' like me." He let out his classic belly laugh. Oh, how I had missed that sound.

Dan set two glasses in front of us, the kind people sip brandy from, with wide globes and short stems. I never drank from fancy glasses like that. I never sipped alcohol either. "Ready?" he asked us.

"Been ready," Dad said.

One at a time, Dan dropped three coffee beans into the liqueur in each glass, saying after each one, "Health, wealth, happiness." Next, he waved the flame of his lighter over the glasses, and a subtle blue flame began to dance on the surface of the liquid. My mouth opened slightly, but I closed it when I noticed they were both watching my reaction. Dad took an empty brandy glass from Dan and tipped it upside down over each glass until the flames diminished then flickered out.

Sliding his fingers around the stem of the glass, the globe resting in his palm, Dad gently pinged his glass against mine. As I brought the glass to my lips, the sweet, licorice-tasting liqueur permeated my nose, then my mouth, then my body as it warmed me from the inside out. Satiated, my body and my cocaine-rattled nerves melted into the heat of the sambuca. We talked about how I had met Jenny, how he had met Suzy, what I remembered most about Miami. At one point, I glimpsed the reflection of Dad and me in the mirror behind the bar. For a fraction of a second, I didn't recognize our images behind the rows of alcohol bottles. They were two strangers sitting at a fancy bar. But after another split second, I was shocked to realize that I was looking at Dad and me. Glowing to be that close to him, all my joy, grief and hope from the past ten years swirled around me, around us. I couldn't stop stealing peeks at us in the mirror, giddy to be together with my dad again.

We finished our sambucas and were escorted to our table. My eyelids felt heavy, and my body was exhausted. I felt as if I were walking through molasses. Cancelling our dinner was not an option, so I excused myself to the restroom for a quick pick-me-up and decided to skip any more drinks.

A woman was in one of the stalls, so I fussed with my hair and washed my hands until she left. I snuffed up a heaping finger-nail's worth of coke—I kept my nails longish for this purpose—in each nostril and waited for it to energize my body. No more booze; I was fighting exhaustion. I cleared my throat and checked my nose in the mirror for any residual powder; I only wanted Dad to know I was using, not everyone else.

We ordered dinner and, luckily, our meals didn't arrive until the coke had started to wear off slightly, so I could nibble some food. But that also meant I was becoming straight. Skipping drinks so I could stay awake left me with no buzz. My awkwardness with Dad returned. We had a stilted conversation about who I was dating (I ignored the fact that "dating" wasn't exactly what I was doing with men), college classes I was taking (I omitted that I rarely went to class) and Dad's job (yeah, yeah, a car polishing company). Our conversation was stupid. I was stupid. I needed more coke if I was going to be a daughter who could impress him.

After eating half my pasta and a bite of Dad's steak, which was truly the most tender and delicious steak I had ever tasted, I excused myself to the restroom once more.

Miserable about our fakey conversation and my inability to tell him what I came here to tell him, I chopped up a big fat line of courage on the metal toilet-paper holder. I snorted the line and rested against the stall, eager for the hit to take effect, to make everything okay again, to make me okay again. The cocaine, and all the mucus that formed in response to it, filled my sinuses and began draining down the back of my throat. Swallowing the bitter phlegm, I relished the exhilaration that was beginning to flow through me. Emboldened, I was ready to get real with Dad. There was no way he could reject me. I was just like him.

I paused in front of the mirror and scrunched my hair so it hung loosely around my face the way I liked. The green silk in the dress matched my eyes—*damn it I wish I still had those emeralds*— and my cheeks were flushed from the coke getting my heart pumping so fast. Pretty good for not having slept in over a day, I thought.

"Want any dessert?" Dad asked as I seated myself at the table.

"I'm stuffed. Can't eat another bite."

His gaze flashed down to my plate, half-full of pasta still. "What, no more hollow leg?"

"That was when I was a kid." I smiled and shrugged as the waiter cleared our plates.

Dad rested his elbow on the table, his chin perched in his hand with his index finger resting on his cheek. He looked at me pensively, like he was making an assessment.

He knows. He has to know. He was an undercover narcotics agent, for God's sake.

"Seen your brother lately?"

I looked right at him. "Yep. Right before I came here. Have *you*?"

"Oh, I saw him, what . . . a month ago. I zipped up for a quick visit. A real quick one. Didn't have time to—"

"Dad! I know all about your visits. You two in business. I know about all of it." I was aiming for wise and non-judgmental, but it came out sounding jilted. He was so cool, the thoughtful look remained on his face, his chin still rested in his hand. I leaned in closer to him and said in as quiet a voice as possible, "I've got a film can of your stuff in my purse."

That got him. The edges of his mouth turned down ever so slightly, and he leaned back in his chair. "Well, okay then."

"Okay what?"

"Just okay. It's good to have that out in the open."

"I agree."

"Anything else?"

"What do you mean?"

"I don't know. Anything else we need to say about that."

"No. I don't think so. Nothing really. Just that, I hope you can be honest with me now. I want you to be. I'm an adult now, and I want to know you, want to know all about work. It's fascinating to me. And"—I leaned in again—"I hope you don't get arrested again."

"That definitely won't happen again." Glancing around the room first, he described in hushed tones how he had it all under control this time, how he was keeping his operation restricted to only a few partners he trusted, Rick was one of them, and how his connection in Colombia had recently introduced him to Pablo Escobar. He wondered if I knew who Escobar was.

"Ah, yes. Doesn't everybody? He's all over the news these days. Sounds like a pretty scary"—Dad nodded—"dude. You're pulling my leg, right? You're not really working for him?"

"*Noooo*. Couldn't even move his bare minimum of a hundred kilos a month. But it was an honor to get that close to him."

The low murmur of the people around us, the occasional clink of a glass or dish, floated away as I became entranced with his story. Rick had always boasted about Dad's coke being uncut, but this was big-time smuggling. I was overwhelmed with the same pride for him that I'd had when I was a young girl, back when I pasted articles about arrests he had made into a scrapbook.

But as the effects from my last snort waned, a gnawing uneasiness crept back into my consciousness. By the time we left the restaurant, the uneasiness had grown into a foreboding, into that something-bad-will-happen feeling. I wanted to warn Dad to be careful so he wouldn't go back to prison, but I didn't want to sound juvenile. I knew so little about his world. All I had experienced was a week in juvey and four years dating a crazy, small-town drug dealer. So, I just kept my mouth shut.

In the morning, Dad offered again to send Jenny and me on a cruise. I said we would think about it just to stop him from offering again. When Jenny and I left that evening, Dad asked if I needed anything for the road.

"No, I'm fine."

"You sure now? Anything?" He cocked one of his eyebrows.

There it was. The offer I had been hoping for. I had his trust and the bond of a shared secret. I was back inside his world, back inside his sanctuary. But I wanted to be cool and didn't want him to think the coke was why I had visited. "No. We're good. Thanks, though."

Besides, I had more than enough of his cocaine to last me the rest of the week.

LEARNING TO FLY

*B*y the end of my first year in college, I was on academic probation and lost my art scholarship. I explained to Mom that college was a lot harder than I had expected, and with the second job I had taken at an athletic club to help pay for rent, utilities and books, I didn't have as much time to study. I skipped the part about all the time I spent getting tanked. She was skeptical, insisting I should have at least a 3.0 grade point average given how well I had done in high school. I argued that Ohio State University would probably be a better choice for me, because it had more degree options, easier classes, and was less expensive. The real reason I wanted to enroll at OSU was I had discovered it had an aviation program. Ever since learning about Dad's work transporting drugs between Miami and Colombia, I fantasized about getting my pilot's license. Dad would be impressed, and I could work for him some day.

"If that's where you want to go, I'll pay for your tuition, but only if you keep your grades up. At least a C average."

"I can help some. Maybe pay for my books."

"I can cover all your college expenses, especially at OSU."

"For the year?"

"For three more years."

"It's like, a few thousand dollars a year."

"I know." I stared at her. That was a lot of money given her salary. "Your father paid me last year for all the back child support he owed. Several thousand dollars. He had to pay it before they'd let him out of prison."

I closed my mouth, which had dropped open with that news, and swallowed. Dad had only one source for that much money. How fitting that his drug money would pay for me to get a pilot's license and maybe join the family business.

With my jobs at the athletic club and the hospital, I worked full-time that summer and started taking flying lessons once a week. My plan was to have several hours of flying time by the beginning of fall semester, when I would take my first aviation class at OSU. To save money, I did most of my drinking at my apartment instead of at bars. This required a lot of sneaking in extra drinks throughout an evening if Jenny was home so she wouldn't realize how much alcohol I was consuming. Rarely did I use cocaine in front of her, because I didn't want her to see how much of *that* I was also using, and so there would be more for me. At Rick's house, we freebased cocaine, but at my apartment, I only snorted it. There was no way I could conceal from Jenny the distinct odor of sizzling cocaine that would be wafting through my bedroom door, and my instincts told me freebasing would be too hardcore for her. She drank and drugged differently than me. Jenny could definitely hold her liquor, keeping pace with me at times, but she could also walk away from it when she wanted to, an ability that was always out of my grasp because I always wanted just one more, which was never just one. She could snort a few lines of cocaine over the course of a day, come down off of it, drink a few beers then go to bed. Me, I would still be awake in the morning, out of cocaine and combing my bedroom carpet for kibbles of coke I may have dropped.

In addition to bars being too expensive, they had become too risky. I could no longer predict what I would do there or, more to the point, with whom. The worst bar incident was the morning I woke up a slut—in a strange bedroom next to a strange man. Strange, as in unknown, because I had no idea who he was. He very well could have been strange in the other way too. A weirdo, a nice all-American boy or a serial killer, I hadn't the slightest idea. As I lay next to him, I tried to piece together the evening before.

I had been drinking at The Garage, a nondescript bar near my apartment where the DJ played good music and most of the bartenders served me tequila without carding me. The twenty-somethings who hung out there weren't the college crowd, more of a blue-collar crowd. The guy who now lay next to me stood out there because he was more like a fraternity boy—clean-shaven, non-smoker, hair spiked with gel—than a construction worker. The bartender hollered, "Last call!" and tipped his chin toward me in question. Out of money, I waved him past me. When I swiveled around in the stool to leave, frat boy stood next to me.

"Hey, I've been trying to get up the nerve to talk to you all night." His voice was much deeper and lower than I expected given his youthful, squeaky-clean appearance. "And now it's closing time. But I wanted to tell you, and you probably hear this a lot"—his cheeks flushed pink—"that you have amazing eyes. I've never seen eyes like yours before. Sort of like Bo Derek's. You're gorgeous like her too."

"I wish." I tried to light a cigarette but couldn't align the lighter with the tip of my cigarette. Frat boy took it from me and held the flame to my cigarette. I caught a hint of sporty cologne or maybe it was his deodorant. Whichever, it was a waft of freshness among the bar odors: ashtrays and smoke and spilled alcohol fermenting everywhere.

"Are you heading home now?" he asked.

"Why? Where're *you* going?"

"Home."

I swayed on the barstool trying to keep his face in focus, but it kept growing fuzzy around the edges, his eyes blurring into dark ovals. His face looked the way Ricky did when I used to open my eyes underwater in the pool, only there was no chlorine sting now. People began shuffling around us, most of them in couples or groups, readying to leave the bar, zipping up purses, chugging the last of their drinks.

"We could go have another drink at my place if you want," he said. "I don't live too far from here."

It was so sweet that he had spent all evening mustering the courage to come over and talk to me. But there was also a nudge of something else—fear or worry or something at the edge of my consciousness. My brain, wooly from several shots of tequila, tried to latch on to that thought and determine whether I should pay attention to it, but the thought disappeared, and I couldn't recapture it. And there was this bashful frat boy waiting for my answer. I had stood and slid my purse off the back of the stool.

That was the last I could recall about the previous night as I now lay there, naked, in bed next to frat boy.

Carefully, so as not to wake him or jostle my head, which felt utterly shattered, I sat up. I tried to swallow but my mouth was too parched. In the dim morning light, I saw my clothes in a pile on the floor. I scanned the nightstand and floor for an empty condom wrapper. Seeing none, fear bolted from my chest out through my body. *I could wake him and ask him if we had sex and if we used a condom.* Admitting I couldn't remember was too degrading. My whole self, not just my head, was shattered. Overwhelmed with shame, and realizing it was irrelevant, at that point, whether we had used a condom, I wanted out of there and fast. Leaning over, gently, I scooped up my clothes and put them on in the hallway, being as quiet as possible.

Relief flooded over me to see my car out front. Asking for a ride home would have been far too humiliating. I had to cruise up and down a few roads until I found a street name I recognized, swearing the whole time I would never drink that much again.

The several days that I waited to see if I would get my period were tortuous, but nothing compared to the six months I had to wait to take an HIV test, or the two panic-stricken days I waited to get the negative results. HIV and AIDS had been all over the news and media in the previous couple of years as the number of infected people soared, clearly not only affecting the homosexual community as had been initially believed. When the new HIV test had recently become available, I knew of several people who flocked to the clinic to find out if they were negative. Having read about the HIV test in a medical journal at work, I knew a person had to wait six months after potential virus exposure for antibodies to be detectable in a blood test. During that nail-biting half a year, I went not once to a bar.

My first semester at OSU, I took aviation, English composition and a ceramics class, all of which I figured would be easy. Turned out that the pottery class required a lot of time in the studio outside of class, but if I wasn't working an evening shift at the hospital or taking a flying lesson, I was drinking.

During the last week of the semester, I stumbled into the ceramics studio, drunk, to work on my final project. The same serious art students, graduate students I assumed, were always there. I was in awe of their focus and talent as they threw sensuous vessels, hour after hour, while listening to mellow music like Gordon Lightfoot, James Taylor and Simon and Garfunkel. As I worked haphazardly at the pottery wheel to throw my final project, which should have been glazed already, I eavesdropped on their conversations. Their easy banter and confidence, their calmness (though they also had finals due the next day), shined a spotlight on my isolation and half-assed attempts at school, relationships and life. As my buzz wore off and their folksy music and warm comradery flowed all around me, the stark contrast between these students and me was glaring. Unable to tolerate my growing self-awareness, I packed up the few wet pieces I had thrown, all of which were too thick and heavy, and decided to finish sculpting them at home.

A note from Jenny on the coffee table explained she was spending the night at her boyfriend's place. Grateful she was gone, I popped open a beer and found my Gordon Lightfoot cassette. After a few beers, I daydreamed about becoming a pilot. Every time I glimpsed my ceramic bowls that weren't going to be dry, not to mention be fired or glazed, by morning, I told myself I would work on them after one more beer, would at least dry them overnight in my oven. I polished off most of a twelve-pack before passing out.

When my alarm went off, I hit snooze until forty minutes before my ceramics class was to start. After a quick shower, I knelt over the toilet and threw up, swearing I would never drink again. I brewed a pot of strong coffee. Its burnt-toast smell caused my gut to churn, so I tried not to inhale while sipping it, desperate for the caffeine. Surveying my unfinished project, the damp clay pieces spread out on a piece of stiff cardboard, I muttered, "I'm such a fuck-up." I loaded the cardboard and pottery into my car.

Gray sheets of rain were pouring from the sky when I arrived on campus, soaking the cardboard as I lugged it into the art building. By the time I entered the classroom, the wet cardboard was bending under the weight of the clay. The teacher—in the middle of critiquing a student project—paused with her hand in mid-air, her pencil pointing at an amazing vertical fish sculpture, which stood somehow from its tail, complete with scales, fins, gills and a thick glaze the color of copper patina. She looked at me with my droopy cardboard and unfired clay pieces, and her hand dropped to her side. Everyone followed her gaze to me standing in the doorway. She pressed her lips together in a tight frown, shook her head slowly and returned her attention to the coppery fish.

I backed out of the room, folded the soggy cardboard in half, smashing the still-moist clay pieces together, and stuffed the entire mess in a trash bin.

On the way home, the rain and the slap-slap of my wipers on the windshield concealed me from the outside world, so I let the tears and snot flow down my face, the salty, ocean taste on my lips and in my mouth. I pictured those graduate students with their flawless earthenware and their friendships and their promising futures. I would never have what they had. Never.

When I trudged through our front door, Jenny was bounding down the stairs. Everything about me was soaked: my hair, my shirt, my shoes. Her hair was also wet but from a shower. Her face glowed with happiness. Even the fruity scent of her shampoo was all freshness and spunk. She paused at the front door, her hand on the knob, and looked at me. "Are you okay?"

I shook my head. "I flunked another class. Ceramics. I flunked my ceramics class. That is so pathetic."

"Bummer . . . " Her lips were parted to say something else, then she wrapped me in hug. "You gonna be alright?"

I nodded.

"Sure? I have to get to class because I have a final. But I can come back after I'm done."

"Go on. I'm fine. And good luck. Hope you do better than I did."

After she left, I slumped at the kitchen table, my chin in my hands, the wood hard under my elbows. I thought about withdrawing from OSU. The patch of a patio outside our glass door was a pool of standing water, and I watched it being pummeled by yet more rain. I opened the refrigerator. Three beers were left from the twelve-pack I had opened the night before. I stared at the beers for a long while. "Fuck it. Fuck those hippie grad students. Fuck the class. Fuck college."

I reached in and lifted one of the beers off the shelf.

That winter semester, I didn't enroll in classes because, I told myself, I barely had time to take flying lessons, which was my priority. Well, my second priority, right after drinking and drugging. I also began dating Lawrence, one of the child psychiatrists who worked at the hospital. He was in his mid-thirties and, by far, the tallest man I had ever dated, six-foot-two and looked even taller because of his lean, wiry build. Lawrence was also the most intelligent and intensely analytical man I had ever known. I was no dummy, but I bumbled around in our conversations trying to keep up with or impress him. That I had snagged the attention of an older doctor bolstered my self-image, but I felt an undercurrent of embarrassment dating him. It wasn't that he was too old for me; it was that I was too young for him. The irony of thirty-five-year-old *child* psychiatrist dating a nineteen-year-old was not lost on me. There was probably a diagnosis for his behavior in that *DSM-III* book on his shelf, but he clearly didn't give a shit.

As Lawrence and I ate lunch together at the hospital cafeteria one afternoon, another doctor—one of the formal older ones who always wore a suit, rarely smiled and never gave me, the lowly mail clerk, a second's notice—paused at our table. "I'm not interrupting anything, am I?" He glanced back and forth between Lawrence and me.

Oh please don't—Lawrence extended his hand toward the empty bench across the table from us—*fuck*. They made small talk while I picked at my salad and tried to think of something intelligent to say. I was way out of my league there. During a lull in their conversation, Lawrence gave my knee a squeeze. I glanced at him, and he smiled mischievously before taking a bite of his sandwich.

The doctor's eyes flitted toward me then back to Lawrence. "So, Lawrence, you know what the legal age is, right?"

Heat coursed up my neck into my face. Not daring to look at the doctor, I locked my sights onto Lawrence's profile. This conversation would most certainly be the end of Lawrence and me; the administration might even threaten him with his job if he didn't stop dating me.

Lawrence stared down the stuffy doctor. "Yes I do. It's eighteen." Without breaking his eye contact, Lawrence took another bite of his sandwich. His defiance was chilling, and I began to have an inkling of what else he was getting from me besides sex—a shocking relationship to flaunt in the faces of the conservative hospital administration, the same administration about which he and his friends, other therapists, were always ranting. Unable to stand the stare-down between the men, I dropped my focus back to my salad until I heard the doctor shuffle to stand, saw his food tray slide off the table and heard his wingtips click away from us.

When I glanced at Lawrence, he winked at me and popped the last of his sandwich into his mouth.

Later that evening, Lawrence said they were just jealous, all those other doctors. He wrapped his arms around my waist and pulled me close. "Because I'm with the foxiest babe at the hospital." We both knew that jealousy was not the driver behind our lunch guest.

I kept waiting for some kind of consequence, but Lawrence was unfazed by the shockwaves of gossip reverberating through the hospital. In fact, the gossip seemed to give him a charge. Secretly, I liked being the focus of all the rumbling. There wasn't a therapist, nurse or administrator on that campus who wasn't familiar with me now. I may have been just a mail clerk, but I was now Lawrence's girlfriend.

Lawrence introduced me to a whole new world: nice wine (though I struggled with the slow pace at which it was to be sipped), snow skiing, jazz on the lawn concerts, golf (I got embarrassingly shit-faced in the clubhouse), meals at every fancy restaurant in town, and a deli that he said was the only true delicatessen in town. He beamed when I agreed, despite not liking fish, that lox and bagels were delicious. "Pretty good coming from a Gentile," he said. I made a mental note to look up the word "gentile" when I got home.

In addition to trying to ignore the stares of people around us at a restaurant, trying to have an engaging conversation with Lawrence was also exhausting. I struggled to find topics I hoped would interest him and certainly didn't want to reveal much about myself and what was happening in my life. Unsure of his opinions about the use of illegal drugs, I concealed my cocaine use and never told him about the family business. I was no longer enrolled in college classes and there was only so much to say about flying lessons. That didn't leave much for me to say. If I had a few drinks before we went out, I fared better, or at least I was more gregarious.

If we were spending an evening at his apartment, I had a few drinks before arriving so the limited amount of wine or beer we consumed together, and at far too moderate a pace, was at least tolerable. Sometimes, I exceeded those few pre-drinks and showed up at his apartment hours late or once not at all because I couldn't tear myself away from the crack pipe.

The longer we were together, the harder it became to hide my drug and alcohol use and the more wary he grew about my erratic behavior and numerous excuses.

One night, I arrived at his house a few hours late and was pretty wired on cocaine.

"Where were you? You were supposed to be here hours ago. To have dinner together. I went ahead and ate without you. You never showed up. Didn't call me. What the hell?"

"Sorry. I just . . . it was Jenny. She broke up with her boyfriend and—"

"Oh, right. And you couldn't call? I don't believe any of this, and I'm sick of it. What the hell is going on here?"

Giving Lawrence one more lame excuse wasn't going to fly, and the possibility of him walking away from our relationship swamped me with powerlessness. Being left by a man was something I never let happen, not once since Dad left me. And I didn't plan on allowing it to happen now. And I was so weary of all the secrecy and evasiveness and trying to limit my drinking around him. The truth, or a small part of it, slipped out of my mouth. "Okay. Okay. I'll tell you what happened. But I don't want you to freak out or think it's something bad or serious, because it's, well, not legal."

A furrow formed between his eyebrows.

"We got some coke. Me and Jenny."

He had a blank, unknowing look on his face.

"Cocaine. We had some cocaine."

"I *know* what coke is. I guess"—he shook his head—"I just didn't know you used it."

"I don't. Not really. Jenny and I pitched our money together and bought a little bit from another student. We were having fun, and I lost track of time. It sounds like the classic excuse, I know, but it's true. I didn't realize how late it was. As soon as I did, I got here as fast as I could."

His expression was sober and stoic. I moved in close to him, but he stood his ground. "So, are you pretty high right now? Still?"

I shook my head and looked directly at him. "No. Do I seem high?"

"No."

I leaned in again. This time he let me kiss his cheek and neck, but he didn't kiss me back. His resistance aroused me, and I pressed my body up against him.

"You're unbelievable."

"You're right. I should've called. I'm sorry." His body relaxed some, and I tugged his Polo shirt out from his pants, sliding my hands up his back.

Finally, he kissed me, and I could feel his penis stiffening. Then he pulled his face away from mine to make eye contact.

Shit, I probably reek like beer. He'll think I'm drunk too.

"You got any for me?"

"Do I have any what for you?" I gave his hard-on a squeeze.

"Not that. Well, yeah, that. But I mean coke."

"Hmm?"

"You got any coke left?"

I raised my eyebrows and paused the hand-job. "You want to snort some cocaine?"

"Sure. Why not?"

I imagined whipping out my film can full of blow. Not exactly "the little bit" I had described. "I've got a few lines left. It's in my car. Are you sure you want to?"

"Yeah, why not. Let's do some. It'll be fun."

"Okay. I'll go get it." I grabbed my purse and dug for my keys while walking out his door. "Be right back."

I shuffled through my glove box for a piece of paper and folded it into a small envelope into which I could put a normal amount of cocaine. I made sure none of the chunks fell in, only powder. No one around here sold coke with chunks in it, though I doubted he knew that. Tucking the flap closed on the small pouch, I slid it in my purse and buried the film can under my billfold and hairbrush.

Back in Lawrence's apartment, I took out the paper pouch and sprinkled some of the powder on the table. He sat next to me, his hand on my back, and watched me. With my driver's license, I chopped the cocaine into a finer powder and formed two scant lines on his coffee table. My mouth watered at the sound of its crunchy texture.

"You look pretty experienced at this."

I shrugged and thought better about pulling out the three-inch straw that I carried in my purse. "Got a dollar bill?" He handed me one, which I rolled into a tight straw.

We each snorted a line, and he put on a jazzy record. I stretched out on his plush sofa. He gave me his sexy look, one side of his mouth curled into a smile. After that dinky line I just snuffed, I needed another one but couldn't figure out how to get the film can out of my purse or get my purse into the bathroom without being obvious.

"Do you have more of that wine? The pinkish wine we had the other night?" Red wine always gave me a headache that lasted the entire next day, and he didn't keep whiskey or tequila around.

"That rosé? Let me see what I've got."

When he went to the kitchen, I slipped the film can into my pocket and ducked into the bathroom. I dumped the big chunks onto the counter to get to the powder on the bottom. I sat on the toilet and made myself pee then took a big pinch of powder and inhaled it as I flushed the toilet. My fingers still had a residue on them, so I slid them along my gums. I quietly opened the cabinet door under the sink and saw a rag in the back under which I could hide the film can. Too risky. Contemplating how to get the can back in my purse, I quickly slipped off my shirt and pants.

This should distract him. I wedged the film can in the pocket of my jeans and rolled them up inside my shirt.

A smile spread across Lawrence's face when I sauntered up to him in only my bra and panties. Two half-full wine glasses sat on the table. *I wish he'd fill those damn wine glasses all the way up.* I dropped my wadded-up jeans on the floor next to my purse. As I leaned over to kiss him, my hair fell around his face. He ran his hands through my hair, down my back then right to my ass. We were fine. Everything was fine now. All I had to do was be truthful and let him see the real me. Well, a sliver of the real me. Only a sneak peek, but it was a start. I was sick and tired of hiding who I was.

His kissing became more urgent, and he mumbled, "Let's go to the bedroom."

I took a few sips of wine and, after he headed for the bedroom, polished off my glass before following him. My confidence growing from the cocaine and the wine and his lust, I stood at the end of the bed and wiggled out of my panties and bra. All the while, Lawrence was watching me as he undressed. He wasn't fed up with me after all. On my hands and knees, I worked my way over to where he lay naked on the bed. Straddling his hips, I rubbed myself over his erection but refrained from sliding down onto him until he began to moan, and his eyes rolled back in his head. As I rocked on top of him I now felt back in control—of him, of our relationship, of my life. Everything was going to be fine. With the amount of coke I had snorted that day, there was no way I could have an orgasm. He would try to bring me to one in some way, but I just wasn't up for the work of it all. So, when he finally gasped and grabbed my hips, forcing himself deep inside me, I writhed on him and let out an ecstatic moan of my own.

I buckled on top of him, and he ran his hands slowly up and down my back. He had the softest hands. I wanted to be able to bask in his attention and, if not his love, at least his warmth. But that wine and coke in the other room were calling to me. After what I estimated was an appropriate amount of time had passed, I slipped off him. "I'm gonna clean up. And I'm so thirsty. I'll get our wine."

Out in the living room, I carefully scooped up my jeans and shirt. Then, running the water in the tub, I snuck another pinch from my film can.

After we finished our wine, he was yawning, but I was amped up. "Sounds like you need another line," I said.

"We don't want to use it all up in one night, do we? You want to save some for tomorrow?"

"No. It's okay."

"You got more?"

"No. This is the last of it." I chopped and formed two thin lines with what was left in the paper envelope. "But I want to do it with you. Who knows when I'll get my hands on any more?" I handed him the dollar-bill straw.

He snorted one of the lines and handed the straw back to me. "Do you do this often? Do a lot of cocaine?"

I slipped the straw from his fingers, inhaled the last line and said, "Hardly ever."

22

ON TOP OF THE WORLD

When Dad moved to the same town in North Carolina where Grandma and Grandpa had retired, the story from Rick was that Dad's parole officer put some pressure on him to get out of Miami because he was suspicious Dad wasn't keeping his nose clean (so to speak). I wasn't sure how he could smuggle if he wasn't in Miami, but, apparently, Dad was still in business. And now he was only an eight-hour drive from me.

Jenny and I drove down to visit Dad for the New Year's holiday. He took us to the 30th Edition, an expensive restaurant on the thirtieth floor of a high-rise building in downtown Charlotte, all black décor, white tablecloths and expansive views overlooking the city lights. Dad ordered appetizers, prime rib, lobster and their most expensive bottle of champagne.

"How about Dom Pérignon, have any of that?" he asked our Italian-looking waiter, with whom Jenny and I had begun to flirt.

"Yes, sir," he said, turning his attention from Jenny and me back to Dad.

"Great. Bring one, no, make it two, bottles of that." He held up two fingers. Then he looked back and forth between Jenny and me and shook his finger at us. "Now, you two leave this poor waiter alone, so he can earn the big, fat tip I'm gonna leave him."

"They're not bothering me one bit," the waiter said, grinning.

We stayed in that dazzling restaurant for hours, eating and sipping champagne. Dad's overindulgence was contagious. Feeling generous, I shared my coke with Jenny (obtained again from some guy on campus). We giggled as we both crammed into a restroom stall and did lines off the lid of the toilet tank. I was certain Dad was doing the same in the men's room. It was such a relief to not be hiding *everything* from Jenny or Lawrence or Dad.

After one of our excursions to the restroom, I was settling back at the table and clearing my throat when Dad leaned over. "You brought some of Rick's stuff down here again, didn't you?" With the free-flowing food, champagne, laughter, cocaine and now truth, my deep love for him surged. I felt so buoyant and free, finally able to be honest with him, to let him see the real me; I was sailing on top of that skyscraper, on top of the world, with my father.

"Sure did." We locked eyes, then I added, "Why, you want some?" At that, we both erupted into laughter.

He wiped his eyes and an easy, contented grin spread across his face. "No, thank you though. I've got plenty where that came from."

As the evening progressed, most of the waiters and even the manager sidled up next to our table, soaking in Dad's boisterous fun. He was, as usual, irresistible. As closing time neared, Antonio —what Dad was calling our waiter even though that wasn't his name—had sat down at the table with us.

The next morning, I was rifling around in Dad's medicine cabinet for a Tylenol or aspirin when he walked up and leaned against the doorway. "You okay in here?"

A familiar feeling of security, of being watched over and cared about, enveloped me. "Well, my head feels like it's gonna explode. But other than that, just terrific."

He chuckled. "Oh man, champagne does that to me too."

"*Now* you tell me. I'm never drinking it again. I may not ever drink *anything* again."

"And that was the expensive champagne too. Not sure what it is about champagne, maybe the bubbles, gives me a splitting headache too." He motioned for me to follow. "I got something that'll help."

I followed him to his bedroom. There stretched out on his dresser was a long line of sparkling cocaine. As he opened his wallet and rolled a hundred-dollar bill into a straw, I realized my mouth was hanging open and closed it, making a conscious effort to smile instead. Dad pointed at the line and offered me the straw. All the times I had visualized this moment, I expected he would share some wisdom first. Wisdom about how to keep my habit under control or avoid getting arrested. And I would impress him with the knowledge and familiarity I already had with coke and would make sure he understood I had been using drugs, all kinds, for years. Our conversation would be natural and bonding. Instead, here we stood, huddled over a big line, neither of us saying a word.

I took the straw and looked at it for a few seconds. "Never snorted through a hundred-dollar bill before."

"Wish they still made five-hundred-dollar bills. That'd be an expensive way to snort nose candy, wouldn't it? Wonder if there's any five-hundreds floating around anymore? I'd like to get my hands on a few."

"I never knew they made bills that large." So much for bonding, I thought. Lowering my face to the dresser, I inhaled half the line in one nostril, switched sides and snorted the rest. Slowly, to minimize jostling my head, I straightened back up. He was watching me with a quizzical look on his face, his mouth twisted in thought.

"What?" I asked.

"That was a huge line."

"Shit!" I slapped my hands over my mouth. "Was half that for you? I am so sorry . . . "

"Well, the whole line was gonna be for me."

We both laughed, and I immediately tried to stifle mine. "Ouch, ouch, ouch. My head. Please. Don't make me laugh."

He shook his head, still smiling. "You sure do take after your old man."

I arrived at Dad's the evening before he was to marry his third wife, Katherine, who was a high school teacher (who knows what happened to Suzy?). When we stopped for dinner on the way back from the airport, his speech and manner were flat, not animated at all, and I hoped it was because he was nervous about the wedding and not because he was out of cocaine. While we waited for our meals, I tried to drum up a conversation. "Hey, guess what I'm doing?"

He was unraveling the paper from a roll of antacid tablets. "What?"

"Taking flying lessons."

"I took flying lessons. Long time ago. You know, I was gonna be a pilot before I became a cop."

"I think Mom told me that. Well, OSU has an aviation program, so I took flight classes there first, but I'm just gonna finish my private pilot license on my own." That I had dropped out of college didn't seem pertinent.

"Single-engine planes?"

"For starters. But I'd like to build up to twin-engine certification."

"Fun, ain't it?"

"It's awesome." Our conversation stalled. He looked bored. I glanced around the restaurant then back at him. I leaned in closer. "What do you guys fly," I whispered. "You know, to Colombia?"

He smiled. "DC-3. Retrofitted to fit our needs."

"That a twin-engine?"

"Yep. Twin-engine prop plane. Can hold a heavy load. We had

extra fuel-tanks put in, so we can fly further without having to refuel."

"I'd like to learn to fly bigger planes next." The conversation stalled again as the waitress slid plates of food in front of us. I munched on my fries, wanting badly to ask if he could use another pilot, if he could help me pay for flight lessons so I could finish sooner, but I felt inadequate, an amateur. "So how come you didn't become a pilot?"

"Was too busy with you kids." He took a bite of his steak. "And with college. And we couldn't afford it. It was expensive."

"Still is."

"I planned to finish when we moved to Miami, but there were so many pilots coming back from Vietnam with way more flying hours than I had. It would've been tough to get a job as a commercial pilot. So, I dropped out of flight school. Became a cop instead." He focused on his baked potato, splitting it open, smashing in butter, plopping sour cream on top.

The rest of the meal was quiet, interspersed with a few questions I asked about the wedding. He finished his meal and didn't once flirt with our cute waitress—clearly straight. How miserable for him. I couldn't fathom getting married without at least a buzz. Hell, I couldn't fathom doing anything without a buzz. This was going to be a long weekend if Dad didn't have any cocaine. At least there would be plenty of alcohol at the wedding and, hopefully, something other than champagne.

"You tired?" he asked, when we got to his condo.

"Not really."

"Well, I'm going to bed. Got to get some sleep before the big day tomorrow." He did look tired and very nervous. My spirits sank to realize he wasn't going to share any coke with me. But he would have some booze around somewhere. Probably scotch, but it would have to do.

"Okay. I'm gonna watch some TV before I hit the sack." I flipped on a new big-screen TV and clicked through the channels, waiting to hear him stop moving around upstairs before I snooped for his scotch. Within a minute or two, his footsteps came back down the stairs, and he tossed a maroon container onto the couch next to me. It was a two-inch-round, one-inch-high disk, flat enough to slide in his pocket and not be too obvious.

"If I have one line, I'll be up all night. And I'm not doing that the night before my wedding. But help yourself."

As he climbed the steps to his bedroom again, loneliness settled around me. The condo was quiet except for the toilet flushing upstairs and the water running. I closed the drapes, dimmed the lights and turned the volume on the TV down low. As I opened the container, my belly fluttered with excitement to see the chunky cocaine inside. I decided to have one thin line, watch a show then crash.

As morning neared, I flipped through the channels trying to find something other than test patterns or evangelical preachers to occupy my racing mind. Only a pinch of cocaine remained, enough for one scant line, and I worried Dad would be mad I had snorted all of it. Having given up on trying to sleep, I waited until I heard Dad stirring upstairs before I went to take a shower. When I came out, he was standing at the kitchen counter sipping coffee. I tried to relax my face, to look cool and not show even a trace of the guilt broiling inside.

"Looks like you could use this," he said, sliding a cup of coffee across the breakfast bar.

I couldn't tolerate black coffee, as my stomach was already acid with worry. "Thanks. Got any milk?"

He pointed at the fridge. After I poured enough milk and sugar into my coffee to make it sweet and creamy, I walked around the counter, so it was between Dad and me again. Wrapping my hands around the mug, I took a few sips. "So, was that ... um ... was that all your blow?"

He smiled. "Why? Is it all gone?"

I slid the disk across the counter. Not wanting to see his reaction, I fiddled with my cup. I heard him click open the lid. *What am I so worried about? What's he gonna do, make me pay him back?*

Ground me for snuffing up all his blow? But it had been a lot of cocaine. If it had been cut into street grade, it would have been worth hundreds of bucks, which I did not have.

"It's okay." He shook his head, his big easy smile spread across his face. How I loved to see him smile like that. "I got a kilo stashed. Just keep it." He slid the container back across the counter.

A kilo! Relief flooded over me. And joy. This was going to be one kick-ass wedding!

An hour before we left for his wedding ceremony, Dad poured two glasses of scotch on the rocks. I took a sip and shivered. "Blech. This is terrible."

He tossed a couple of Rolaids in his mouth, crunched them up and took a sip from his glass. "You kiddin'? This is as good as it gets." Standing there in a tuxedo with a crystal tumbler of scotch in his hand, he looked so classy, so in command of his life. However, he *was* washing antacids down with scotch. Maybe that was the key to drinking this alcohol that was scorching my throat: a chaser of antacid. I tried to find the rich, smoky flavor Dad described, but to me the scotch tasted bitter and combustible. It was like drinking something mentholated, fire all the way down my esophagus. Holding my breath for each swallow, I drank it anyway, not wanting to waste an opportunity for comradery with Dad and hoping it would take the edge off coming down from the coke.

Dad refilled his glass and asked if I wanted another.

Looking at the clock, I said, "Don't we have to go?"

"Yep. This one's for the road."

Pointing at the bottle, I said, "Is that the only thing you have?"

"I've got some Dewar's White Label."

"Is that scotch too?"

"Yeah, but it's not as good as this stuff."

I crinkled my nose. "Okay. Pour me another one."

"I better reload our stash too before we go." He made a gimme motion. "Soon as this ceremony's over, I'll be havin' some of that nose candy myself. But I'll have you hold on to our stash. Don't want it rattling out of my tux when I'm puttin' Katherine's ring on."

Our stash. I loved the sound of that.

When we pulled into the church parking lot, I barely noticed the scotch's pungent flavor or the sting in my throat anymore. Instead, I was buzzing from the scotch, Dad's company and our stash, which I was carrying in my purse. Just like Mom used to carry Dad's PPK in her purse! Like mother, like daughter. Sort of.

It was Katherine's first wedding, and the ceremony was elaborate and formal. But the champagne and scotch were free-flowing during the reception. The booze and Dad's joviality loosened things right up. The stash slipped hand-to-hand between Dad and me all evening. I'd like to think the entire day was glorious, but I drifted in and out of blackouts so I can't say for sure.

Here's what I knew happened. I flirted shamelessly with the young limo-driver while he waited to take Dad and Katherine to their honeymoon suite. Dad's real estate agent, whose name I had forgotten, drove me to the private party at the honeymoon suite after the reception and kept glancing at me from the driver's seat with a sloppy grin exaggerated by his large jaw and slight underbite. There was another spread of food at the party, but I was too wired to eat anything. Katherine sat in a chair looking stunned and still wearing her full bridal regalia until Dad said, "Why don't you take that thing off and relax darlin'? Wedding's over." The nameless real estate agent drove me to my grandparents' house, though I'm not sure if this is a vague recollection or simply a deduction. The rest was lost to me.

The day after the wedding, Dad's real estate agent showed up to take me to the airport. As soon as I sat in his car, that same sly smile from the evening before crept onto his face. I was mortified to think we may have fooled around. The thought disgusted me, since he wasn't that attractive, was married and was my father's age. We had been in Dad's hotel suite with several other people all evening. Certainly, Dad wouldn't have allowed anything like that to happen. I mumbled to the nameless real estate agent—I was too embarrassed to ask him his name again—that I was wiped out and hoped he didn't mind if I snoozed on the way to the airport. Then I leaned back against the headrest and pretended to sleep.

Whenever I visited Dad, I returned home with a hefty stash of coke. This was happening frequently enough that I was back to hiding it from Jenny so she wouldn't see how much and how often I was using. So much for being my true self. I would disappear into my bedroom or go for long drives, which required some preparation. First, I called Lawrence and told him I was staying at my father's an extra day or was going out with friends. Then, before Jenny came home from work, I wedged a cooler full of ice and cheap beer behind the passenger seat where I could reach into it from the driver's seat. Finally, with my film can tucked in my purse, I drove around for hours, drinking, listening to upbeat tapes like the Eagles or Tom Petty and daydreaming about my future. Every hour or so, I pulled over in an inconspicuous location and scooped coke to my nostrils with my fingernail. It took too much time to make lines and use my straw. Through the bliss of cocaine, my life seemed full of promise. I visualized myself flying into Colombia with Dad and his partners, imagining what the jungles there were like, maybe similar to the mangrove forests in Miami. I could see the look on Dad's face, flush with pride, when he would introduce me to his partners, telling them that whenever they needed a co-pilot, I was the best around. And trustworthy, he would say, explaining how I was already in the family business. I pondered what portion of the blow and money I could get for co-piloting a plane. *Forget a college degree. If I can make the same kind of money Dad's making, who needs a degree?*

On one of these drive-abouts, I cruised by Mom's condo. The lights were out, and the place looked calm and quiet. Images of all the tumult that occurred in that condo flashed through my mind: Mom and Rick screaming at each other, Rick terrorizing me with a butcher knife, Mom crushed, again and again, about my drinking, Mark and I having sex in every room of that condo. That's probably where we conceived the baby, I thought. Next, I drove by Mark's mom's house, slowing as I neared to ensure his car wasn't out front. Thinking about Mark soured my buzz, and no matter how loud I cranked the music, I couldn't get him out of my mind —"Hotel California" was no match for a force like Mark. I couldn't get out of my mind how fiercely he had loved me (at least that's what my brain, in a drunken stupor, was telling me). But everything had gone to shit because I wanted to go to college instead of having a baby at seventeen, and I wasn't even in college anymore. After driving past his mom's house, I checked my rearview mirror and shivered to remember the last time I had seen him in my mirror.

Next, I drove by the old church I used to attend with Mom. Pulling into the empty lot, I remembered the church kept an open-door policy, always leaving the chapel unlocked, so I decided to go inside and say hi to God or Jesus or whoever might be in there. I polished off a beer and groped around for the door handle. My unsteady gait walking up to the church made me aware of how intoxicated I was. That was the thing about cocaine, its stimulating effects masked the depressive effects of alcohol. When I pushed open the church's heavy front door, the hinges creaked, the sound echoing against the ceiling. The chapel smelled of candle wax and dust and sulfur from matches. Despite my not having attended church for close to a decade and finding religion mostly irrelevant by that point in my life, the stillness in there felt sacred—undisturbed and patient—as if something had been waiting and now turned its attention toward me. I stepped deliberately, one foot in front of the other, intent on not falling over.

Sitting in the front padded pew, I heard only my breathing and my heartbeat in my ears. In front of me was the red-wine colored carpet, the minister's podium, the cross, the stained-glass arched windows. Its familiarity reminded me of the connection I once shared with Mom. In that emptiness, I glimpsed myself sitting there alone in a church. Then my mind zoomed out to the past few hours, and I saw myself driving around and drinking alone.

Out further to the past few years, and I witnessed all my hopes and plans and anyone I cared about peeling away from me until I was left with only drugs and alcohol. Those sobering images crashed through my buzz and left me feeling pathetic and small and as hollow as that church.

"Okay, God, if you exist, why don't you tell me, show me, how to get my life straightened out? Huh? Why don't you just fix me? If you really exist, why don't you let us all know? Screw all that you-just-have-to-believe-in-me faith crap." Sitting on the pew, I waited for an answer, guidance, solace, forgiveness, anything. The result was a quiet so devoid of any sound that it screamed in my ears. Nothing came but the craving for another beer, so I trudged back to my car. *Well, if there is a god, I just screwed myself in there.*

When I awoke, I glanced around to see where I was, relieved to see my rickety bookcase, my closet doors, my gaping curtains, which I wished I had closed the night before because sunlight was blasting into the room. Shutting my eyes tight, I lay there trying to piece together what had happened after I left the church. Hoping to relieve some of the pain pressing against the back of my eyes, I pinched the bridge of my nose. I couldn't even remember driving home. I sat up in bed and it felt like my brain slid against the inside of my skull. More carefully, I swung my legs over the edge of my bed. Squinting against the sunlight, I saw my car sitting in the parking lot. No dents that I could see.

That afternoon, I was still walking delicately and only able to tolerate sips of water or black coffee.

"You look like you don't feel so hot. What'd you do last night?" Jenny asked.

I was aware that drinking and using drugs by myself wasn't normal, that driving by the house of an old boyfriend who had raped me was bizarre, that wandering into a church drunk off my ass was pathetic. The worst of my behavior though was the lying I was about to do. I told Jenny I had gone to a party with some high school friends. What a joke—that drive-about was no party. And I didn't have any high school friends. So desperately I wanted to blurt out the truth to Jenny. And why not? The previous night was nothing compared to my self-destructive, socially unacceptable behavior of the past. I felt so much shame associated with whatever I did when plastered that I lied when the truth would have been just fine. I recalled Tom, my previous drug counselor, saying normal drinkers don't usually lie about their drinking or hide it from others or get shit-faced alone. Normal drinkers, he had said, don't wonder if they have a problem with drinking.

Go to hell Tom, I don't have a problem. I just have to drink slower or stop at five drinks. Next time, five is the max.

23

DROWNING

After Dad married Katherine, he and I did all our drug use in his auction barn—Dad's latest "business." Antiques were all the rage in North Carolina, where people had furniture that could be a hundred years old, or older, in their houses and barns. Some of it worth serious money. An antique auction company was a superb cover for Dad's smuggling operation because lots of inventory coming and going meant heavy cash flow. His auction barn was a rustic wooden warehouse, big enough to store antiques and seat two hundred people. Dad's office was off a hallway at the back of the building, behind the concession counter. While the main part of the auction barn had a high ceiling, the office had a drop ceiling, and Dad positioned a heavy antique oak desk so that, when he stood on it, he could reach the ceiling tiles, push them up and over and stash cocaine up there. He sometimes had twenty kilos spread around on those ceiling panels.

Whenever I could get a weekend off from work, I drove down on a Friday to help Dad set up for a weekend auction. Between warming the concession food, setting out a couple hundred folding chairs and queuing up items to be sold, we laid out long lines on Dad's desk. By the time the crowds were milling around, and the auction barn reeked of furniture polish and hotdogs and the haze of cigarette smoke that accumulated at the ceiling, I was flying. Dad and I were connected like never before, the love and the humor and the trust coursing between us like the blood, his blood, his DNA, that coursed through me. And the cocaine was flowing between us, gluing us together.

Just before an auction was about to kick off, the conversations of hundreds of people eager to start the bidding reverberated through the building. I kept the concessions moving: sodas, beer, hotdogs, nachos, soft pretzels. Then Dad and a few of his teenaged employees hustled items up to the stage, while his partner, Martin, auctioned them off. Martin's stream of bid-seeking was so fast and fluid, and his Southern accent so strong, I could barely make out anything he said except when he accentuated the dollar amounts each time a bid was made.

At those auctions, my life was perfect. Until my euphoria from the last line dulled, and the noise and crowds and strangers pressed in around me, rattling my nerves. And worse, the energy flowing between Dad and me dissipated along with my buzz. Then I began questioning what I was doing using coke with him. The more sober I became, the more the terror and bizarreness of what I was doing sank in. *What if Dad's parole officer shows up? Would I get arrested too? Dad would definitely go back to prison. This is fucked, snorting with my own father.* Desperate to shut up the conversations in my head, I became vigilant of Dad's whereabouts, waiting for him to head back to his office, then after a few minutes, sauntering after him.

I rapped on Dad's office door. "It's me." Underneath Martin's ceaseless calling, I heard Dad unlocking his door. "Got a hundred, a hundred to the bidder over here, do I hear one-fifty, one-fifty anywhere, for the roll-top desk, there's one-fifty, now we have an auction going, do I hear—" The door clicked shut behind me, finally shutting out Martin's grating voice.

My body buzzed to see spread out in front of Dad an open gallon Ziploc bag full of chunky, sparkly cocaine and a mirror with a dusting of powder on the surface. Trying to act nonchalant, I tipped my chin toward the bag and said, "Can I have some more of that?"

He cleared his throat and swallowed. "Sure. It's all yours." He nudged the mirror toward me.

"Really? All of it?" I raised my eyebrows in mock surprise.

"Figuratively speaking. For such a slim thing, you sure can keep up."

I blushed with pride. "You want me to help you out there"—I thumbed toward the door—"then keep the lines coming, because I can't be in front of all those people when the coke starts wearing off." Sliding the mirror closer, I picked up the rolled hundred-dollar bill. Someday, I planned to use a hundred-dollar bill to snort blow, instead of the plastic straw I carried in my purse.

"Tell me about it. It gets crazy out there. They love an auction down here, that's for sure. It's a great cover too. I tell my parole officer and Katherine I need to go on a road trip to scout out some antiques, I deliver a few kilos, bit-a-bam, I'm back with a load of money. And a few antiques."

I tucked my hair behind my ears, snorted the entire line then dropped the hundred-dollar tube on the mirror, anxious to feel normal again. It didn't take long. When the bitter, medicinal-tasting cocaine began trickling down my throat, something terrific was about to happen again. Any minute. *There's nothing wrong with this. I'm an adult now. This is fine. This is a blast.*

As long as I stayed high, I floated around the auction barn full of love for Dad—great, big waves of love. We were family again. I was safe and protected again. Dad didn't want anything from me in return for the cocaine. Ever. He didn't ask me to pay him, didn't even ask me to work the auction with him. I just wanted to be there with him, near him, near the coke.

But nagging at the periphery of this deep, reestablished bond was an uneasiness when we were straight. I attributed our stunted conversations to the fact that we were getting to know each other as adults. All we needed was more time together. And we weren't straight that often or for very long, so I pushed that discomfort out of my consciousness whenever it popped up.

*T*hat spring, Lawrence told me he was moving to New York for a career opportunity that was too good to pass up. He didn't say anything about me moving there with him. A week later, I began flirting with Brad, who worked with me at the athletic club. Brad had been a high school football player and had that tall, beefy build, now with a little extra weight around his waist. He had a boyish face, despite his receding hairline, and skin so fair I could watch the red rising into his neck and face when he became angry or embarrassed. He drank as much as I did, though he had a take-it-or-leave-it attitude about booze. For me, not drinking was no longer an option. Brad and I often went out to a bar after closing the athletic club on Saturday nights, and Brad became smitten with me so quickly I felt almost sad for him. I told him I wasn't free until Lawrence moved away in a couple of months, and he said that was fine with him, he would wait. And he did wait, most patiently, though one night we were slamming tequila shots for hours in a dark corner booth of a bar and began groping each other so intensely the bartender suggested we go get a room.

During the weeks leading up to Lawrence's departure, I drank heavily every night. I could tell he was concealing his excitement about his new job, but there was an exuberance to his demeanor as he tied up loose ends, talked with a realtor about a place he would rent in New York and packed up his apartment. A couple of times he raised the topic of our pending separation, but he made no promises about what would happen after he relocated. During those conversations, I didn't have much to say. I wasn't enough to make him stay, and he didn't want me enough to take me along. Whenever I did try to talk about his leaving, I felt I would choke on my words, on the sense of abandonment welling up inside. When he asked me how I was doing, I felt like weeping, but the idea of crying in front of him like a helpless little girl or, worse, one of his patients, filled me with self-loathing.

The week before he left, he invited me to drive with him to New York and offered to pay for my return ticket. I guzzled a beer and started on another one, my sixth or seventh that evening. This loss was engulfing me. Lawrence was leaving me just as my father had, and I could do nothing to stop him. And, like Dad, he didn't seem to be having any difficulty walking away from me.

By ten o'clock that night, I had to get out of his apartment. As we hugged goodbye in his doorway, he tried to hold on to me for a moment. Now he pitied me, which was worse than being discarded. I pulled away and headed down the sidewalk.

"Hey, are you okay?" he called after me.

I nodded and waved over my shoulder without looking back.

"Call me if you want to talk."

As soon as I closed my car door, sobs jerked out of me so I couldn't catch my breath. This wasn't just about Lawrence; this was bigger than him and all tangled up with Dad walking out a decade earlier. I cried about Dad, I cried about Lawrence, I cried about Brad. I cried until I was drained. The car was so silent I could hear my breathing slowing down. In the stillness, memories of Dad rolled through my mind: him disappearing, the divorce, no-show weekends, the years I didn't hear from him while he was in prison and now us using drugs together. Mixed up with my loneliness and despair was the awareness that it was fucked-up for a father to use drugs with his own daughter. I scrounged for some napkins in my glove box, blew my nose and wiped my face.

My car was on autopilot. The next thing I knew, I was at Brad's apartment. As soon as he opened his door, something in me let loose. I pressed my body against his and started kissing him, my need for him was savage. For once, he didn't resist. I wrapped one of my legs around his thigh and slid my hands under his shirt, across his chest, around his back, clutching his shoulder blades.

He backed us into his bedroom and followed my lead as I began shedding my clothes.

When I awoke the next morning in Brad's bed, both of us naked, my guilt was staggering. It so consumed me, I couldn't tell who I felt worse about, Brad or Lawrence. My throat was raw, my body dehydrated and aching everywhere. As usual, my head was throbbing with pain. *I am out of control. Something has got to give here.*

He rubbed my back. "I sure enjoyed last night."

Another smack of shame. I pulled on my shirt. "Me too." His gaze followed me as I moved around the room, collecting my clothes and getting dressed.

"You don't remember." His words hung in the air between us while I focused on working my shoes on, avoiding his gaze.

"Of course I do." I sat back up, slow enough to avoid sloshing my brain around but quick enough that it wouldn't be obvious how sick I was. He followed me out to the living room where I was searching for my purse. Putting his hands on my shoulders, he gently turned me to face him. His eyes were blue and liquid and soft, reminding me of the color of the deep end of my pool in Miami; they were little pools waiting for me to jump in. For a long moment, I wished I could jump, wished I could free-fall into his arms. But in his sad eyes, I saw how I would only ever disappoint him.

"I can't believe you don't remember the first time we made love."

My body tensed, ready to bolt. I couldn't comprehend what love was, and I certainly didn't know how to make it. "I kind of remember. It's a little fuzzy."

He shook his head, shaking loose something he no longer wanted in his mind. Me, probably. I stretched up to nibble on his earlobe and murmured, "Guess I had too much to drink last night."

"You think?" He leaned back, his face just out of my reach.

"C'mon. It's not like it's the last time we'll have sex."

He pulled me so close I could no longer look at him, nibble his ear or kiss him. In that embrace, I knew he wanted far more from me than I could ever give him. He wanted closeness and warmth and love, and before long, he would want me to cut back on my drinking. Who knew what he would think about my drug use? If he truly knew how fucked-up I was, he would walk—no, run—away from me as fast as he could. I was broken, desperate, no good for him.

That afternoon, Lawrence and I had lunch together in the cafeteria. Neither of us were eating much, just looking at each other then glancing away. I was shaky hungover and too emotionally battered to trust what would come out of my mouth. "You seemed pretty upset last night. You feeling any better?" he asked.

"A little, I guess." What bullshit. And from the look on his face, he knew it too. "Actually, I'm not doing so hot."

"Why don't we just see what happens after I get settled in New York?"

I nodded. My eyes stung and my nostrils flared as I held back my tears.

"Is there anything I can do? To make my leaving easier?"

If I spoke and my voice faltered, those floodgates would open again, racking my body with sobs in front of the co-workers all around us—the stodgy old doctors and administrators and sexy, thirty-something nurses who Lawrence should have been dating. I shook my head.

I was disgusted with myself for sleeping with Brad and for getting hooked on a man like Lawrence whose interest in me was fleeting. Since Mark, I had known how to spot a man who wouldn't leave me. Lawrence wasn't one of them. Yet something in him had triggered me to pursue the unattainable. *This is exactly what I'm doing with my father, still. I'm treating Lawrence like—what do the shrinks at the hospital call it—a surrogate father.* The possibility revolted me, and I wanted to claw and kick and thrash at the thought, to push this craziness out of my consciousness. I was becoming untethered, like I was detaching from . . . from what?

Reality? Sanity? To distract myself from my spiraling fears, I started bopping my foot up and down rapidly until I noticed it was vibrating the entire bench and table. I recalled a teenaged girl who was a patient on Lawrence's unit. She was stunningly beautiful and crazily, ceaselessly talking, tapping, eating, laughing, pacing. A manic (I had to stop reading that damned *DSM-III* book!). I steadied my foot.

Lawrence waited, saying nothing, probably wondering what to do with this nutcase of a girl sitting across from him. Then a look of concern, or maybe it was pity, came over his face, and something inside me deflated and crumpled around itself.

"I think I need to see someone. You know, a therapist," I said.

He didn't look surprised at all, and I hoped it was because he believed in therapy. "Well, you know I support that idea. Everybody can benefit from a therapist." He pulled out his wallet and sifted through some business cards. "If it's a good one." He slid a business card across the table to me. "She's the best psychologist around."

I stuffed the card in my purse.

Lawrence's departure left me feeling worthless. Brad was ready to start our relationship for real, but, instead of diving right in there with him, I found myself pushing him away. Far away. What he wanted from me, a loving relationship, was overwhelming. If I was honest and open about who I really was, he wouldn't stay with me. And if I wasn't honest, he wouldn't be satisfied. It was a no-win situation. There was also my using. I was exhausted from hiding my coke habit from Lawrence, and I was certain Brad wouldn't tolerate my addiction. Not for long.

For two weekends in a row, I gave Brad excuses as to why I couldn't go out with him, then I stopped returning his calls, hoping he would give up on me. One afternoon at the athletic club, he asked me to take my lunch break with him. Cornered, no way to avoid him there at work, I decided to finally face him.

As soon as I slumped down at a table in the back of the café, he jumped right in. "What's going on with us? I thought we could be together once your boyfriend moved away?"

"It's been harder than I expected . . . him leaving. I'm confused. I care about you. A lot. But I don't think I can—"

"What? You can't what?"

"I don't think I can make you happy."

He stared at me for a moment. "You don't know what will make me happy. Let me"—he tapped his chest—"decide that. I wanna be with you. I've been waiting for months to be with you."

"My life is a mess, an absolute mess. I'm falling apart. I dropped out of college. I just got dumped after an eighteen-month relationship. I'm getting deeper and deeper in debt. And you know I need to cut back on my drinking."

Clearly, he was hurt, which left me full of guilt. I promised myself I would take a break from men and then never again get involved with a man who wanted so much closeness. Or a man like Lawrence who could walk away without a glance back.

Without the attention of a man, I soon realized how alone I was. By this point, I was avoiding Jenny regularly and had no other female friends. Hovering at the edge of that bleak nothingness that was always pressing in around me, I consumed more and more alcohol and coke. My hangovers became worse. One was so brutal, and I had slept so little the night before, I could barely drag myself to work. Using cocaine at a psychiatric hospital was a bad idea, especially one with a drug treatment unit —I hated delivering mail to that unit. The drug rehab patients looked more downtrodden and broken than the psychotic patients who shuffled around on Thorazine with their vacant stares and twitchy faces. But that morning, I snorted a few lines to revive myself before heading in. No one seemed to notice, so I did that a few more times. Then I took some cocaine to work for a little pick-me-up during my lunch break. Eventually, I was snorting a few lines at work whenever I had any. On those days, I was able to sort mail faster than ever. Snorting and sorting, I called it. The way I figured, if Dad could fool a parole officer, I could easily fool those nurses and doctors. All I needed to do was stay cool and follow Dad's motto: be like the wind at night. Invisible. Illusive.

Just like after Mark raped me, my commitment to stay away from men didn't last long. It just had to be the right kind of man, only that range was getting smaller and smaller. I avoided possessive men (at all costs), men who didn't drink (too exhausting, all the secrecy), needy men (major turnoff), aloof, career-driven men (too likely to leave me) and men that wanted to genuinely know me (I would always let them down). A couple of months after I broke it off with Brad, I dated a medical student, but not for long because he was innocent, possibly still a virgin and overwhelmed by my advances, which caused me to feel slutty. Then I turned my attention to my flight instructor, but he seldom drank, so I let that fizzle. It was getting difficult to find a man who drank as much and as often as I did, but who wasn't stumbling and slurring as he flirted with me, or so wasted that his eyes were glassy and vacant, or worse yet, loud and picking fights like Mark—I gave wide berth to that type. And I never found a man who used as much coke as I did. No one I knew even had access to that much blow, except Dad and Rick.

Unable to connect to anyone, swinging wildly between hiding in my bedroom alone and hooking up with one man after another, I began to feel as if I were sinking, barely keeping my head above water. Several times since Lawrence had moved, I thought of calling the counselor he had recommended, had even checked my insurance policy to see what my portion of the fee would be. But I hadn't mustered the courage to pick up that phone, especially to call a woman. Talking to a therapist would be difficult enough, but talking with a female therapist would be excruciating. The space between a woman and me was always encumbered and confusing, because I couldn't read a woman the way I could a man. I never knew what to say to women or how to capture their attention or figure out what they wanted from me.

But Lawrence had told me this lady was the best psychologist around, so how hard could it be to talk to her? He had also said she was sexy. A sexy, female therapist sounded better than the few female counselors I knew from the hospital who were frumpy or stern or downright rigid.

The morning I dug through my purse and found Dr. Adler's now dog-eared business card, I wasn't any more hungover or remorseful than any other morning. In fact, all I had done the night before was drink myself into a stupor, pass out, come to in the morning and go to work. All of that alone in my apartment. It was that very isolation, my world closing in around me, that finally compelled me to reach out, as only the drowning will do.

ANOTHER WAY

*a*s Dr. Adler—she said I could call her Miriam—and I settled in opposite each other, I was relieved that she was, initially, flipping through my paperwork instead of looking at me. I was uncomfortable just sitting there face-to-face with a woman, and I was supposed to talk to her about my life, my pain, my secrets? Simply being in her office confirmed that my life had turned to complete shit. When she did look up, I surveyed my hands, the furniture, the floor, the artwork. Behind her hung a large, framed photo of a seal pup with snow-white fur and huge, glossy, sad eyes. The pup appeared helpless and vulnerable, and I wondered if that seal had since been clubbed to death.

"Were you a patient of Dr. Segel's?" she asked.

Confused, I tipped my head to the side.

She glanced down at my paperwork and back at me. "You wrote down Lawrence Segel referred you here."

"No. I work at the hospital where he works . . . worked. Where he used to work. He just moved to New York. We are, or were, dating."

Her eyebrows shot up with surprise then quickly returned to neutral. "Oh. I see."

It dawned on me that Lawrence didn't only know of Miriam,

he knew her, they were colleagues, had worked together with patients from the hospital, probably went to the same conferences. *Oh God, maybe they're friends, and he talked to her about me already.* My cheeks grew hot.

"Well, then. I won't send him a thank you card for his professional referral," she said, smiling.

"Do you know him?" *Of course, she does you idiot!* "I mean, do you know him well?"

"I know most of the psychologists in town because I've been in practice here for over ten years. He's referred a few patients to me. I'd say he's a colleague and an acquaintance. I wouldn't tell him that you've come to see me, now that we have that referral issue cleared up." She smiled again. "And you know everything you say in here is confidential."

She set the paperwork down, stopped talking and regarded me. It was all I could do to make eye contact with her. *I hate this. I hate this. What the hell am I supposed to say?*

"Do you want to tell me a little about why you're seeking counseling?"

I took a deep breath and stared out the window. A massive sycamore tree grew at the far end of the parking lot, its mottled trunk sinuous and reaching far above her third-floor office. Bringing my attention back to her, I said, "Well, Lawrence moved to New York." *Stupid, you just said that.* "As I said a minute ago. But you already knew that, right? That he moved away?"

"I had heard that he was leaving." She took a sip of coffee from a Styrofoam cup. I couldn't read her, but she didn't appear uncomfortable. She was probably being honest.

I can't do this. What am I supposed to do, blab to her about everything? Dad? The coke? The drinking? All the men I've slept with? "We've been dating for, oh, about a year and a half. And I didn't move up there with him. Obviously."

Another coffee sip. "And what has that been like for you?"

I pondered that question. While I did miss spending time with him, the worst part was the void inside me when he left. That sounded so narcissistic that I couldn't bring myself to say it; that it didn't hurt because he was gone, it hurt because he left me. *I need a drink. This would be so much easier if I'd had a few drinks before coming here. As soon as we're done, I'm going straight to a bar.* "I guess it was hard when he moved away, and I do miss him, it's . . . "

More sips. She wasn't filling any awkward silences in that office.

"It's more that he . . . left. That he just left." I wasn't making any sense. I gazed outside to the tree again, then up the wall to the seal photo, over to the cup in Miriam's hand, then followed the cup as she moved it to her lips. She wore pale pink lipstick like Mom. No other make-up. How could she do that and still seem so sure of herself?

"Can you say some more about that?"

All I could think of was how his leaving reopened the vast emptiness that was, apparently, still inside me in the exact shape of my father. I wanted to dive right out of her office and soar over to the sycamore tree, but something in that expression of hers— not a blank slate but soft and patient and, sort of, open—kept me planted on that chair. "It seemed so easy for him to leave, to move away, without even thinking about taking me with him. He never asked me to move there or anything. He told me he found a job, and, poof, he was gone."

She gave a slight lift of her chin in acknowledgement of what I was saying.

I stole a peek at the clock. Ten minutes left. To my consternation, tears were building up in my eyes. Reaching for my purse on the floor, I blinked a few times. When I sat back up, she wasn't making any move to escort me out of her office. In that pause there, she and I facing each other, the words slipped right out of my mouth. "That's exactly what my father did. Just walked out on my family."

"And Lawrence leaving has stirred that up again for you?"

I nodded and slid my purse over my shoulder, scooting to the edge of the chair to stand.

"We still have several minutes left," she said.

"Ah, I know, but I gotta go. I have another . . . thing right after this."

"Okay. If you want, we can talk some more about this next week." She gave me that soft smile again.

I had no intention of going back to her office. But as the day of the next appointment neared, I found myself planning what I would tell her, rehearsing my words, playing out our conversation. Within a few weeks, I came to both dread and anticipate our weekly appointments, knowing how uncomfortable and exposing our conversations were but getting relief from each session. After a couple months, I came to anticipate those appointments, then came to need them almost as much as I needed a drink. If I could have, I would have seen her every day. Our appointments were the only time and place where my outside world matched my inside world, and she was the only person with whom I was beginning to be even slightly honest. Even Dad, with whom I could at least drink and use drugs without reserve, was oblivious to how desperate and isolated I was or how out-of-control my behavior had become.

Gradually, I told Miriam all about Dad walking out on us, about our family life after that, about my teenage years and my drinking and drugging. But I held back that Dad was a smuggler and I was using coke with him. I knew counselors weren't allowed to divulge to police any information they learned from clients except in cases of homicide, self-harm or child abuse, but Dad was still on parole. I didn't want to risk blowing his cover. Besides, the cocaine was *our* little secret, just between Dad and me.

It took me much longer to tell Miriam about my abortion and the rape. We talked a lot about my promiscuous behavior with men, me blaming it all on the booze. "I wish I could just stay away from men when I drink. I'm not sure why I do that. I used to wear my mom's old wedding band on my left ring finger when I went to bars, you know, to discourage men from hitting on me."

"That's clever. Did it work?"

I shook my head. "I don't know. Sometimes. Once I'm loaded, all bets are off with me and men, wedding ring or not."

"Are you attracted to these men?"

"No." I waved my hand toward her, brushing away her suggestion. "I mean some of them. And some were sweet. I don't always sleep with them, and some I don't even know if I did. Some are older than me, like at my dad's wedding, I'm pretty sure his friend was hitting on me." I shuddered. "I mean, he was my dad's age. I don't think I did anything with him, thank God. Once I have a few drinks, my radar is flipped on, and I'm scanning for a man I can have. And the more I drink, the flirting turns into seducing, and next thing I know, I'm in bed with a guy. The booze unleashes this seductiveness in me."

"What does seducing a man get you?"

"A lot."

"Like?"

"It makes me feel sexy and desirable. Adored. Sort of like I'm . . . in control." As soon as that last word slipped out, I wanted to shove it back inside my mouth, back into the deep end of my psyche, but it was too late.

"In control of what?"

I knew she would latch on to that word, and she probably already knew the answer. It was absurd, of course, that being promiscuous had any connection to being in control. "Maybe secure is a better word. Secure or in charge of what happens with men, with a man. You know what I mean."

She shook her head and was silent, waiting for more. In the silence between us, the truth came into focus for me. I saw it in the way I had latched on to Brad the instant Lawrence told me he was leaving. Saw it in the string of men whom I pursued after I walked away—no, escaped—from Mark. Saw it in my preoccupation to reconnect with Dad at any cost. The truth was so clear that I could reach out and touch it. I turned to the calm of my sycamore tree, but even that sentry couldn't shelter me from the truth. Being left by a man was intolerable to me. Capturing the attention and holding on to a man was my primary focus in life. And sex was how I tried to tether a man to me. Or in the case of Dad, impressing him with whatever means possible.

I shook my head. "I just wanna be able to drink and not go home with some guy."

She pursed her lips together, pensive but nonjudgmental, and kept her eyes on me long enough to make me feel squirmy. Studying her desk, I noticed the lack of photos, and I wondered if she had any kids. She wore a wedding band, so she was at least married. *She's probably been happily married to the same guy for twenty years. Probably the only guy she's ever had sex with.*

"How could you keep that from happening?"

"What?" I glanced back at her.

"Drink and not go home with some guy?"

"I guess I would have to drink less." Just the mention of cutting down sent a shiver down my back. *There has to be another way.*

MIDNIGHT CALLING

*W*ay too early on a Saturday, Rick called me talking fast in a raspy, dry whisper. "Lynn, I gotta bring some stuff over to your house. Right away. You gonna be around this morning? Like ten, fifteen minutes?"

"What stuff? I don't even know what time it is." I was still bleary from booze the night before.

"I got helicopters flyin' over my house. I can't talk. I'll explain when I get there."

Clearly he'd been smoking crack for who knows how many days in a row. "Maybe you just need some sleep. Why don't you go to bed and call—

"No can do. I really need to come over. Like now. We'll talk when I get there, okay?"

"Alright. Come on over."

Rick knocked on my door ten minutes later. As soon as I let him in, he ducked inside, glancing over his shoulder before shutting the door. "Is your roommate here?"

"She's at her boyfriend's for a few days." In fact, she rarely stayed at our apartment anymore.

"Listen, the cops are watching me. There were helicopters over my house all night long. I need to keep something here." He demonstrated by pressing a finger to one nostril. He was grinding his jaw back and forth and pacing around my living room.

It didn't make any sense that cops would fly over his house all night but not pound on his door and arrest him or follow him here. He was just freaking out. "How much are we talking about?"

He lit a cigarette and took a few draws. Balancing his cigarette in the ashtray, he pulled from inside his jacket a gallon Ziploc freezer bag full of chunky powder.

My pulse quickened with anticipation and a tinge of fear. "For how long?"

"Just 'til things cool off. A few days, tops."

I swallowed hard. "If they're watching you, why haven't they arrested you?"

He dragged his hands over his face, from his forehead to his neck, stretching the gray skin under his eyes downward. "I don't know. Nessa says I'm paranoid as shit."

I stared at him for a few beats, not sure what to say. "You do seem pretty wired. Maybe you're imagining things. How many days've you been freebasing?"

"Oh, man, let's see . . . two, maybe three."

"Yeah, I think Vanessa's right, you're probably imagining things. Leave it here. Go scarf some food down and get some sleep. Come back when things are cool."

As soon as he left, I scooped a small pile of coke onto a mirror. The flakes crunched under my driver's license as I chopped the mound into a fine powder then formed a line. I inhaled, watching the line being vacuumed up. I fell back against the chair, smiling. "This is gonna be a great weekend."

By Sunday evening, I hadn't left the apartment or slept or eaten anything except peanut butter and cheese crackers that I devoured the few times I came down from the cocaine enough to realize I was ravenous. I kept telling myself I was snorting my last line, absolutely my last, but when the elation from the last line faded, despair rose up in my chest again. And that huge bag of coke, at least a half-kilo, kept calling to me, luring me back to that fleeting moment, to that place of perfection, to that illusive space where everything was right and true and I was a beautiful person. Only the coke, just like the booze, pulled me too far, drew me into racing, manic paranoia.

I tried to go to work on Monday, driving into the parking lot before desperation overtook me, before I was straight again. Even armed with my film can in my purse, I couldn't face those doctors and nurses or even the flirty psych techs or maintenance guys.

Back at my apartment, I snorted another line before calling in sick, promising myself I would go to work on Tuesday.

Mom called that afternoon. "You usually work on Mondays. Everything okay?"

"I'm a little sick. Intestinal bug or something I ate didn't agree with me."

"You're not pregnant, are you?"

"God no!"

"Are you hungover?"

"Give me a break. I'm just sick today."

"Okay. Why don't I come over after work and check on you? I can bring you some soup or some vitamin C."

"I'll be fine. I got soup in the cupboard, and Jenny's here. I'm sure I'll be at work tomorrow. See you then."

Several hours later, long after the TV stations went off the air, I dropped onto my bed and squeezed my eyes shut. If I slept for a couple of hours, I might be able to go to work. As I lay there, the birds outside began to stir, a few singular chirps here and there. The pre-dawn light seeped pale and gray around the edges of my curtains. I scooched deeper under the covers. *If I call in sick again, I might lose my job. I hope Jenny doesn't come home and find me wired out of my mind here. How long can a person live without sleep?* The bird songs outside intensified. *If I go to work, people will know I'm wasted. Definitely can't deliver mail to the drug treatment unit today. Fuck, I can't breathe.*

I threw the covers off. Morning light was now fuzzing in all around the edge of the drapes and through the slit between them. To my ears, the birdsong outside my window was ominous; the day would come, whether I was ready or not. Soon, most people, most normal people, would be getting ready for work or school or to take care of their children, while I hung on to life by a thread.

A shower and some food, I thought, and no more coke. Then I'm going to work. As I started to slide open my curtains, I could make out a car parked behind the gas station in front of my apartment. When my eyes adjusted to the light, I saw it was a police car. I closed the drapes, overlapping them so there was no gap, and forced myself to take a few long, deep breaths. Still, my heart pounded in my chest. I had heard of people going into cardiac arrest from snorting too much cocaine. More slow deep breaths, but I could not slow my heart rate.

After several minutes of pacing around my bedroom, I peeked out the window again. The cop car was still there. Panicked, I grabbed the phone.

"Hey, Dad. Sorry to call so early."

"You alright?"

"Uh, sort of. But . . . you know if Rick's okay?"

"Think he's fine, why?"

I hated to cause a rift between them. "Well, he asked me to take care of some stuff for him. For a little while, but it's been a few days since I've heard from him. Not sure how much longer I can watch his stuff." The phone line hummed with silence. I didn't want to say too much in case police helicopters *had* been flying over Rick's house and my phone line was tapped, though that didn't seem likely as I hadn't been out of my apartment for days. "You have any idea what's goin' on?" I had to say it. "Cause now there's a cop car parked across the street this morning."

"I don't know nothin' about this, darlin'."

All I heard were my jeans scraping on the wall as I slumped to the floor. Those words had always been Dad's tell—"I don't know nothin'." Those were the words he used when he definitely *did* know something but did not plan on incriminating himself. His words pierced my muddled thinking, and I saw my situation with blazing clarity. The reason Rick brought the coke to my house in the first place was because he didn't want to get busted with it. If I got caught with this cocaine, he wouldn't run over to the police station and tell the cops, *No, no, that's my blow. Leave my sister alone.* Hell no! If I got caught with this half-kilo, no one would rescue me. No one. Not Rick and certainly not Dad. This wasn't a family business, and Dad wasn't protecting me anymore.

"But I'll give Rick a call. See if he needs anything." His words were hollow and meaningless, just like every time he told me he loved me over the past ten years. But they snapped me out of my trance.

Hanging up the phone, I went into action, stashing the coke inside a canvas mail bag, cinching tight the rope and crimping shut the clunky, metal clasp. I surveyed my closet for the least obvious place to hide it. There was an attic door in the ceiling of the closet. I pushed on the built-in wooden shelves at the end of the closet to sure they were sturdy. Climbing up the shelves, sweat trickling from my armpits, I nudged open the panel in the ceiling. Heat gushed down on me from the attic. I slid the mail bag into the attic and shimmied the panel back in place.

After calling in sick at work, again, I took a shower with the water as cool as I could stand it, then crawled to my bedroom window again and peered over the sill. The cop car was still there, and I could now make out the two cops sitting inside.

I plotted how to get the cocaine out of my house and back to Rick. None of my purses was large enough to hold the Ziploc bag. *My backpack. It'll fit in my backpack. I'm a college student or was one. For God's sake, I can walk out of my house with a backpack on. That won't look suspicious. They'll have no justification to search my pack.*

As I climbed the shelves again to get the bag, it occurred to me that the attic would be the safest place to snort one last line. I grabbed a mirror and straw and hoisted myself into the attic. I perched on the two-by-four rafters, my butt on one and my feet on another. The closet light beamed a column of light above the attic opening, enough that I could see to balance the mirror on my lap and chop up a line. I was careful not to spill any on the pink insulation; there would be no way for me to recover any that I dropped there, and even if I could, I wasn't putting *fiberglass* up my nose.

Once the cocaine entered my bloodstream and the exhilaration spread through me, I told myself everything was fine, the cops were just taking a break back there. The coffee and donut thing. Replaying my conversation with Dad, I was certain he only responded the way he did because he was worried my phone line had been tapped. I tried to remember if I had said "coke" but was certain I had only used the word "stuff." He was probably calling Rick right now telling him to get over here and pick up his product. I hunkered there until my legs itched from the pink insulation and my sweaty shirt clung to my back.

When I inched back down the closet shelves, the cops were still there. Mother fuckers! I sat on the floor of my bedroom for several minutes, thinking of who else I could call. Not Mom, that's for sure. Not Rick, in case his phone line *was* tapped, which might further connect me to him. But I could take the coke to him, could drive over there, knock on his door, set it on his coffee table and walk back out. No, there was no way I could saunter out my front door with a half-kilo of blow in my backpack while a cop car sat a couple-hundred yards away. I could call Miriam, but I would have to explain how I had been withholding information and lying to her. Then my old drug counselor popped into my mind, his gruff face and voice as vivid as if he stood there before me.

I crept down the stairs, scanned through the yellow pages, muttering, "Please, please, please." There it was, Tom Donaghy was still listed.

As soon as I heard his New York accent, I stood motionless pressing the phone to my ear. *What the hell am I doing? I can't tell him what's going on. And do I really want to get rid of this blow?* "Hi. I'm not sure if you remember me, Lynn? My mom, Linda, brought me there a—"

"Of course, I remember. How are you?"

"Good. Well, actually, I've been better. And when I last saw you, you said I could call you again if I ever needed to talk."

"What's goin' on?"

Tom's voice was like a tenuous connection, a thin thread between me and the one person in this world who might be able to help extract me from this situation. Desperate, I decided to lay it all on the line and describe precisely what was happening. So what if the cops who *might* be watching my apartment *might* have tapped my phone line. I had to end this. So I rattled the whole story out to him. All of it.

When I finished, he said, "Still think you got this drug use under control?"

The question was so absurd after everything I had relayed to him, but I was in no position to be sarcastic, and I didn't feel like joking. "No. My life is fucked, and it's all because of the drugs."

"Good. Maybe you've hit bottom. Maybe not. Here's what I would do. Call your brother. Tell him to get over there and get his stuff, or you're flushing it."

"Flushing it? There's no way. I can't flush it."

"Well, it don't sound like you're ready then to—"

"No. Wait. Wait. I mean, literally, I *can't* flush it. Well not at once. There's too much. It would clog the toilet."

"How much coke are we talking about?"

"A Ziploc bag full."

"Like a sandwich baggie?"

"No, one of those big ones. The gallon size. I think it's at least half a kilo. I don't have any scales, so I don't know."

"Holy shit! You've got yourself in a risky position if you get caught with that. Well, tell him anyways. He'll get the gist of it. And then you need to stay the hell away from him. And your father. Don't call them. Don't visit them. If they call—"

"They won't. They don't." The old loss I had come to associate with Dad washed over me as I imagined drifting further and further apart again. This time it would be *me* walking away from *him*.

"Stay away from them or you'll be using again in no time. Here's the last thing I want you to do. You know the church on Dublin-Granville Road? Big brick one? There's a recovery meeting there tonight at eight o'clock. Meet me there. Okay?"

I was leaning on the armrest of the loveseat, but with his suggestion, I flopped backwards, lying on it with my legs draped over the armrest. I stared at the ceiling. I had gone to those meetings years earlier, and I didn't see how they could help. But as I talked with Tom, being truthful with him felt like I had grasped a life preserver right when I could no longer tread water. My life—both what had come before and what I predicted might come after—spooled out in front of me like a movie: year after year after year, chasing oblivion, losing control, never having friends or love or even a healthy relationship, only a string of desperate encounters with other drunks, despising myself every morning and drinking myself into being "okay" every afternoon. It was that vicious cycle I couldn't endure any longer.

"Okay. I'll see you at eight tonight."

As soon as I hung up the phone, I peeked out the window. The cop car was gone. For just a few seconds, I considered that all my panic and despair of the past couple of hours had been fabricated by my booze- and cocaine-saturated brain.

Before my resolve waned, I dialed Rick. "You've got to come over. I'm having some . . . trouble with your stuff here, and it looks like I might have had a cop watching my place. So, you gotta come pick it up or I'm gonna get rid of it."

"Whoa, calm down. What's up?"

"I don't know what's goin' on, if someone's watching my house or not, but for a while this morning a cop was parked behind the gas station in front of my apartment. They're gone now, I think. Least I don't see the car now."

"You had people over there, coming and going, partying?"

"Hell no. I've not even been outta my place all weekend."

He chuckled. "I know how that goes. I'll be right over."

"What if the cops are still out there? Somewhere I can't see?" Now who was the basket case?

"I don't give a shit. A brother's not allowed to visit his baby sister? What do they got on you or me? They got no reason to bother us. I'll be right over. Just sit tight."

Racing into the kitchen, I shuffled through the cupboards for some kind of white powder I could use to replenish the Ziploc bag. I couldn't even guess how much I had used or if Rick would charge me for it. Snatching the box of baking soda, I lurched up the steps two at a time and climbed into the attic. As I sprinkled the powder over the coke, I held the bag above the light coming through the attic opening, eyeing the level, trying to remember how full it was a few days earlier. I zipped the bag shut and was scrunching the soda into the cocaine when the doorbell rang. I flinched.

I scrambled down the closet shelves and glanced out the window to confirm it was Rick. When I opened the front door with the chain still on, Rick said, "Haven't seen one cop car anywhere between my place and here."

I let him in and scanned the parking lot. He set his backpack on the floor, unzipped it and pulled out a scale.

"You've got to be kidding! I've been sitting on this shit for you for days, putting my ass on the line, cops sitting outside my place all morning and all you can think about is how much I've snorted?"

He had a smirk on his face. "Hey, I'm just tryin' to see what the damage is here. Chill out." He cleared a space on the coffee table among the ashtrays, old mail and empty beer cans.

Hovering over him, I scraped and chewed on my fingernail cuticles, which were already sore from being gnawed on for days. Rick placed the bag on the scale and tapped the weights as the beam teetered up and down. Bracing myself for an argument, I practiced my alibi. *Hey, you never said I couldn't snort any.* Tap, tap, tap and the beam came to rest.

"Ah, shit, you had me worried for nothin'. I figured it'd be worse than this. This ain't no big deal." He leaned back on the couch and looked at me for a few seconds. "Hard to put down, huh?"

I dropped into a chair. "Too hard. Man, I can't do this anymore."

"It's cuz it's uncut. It's so intense, the buzz *and* the crash. It's way worse when you're smokin' it."

"What about—" I pointed in the direction where the cop car had been.

"Well, I'm gonna finish visiting my sister, then I'm goin' home."

We sat there, each having a smoke and staring at that bulging Ziploc bag. It was a curse to us, a load of bad business that Dad had plunked down into the middle of our lives. And I think we both knew it. This drug was the absolute best and worst thing our father had to offer us.

Rick crushed out his butt, took a big pinch from the edge of the bag where there were fewer chunks and sniffed it up his nose. Wincing inside, I hoped that pinch was more coke than baking soda and watched him in my peripheral vision while I dawdled with my cigarette, tapping the ashes off the glowing tip then extinguishing it.

He cleared his throat and swallowed. "Ahhh. I missed this stuff."

"Not me. Not yet anyway."

He stood, situated the bag and scales in his backpack, covered it all with a jacket, zipped up the pack and strode out the door. As he walked out with his cocaine and his scales and his renewed hope for keeping it under control this time, the bond that existed between Rick, Dad and me began to unravel.

*A*s promised, I met Tom at a twelve-step meeting that night. He marched me right over to a group he referred to as some "great women" who could help me. I was thinking more along the lines of, "Great. Women." Without any mood-altering substance to ease my self-consciousness, it was excruciating to be around a bunch of recovering alcoholics who probably saw right through my veneer and knew I was in sorry-ass shape. Even worse was a group of women. Women didn't usually like me. I was getting better at talking with Miriam, but I paid her to talk to me.

The three women were in their late twenties. The tallest one asked me if I was new.

I had no idea what she was talking about—new to drinking and drugging, new to *not* drinking and drugging, new to the meetings. Well, two out of three applied. "Yeah."

"You picked a good one to come to," the chubby woman said.

"It gets easier. Just don't drink, go to a lot of meetings, and things'll start getting better," said woman number three.

What the fuck? Just don't drink? If I could "just not drink," I would . . . or wouldn't . . . whatever. And I certainly wouldn't be at a recovery meeting. I nodded.

They all scribbled their phone numbers on the front of a small booklet then passed it to me. Woman number three said, "It's got all the meetings listed, where and when they are. And our phone numbers so you can call one of us, you know, if you're thinking about getting drunk. When I feel like drinking, I have to get to a meeting or call someone."

Now I was bewildered. How on earth could calling one of these women help me not drink? I slid the booklet in my purse. "Sure. I'll do that. Thanks."

Back at my apartment, I fell into bed in my clothes and slept for ten dreamless hours.

JUST ONE

When my alarm went off at seven, I was amazed to be clear-headed for the first time in—I couldn't remember how long. For breakfast I made scrambled eggs and toast—another first, being able to eat in the morning. I offered to make Jenny some eggs and tried to chat with her about her plans for the day, but she declined my offer and spoke tersely to me about the last check I wrote her for my half of the rent, which had bounced. To make matters worse, the last several times we had both been home, I pretty much avoided her, hiding in my room with my cocaine or leaving to go do something with "friends." Embarrassed about my behavior, it felt like my covers had been pulled. She could see me for the loser I was. The next thought that came to me was that I needed a drink. It popped into my mind with no warning, my solution to everything. *No way. I'm going to work today before I lose my job. This job's all I have left.*

I was relieved when Jenny left for class, and I was no longer faced with her disappointment and anger. I couldn't even offer to write her another check, as I had even less money in my account now than when my last check had bounced. After a shower, I opened the closet door to get dressed, and my stash place in the attic zoomed into my mind, the canvas mail bag lying there, just above my head, in the dark, itchy attic. There was probably a chunk or two of cocaine in that bag—at least some powder—that had fallen out when I was scooping coke out of the Ziploc. My mind locked on to that possibility the way a dog locks its jaws on to a bone. Stay the hell out of that attic, I told myself. I snatched a pair of pants and a shirt from my closet and pushed the door shut. Leaving the damp towel on the floor where it fell, I dressed and raced downstairs. *Just go to work.*

By the time I pulled into the hospital parking lot, I wanted nothing more than to return home, climb into the attic and snort anything I could find on the bottom of that mail bag. The craving was physical, starting in my hands, which were locked on to the steering wheel, coursing right through my solar plexus and ending in my foot, the one that was hovering over the gas pedal. *Just shut the car off.* I twisted the ignition off and checked my appearance in the rearview mirror, wondering how I could weigh a little over a hundred pounds yet look so fat, so puffy. One good night of sleep and one breakfast couldn't undo the damage I had done to my body over the past several years. If I could have one line or one drink, I would feel better. Hell, I would *look* better. Bullshit, I told myself, it's the booze and drugs making me all puffy. Just go to work.

When I came home from work, the apartment was empty and the craving for a drink permeated my being, my every thought, my every action. Just one, the craving told me, two, max. I dug out of my purse the recovery meeting schedule with the women's phone numbers on it. There was a meeting at eight o'clock not too far from my place. I boiled pasta and heated up some spaghetti sauce, grateful there was no beer in the fridge. Jenny had long ago stopped leaving any in there. When I finished dinner, I glanced at the clock. It was only six. Turning on the television, I flipped through the channels. Nothing but news. I hated the news. It was all child abuse and violence and rapes. I clicked off the TV. The bag in the attic called to me, beckoning me to turn it inside out and salvage any residual cocaine

and the ecstasy that crusty powder promised. I imagined dragging that cursed bag down from the attic and chucking it in the
dumpster. The thought alone triggered panic as I envisioned
myself later, after I changed my mind, digging through the
dumpster for the bag and scouring it for any kibbles of cocaine. I
forced myself to sit down and have a cigarette, watching the
smoke from each exhale swirl toward the ceiling and dissipate. If
only I could make my craving for a drink dissipate like that
smoke. Music, maybe music. I jumped up and turned on the
boom box, but that goddamned mail bag was screaming for me. I
snapped the boom box off, grabbed my smokes and went for a
drive.

My intention was to drive around until the recovery meeting
started at eight, but my car was, once again, on autopilot. This
time, it went directly to the liquor store. I never made it to the
meeting.

***

*W*hen Rick moved to North Carolina to be closer to
Dad and, I assumed, to the coke, I hoped this
would make it easier for me to stay away from the blow. But I was
arranging a visit with Dad and Rick within a few weeks. I told
myself they were family; it was fine to visit them whenever I
wanted. And Vanessa and Rick had a new baby boy who I wanted
to meet. Or so I told myself.

As soon as Dad pulled out of the airport parking lot, the usual
niceties and hi-how-are-yous out of the way, a vast emptiness
yawned between us. Despair about our relationship seeped in
through the façade I was upholding, shining a thin beam of light
on the lies I had been telling myself. We weren't connected again;
we were just fellow drug addicts. And I was never flying a plane
to Colombia for Dad and his partners (besides, I needed money
for counseling far more desperately than for flight lessons). He
passed me his stash. When I popped open the lid and saw the

pale pink crystals clumped together, the finer powder around the edges, none of that other stuff mattered.

We went directly to the auction house and spent most of that long weekend there, just the two of us, avoiding Katherine. On our way back to the airport at the end of the weekend, Dad and I didn't speak a word. It was late morning, and I wasn't sure if he'd already snorted a line, but I hadn't. Our silence pressed down on me until I wanted to scream. Just when our lack of conversation was becoming unbearable, Dad slipped a cassette into the slot of the stereo system, and Neil Diamond's voice purred out. Studying the cover of the case, I said, "Hmm, that's funny. I have the same album. I love Neil Diamond."

"Me too. One of the few things I can listen to when I'm snortin'. Mellows me out." He glanced over at me. "Know what I mean?"

"Yeah." I stared at the cars in the lane next to me, trying to think of something funny or clever to say. When I glanced back at Dad, he stared at the road, his mouth turned down.

After several minutes, he reached into his pocket then tossed his stash container in my lap. I stared at it there, at the one thing Dad had to say to me, then gazed out the window, aware of that small plastic disk resting on my leg. It held 25-30 grams, about an ounce, but in our unbearable silence that morning, it felt like it weighed a pound. When I looked back at Dad, his eyes were still locked on the road. I flipped open the lid and snorted a pinch of bliss, a pinch of instant comradery.

When I returned to my apartment late that afternoon there was a curt note from Jenny. She had moved out, leaving only the boom box and a cat-shredded recliner someone had given us. The note listed how much money I owed her because yet another of my rent checks had bounced. I slumped onto the floor. I couldn't afford the rent myself, hell I couldn't even afford half of it, and didn't know anyone else who could move in with me. The apartment was still, and I listened to the leaky faucet dripping in the kitchen, the sound reverberating through the deserted apartment.

I slid out my stash. One line would clear my head, and then I could decide what to do next.

Several hours later, I lit the last cigarette in my pack. The gas station across the street was open all night, but the idea of walking over there and standing in the glare of the fluorescent lights, facing another person, even a night-shift cashier, sent chills down my back. I went to the bathroom to see how wired I looked. Staring at my image in the mirror, I hated myself. My pupils were huge, my eyes glassy, my skin clammy and pale. *There's no way I can go to work in the morning. I can't even go to the fucking gas station.* Waiting for the coke to wear off so I could go to sleep, I went down to the kitchen and pulled out the trashcan, grateful Jenny hadn't emptied it. Rifling through the top layer, I picked out a few of the larger cigarette butts. A couple of hours later, I dragged the wastebasket back out, shook some garbage onto the floor and sifted through the damp paper, wilted lettuce, empty beer cans, coffee grounds and stiff bread crusts, picking out the butts that weren't too soggy to light. As I shoveled all that crap back into the can, I imagined how I must have looked sitting on the floor scrounging butts out of moldy garbage.

I got one or two tokes from each butt before the filters started to burn. The inside of my nose was sore, and when I blew it, the tissue contained streaks of blood. I put what was left of the cocaine in the mail bag, took it to my usual hiding place in the attic and shoved it as far from the opening as I could.

"That is *it*," I said. "No more blow tonight." I knew if I could make it through the worst part of coming down off the last line—when my spirits and my endorphins crashed, when my life felt like it was skidding to its pathetic end—I would be able to fall asleep. It was the first fifteen minutes of coming down that always sent me back for more. A fresh, full cigarette would help me through the worst of it. I peeked around the edge of my curtains at the glow from the gas station. "Just walk over there and buy a pack," I said aloud. "No one's gonna know how wasted you are. And who cares if they do? It's some night-shift cashier." I stood with my hand on the front doorknob. A picture formed in my mind of that police car parked behind the gas station a few months earlier.

I walked to the kitchen then back to the front door, hand on the knob again. The euphoria from the last line was waning, and the empty apartment mirrored how I felt: hollow and lifeless. Glancing at the clock, I promised myself I would go fifteen minutes without snorting. If I could make it fifteen minutes, through the worst of the craving, I could stop. Dropping into the chair, I rocked back and forth with my hands wedged between my knees. I was slipping into an abyss, my puny, pathetic life closing in around me.

I ran upstairs, scrambled into the attic and shoveled with two fingernails at once as much coke as I could into my nostrils. I forced myself to take a few long slow breaths. My nasal passages were raw, my mouth tasted of sour yeast from drinking cheap beer all day, and my armpits stunk. Finally, the effect of the cocaine kicked in, and balanced there on the attic rafters, everything was fine. My life wasn't *that* bad.

Forty minutes later, I was rummaging through the trash for the next biggest, least soggy butts. Slouched on the floor, I got one or two puffs from each stubby, damp butt. "God," I mumbled, "what kind of life is this?" That horrific morning months ago, when I had hid in the attic from cops while shoveling coke up my nose, should have been all I needed to admit my life had turned to shit. Instead, a wretched night alone scrounging through the trash was what allowed me, finally, to face the truth about myself. There I was on the floor hunched over a pile of garbage. This must be what Tom meant when he had asked if I'd hit my bottom yet. How could I get any lower?

Remembering that Dad had said Neil Diamond was the only music he could listen to when he was high, I dug through my box of cassettes until I found Neil buried near the bottom. There he was on the cover, jamming on his guitar, wearing a total seventies shirt: deep, V-neck with sparkling strands dangling all around. I pulled the boom box over to the recliner, the volume just loud enough for Neil's soothing voice to block out the screaming emptiness of the apartment. As I stretched out in the chair, I finally crashed—asleep or unconscious, it didn't matter which, as long as it was away from myself.

When I awoke around noon, I was a shell with nothing meaningful inside: no feelings, no love, no hope. What scared me the most was my belief that I would always feel that way, that my life would continue unraveling, that same movie spool of loneliness, oblivion, self-destruction and self-loathing, on and on for decades. If there was any mercy, I would just die. I contemplated killing myself, deciding that pills were by far the least violent option. But I recalled the medical history of a patient who had both her feet amputated after a botched suicide attempt. The pills she took were only enough to knock her out for several hours, her legs folded underneath her restricting the circulation. I imagined the horror the woman experienced, not when she lost her feet but when she regained consciousness the next day, still alive. Given my track record, that would be me, trying to overdose but waking up instead. Then I recalled Mom once describing suicide as a permanent solution to a temporary problem. Permanent. The thought of Mom's heart breaking again was intolerable.

Still without cigarettes, out of cocaine and beer and far too sick to eat or drink anything but water, I wandered from room to room as my body shrieked for some kind of escape. Tequila was what I needed, but at twenty-years of age, I was still unable to buy a bottle at the liquor store and there was no way in hell I was walking into a bar in my condition, even the one where I had always been served tequila.

By two in the afternoon, I had taken a shower and walked to the gas station, hoping my credit card wouldn't be declined. Purchasing a pack of cigarettes, I didn't even look at the beer shelves. Those rows and rows of beer were my problem. Every single time something bad happened to me or I did something I was ashamed of, I had been intoxicated. For years, I bullshitted myself that I had everything under control, despite flunking classes and getting arrested and going home with a stranger. As things worsened, I winnowed out of my life those things which caused trouble for me—bongs, college, bars—everything except the mood-altering substances. And men—they were a persistent, perplexing, unsolvable problem too. My world had contracted to my job, my apartment, booze and drugs, and whichever man I could fit in my life for a few months.

I no longer had any doubt. I couldn't live with drugs and alcohol anymore.

TRASHED

That evening I showed up at Mom's condo. We made dinner, and it was like old times, the two of us moving about the kitchen, me stirring at the stove and her setting the table. After we ate, I blurted out, "Mom? I'm in serious trouble."

Her face went rigid. "With what?"

She was the one person who hadn't given up on me yet, besides Floyd and Bob, but they couldn't give me a place to live, a place to crash land, which is what I needed. She was my last hope. This was my last chance to dive in before she gave up on me too. And I didn't care about the sharks anymore, I'd been swimming with them for years.

"With drinking. And drugs. It's gotten . . . out of control. I can't stop. I try. Every day, I say I'm not gonna drink or use anything, but I do anyway. Every day. I can't keep living this way. But I can't stop." It was such a relief to admit that, to let it out at last. All the fight and hiding and resistance, all the illusions and secrecy, melted away, and it was me and that simple truth. I was unable to stop using.

She watched me while I talked, her brow creased with concern. "How much are you using? Exactly?"

"I've been drinking a lot. Like a twelve-pack or several shots of tequila every day. More if I start earlier in the day. And using a lot of coke when I have it. With Dad."

Mom groaned. "Oh, God. That son of a bitch!"

"If it wasn't from him, I'd get it from someone else. And then I might be in worse shape. At least I'm not getting drugs off the street or selling my body for them, shit like that." She stared at me, the distinction lost on her. "It's safer to use drugs you got from your dad or your brother . . . from someone you know"— she was still staring at me—"Never mind. I know, it's all screwed up. Me, Rick, Dad. All of it. But please don't try to get Dad in trouble. He's still on parole."

"What do you want to do? What's your plan?"

I had nothing left to lose. "Well, first, I'm gonna stay away from Dad and Rick. I can't be around them. Then, I was hoping I could move back in with you. Just for a little while. A month or two. 'Til I can get on my feet again. Pay off some bills. Eventually, I could go back to OSU."

"I need to think about this a little." She started to clear the dinner dishes. I helped, working next to her, scraping the plates, rinsing them and stacking them in the dishwasher. All the while I watched her from the corner of my eye, hoping for a sign that she was softening, that she was going to help me. A sign that she hadn't given up on me yet. After we finished cleaning up the kitchen, she sat back down, and I leaned against the counter where I stood, bracing myself for her decision.

"I have two conditions." She raised her index finger in the air. "One. You are *never* to use or drink in my house. First hint of you being drunk here, and you're out." She raised a second finger. "And two, you have to get some kind of help. Drug and alcohol treatment, recovery meetings, an alcohol counselor, something."

I felt like I was levitating and could have floated right up to my old bedroom and nestled into my old bed. At that point, I would have agreed to any of her conditions, but was grateful they were so reasonable. Just my luck, I remembered right where I put the recovery meeting schedule with the women's phone numbers scribbled on it.

The next day, I shoved my meager belongings—clothes, a handful of books, a few pots and pans, my telephone and toiletries—into boxes and shuttled them, along with my bookcase and dresser, to Mom's condo. When I went back to the empty apartment one last time to clean it, lingering there was all the despair and desolation I had experienced over the previous two years. While my waterbed was draining through a hose hanging out my bedroom window, I vacuumed the carpet and scrubbed the sinks, toilet and shower. At last, all that remained was for me to put the waterbed frame and the collapsed mattress in the dumpster. I didn't want to keep it or try to sell it. I just wanted to get rid of that bed and all the memories it held: the hangovers, the nights sitting on it drinking alone, the blackouts, the men.

With the residual water still sloshing around inside of the mattress, it was much heavier than I expected. After I dragged it to the top of the stairs, I tried to push it down, but instead of the mattress careening down as I had hoped, it only slumped onto the first few steps. Sitting at the top of the stairway and pushing it with my feet produced mere indentations in the rubbery mattress. Out of options, I dragged it down the stairwell, stopping to rest my back every few steps. Panting and sweating, I tugged it to the front door and heaved it onto the porch. I stared at the dumpster at the other end of the parking lot. I tried to think of anyone who could help me, anyone besides Mom, who was at work. The one person I could think of was a karate instructor who lived a few apartments over. But I hadn't talked to him in months, not since we had gone on a few "dates" and ended up in bed at the exact moment his girlfriend, whom he hadn't told me about, called. I drew the line at having sex with someone else's boyfriend—that was uncool and kind of gross. I wasn't about to call karate man now.

After catching my breath, I resumed dragging the mattress toward the dumpster. When I finally had the unwieldy mass next to the dumpster, I had to somehow get it inside. One bit of good luck, the dumpster was the type with a front instead of a top opening. First, I lifted one end of the waterbed mattress into the dumpster, but when I tried to lift the other end, where all the water had rolled, that first end slopped back out. After a few tries, I was grunting with frustration and crying at the realization that I couldn't do this alone. I contemplated leaving it in front of the dumpster but worried the landlord would figure it was mine, and I needed that security deposit to help pay Jenny some of the money I owed her. In one last desperate attempt, I hoisted the middle of the floppy mattress over my head and shoulders then careened forward into the dumpster door. Enough of the waterbed mattress fell into the dumpster so the weight held it there while I slid out from under it. I humped the rest of it inside. When the last of the waterbed, mercifully, dropped into the dumpster, my upper body was partway inside the dumpster too. It was dank and had a stench like something died in there a long time ago. This is what my life had become, me halfway into a heap of stinking, rotting trash.

As I drove away from that apartment toward Mom's condo, I let go of everything and wept. The exhaustion, loneliness and fear poured out of me. By the time I reached the condo, I felt lighter than I had felt in years.

Later that evening, no longer preoccupied with moving out of my apartment, I was settling into my childhood bed when the craving for a drink hit me hard, overwhelming me. Mom was home. She would know what I was doing if I went out. And I was exhausted and sore from packing and unpacking and cleaning, so I nestled deeper into my narrow bed and told myself I would have to wait until the next day to have a beer.

In the morning, after resisting a drink the previous day, at least for that one day, a blip of triumph fizzed inside me. *I went all day without a drink. All day! Maybe I can do this.*

Despite my day-one victory, the first few weeks without any mood-altering substances felt like my nerve endings were exposed and dangling. Having been numb for so long, I had no skills for coping with the emotions that kept knocking me on my ass—shame and pain and embarrassment and sadness about my past. But deep inside me, in my core, I knew if I kept myself numb, I would never feel any joy or happiness either.

Unfortunately, this knowledge did nothing to diminish my cravings. Dozens of times each day, I would think that it would be fine for me to have a few swigs or snorts. When my cravings became intense, I imagined Mom catching me drunk—for I knew that I wouldn't have only a few of anything. I could see her escorting me right out the front door and me wandering around looking for a place to sleep. With nowhere else to go, I would likely end up in a bar and go home with some man. In the back of my mind, there was always Dad, but I knew his cocaine would take me down again, and fast. Minute by minute, day after day, I pushed the impulse to drink or use drugs out of my mind. I was jumpy and edgy, smoked way too many cigarettes and ate like a pig—big bowls of ice cream, French fries, anything that promised to soothe my body and shut my mind up. I kept my schedule regimented: work, a weekly appointment with Miriam, home for a quiet dinner with Mom and attending twelve-step meetings.

Initially, I attended meetings in the suburbs near Mom's condo, but there I felt less-than and slutty compared to the women who attended those meetings. None of them had done the things I had done when drinking, or if they had, they weren't talking about it. The meeting at which I was the most comfortable was downtown, just at the edge of The Bottoms. The meeting began right after work when my temptation to drink was greatest. I drove there with the same urgency and anticipation with which I had driven to bars or the liquor store or to Dad's. The cast of characters at that meeting swooped me up in a safety net. There was an imposing, six-foot-something man who had been a pimp ten years earlier, and every time he saw me, he said, "Has anyone told you today that they love you? Well, I do." That's it; he never even tried to hug me. And there was a bitter, shriveled old man with nicotine-stained fingers who called himself a mother-fuckin' alcoholic but who always had a big hug for me. "Come sit over here, Baby Doll," he would say, patting the chair he always saved for me. A poetry-writing Vietnam vet with a bushy, unkempt, gray mustache would scratch a poem on a slip of paper and slide it across the table to me during meetings. Those poems were amazing and would give me a dose of hope right when a drink was calling to me. One woman cautioned me that the men at the meetings hadn't changed just because they weren't drinking anymore. She was in her fifties and had drunk and drugged herself into prostitution before quitting. "Whatever you do, don't get involved with any of these vultures for at least a year if you can help it. It's the women who are gonna save your ass. This early in recovery, the men will take you right back to drinking. Trust me. I tried that route."

I did not heed her advice initially. Men still served as a strong diversion from whatever was going on inside me, one more way to boost my sense of self, which was still back in that dumpster. Some days I wanted to hunt down my next "boyfriend," take him hostage, make him want me, wrap my legs around—No! I would tell myself, over and over. I'm not falling in bed that easily anymore. Not with this guy. Not today. Some other time. About face. Good-bye. Other times, I regressed right back into my same old behavior, pursuing a man right into the bedroom. The problem is that addicts who have recently stopped using have brains that are screaming to be flooded again with dopamine and endorphins and will use almost anything to bathe those "feel-good" neurons—sugar, cigarettes, food, sex. Not a great time to start a "relationship."

The advice I *did* take was to attend as many meetings each week as possible—I made it to four or five—and to hang out between meetings with people also in recovery. So, where my evenings had previously been filled with drinking, they were now filled with meetings and often dinner or ice cream afterwards with my new associates, now in small groups of men and women, to avoid any one-on-one time with men. The less time I spent alone, the better I began to feel. One night, I found myself at Denny's at midnight sharing baskets of onion rings and French fries with a group of other recovering addicts and alcoholics and laughing so hard the muscles in my abdomen were cramping up. I couldn't remember when I had last laughed like that, genuinely, without any mind-altering chemicals. That gave me a glimpse of a part of life I had been completely missing out on, and I wanted more.

That fall, with six months of clean time, I enrolled in college classes again and found they were easy when I actually attended them. The social aspect of university life was more of a struggle. Without the dulling effect of being high, I was self-conscious around my peers. All the women seemed superior to me: smarter, prettier, more confident. I simply had no clue what to say to them, and they didn't seem to want to talk with me. My response was to get attention from the men, but by that point, being seductive with men left me feeling even more lonely and empty.

One morning, I showered, spent half an hour applying make-up and styling my hair, drove twenty-five minutes to campus, pulled into a parking spot and checked myself in the mirror. I don't know what about my appearance was intolerable to me, but I couldn't face those college students that day. I wasn't good enough—wasn't pretty enough—to even walk onto campus. All the worrying and wondering what others were thinking of me was exhausting. I needed to shut my mind up. Disgusted with myself and how screwed up I was, I drove back home.

For the first time since starting to see Miriam, I called her outside of our regular appointment. She had always told me I could call her if I ever needed to talk between our sessions, but it seemed so desperate to not be able to go one week without talking to a therapist, so I had refrained. While I awaited her return call, I paced back and forth in the living room, hatching a plan to get a six-pack, just enough to take the edge off and relax, enough to make me feel pretty and irresistible. Then it dawned on me that I was now twenty-one and could walk right into a liquor store and walk right back out with a bottle of tequila! A small bottle, only a pint. And I would only drink one or two shots, enough for a buzz but not enough to make me stumble home with some guy or for Mom to tell I had been drinking. My craving intensified as I recalled drinking shots: the salt crystals dissolving on my tongue as I licked them off my hand, the earthy burn of the tequila, the puckering juice sucked from a wedge of lime. I remembered how quickly tequila hit my blood stream. In fact, it was more like a drug in how quickly and powerfully it intoxicated me. Right after cocaine, tequila was my drug of choice. Then came the memory of Dad's cocaine, the crusty flakes glinting pale pink.

The phone rang, jolting me out of my pipedream. Miriam's voice was calm but concerned.

"I can't do this anymore," I said.

"Do what? Tell me what's happening."

"I can't even walk onto campus without feeling like a piece of crap. I look like crap. I can't stand myself, and I want to get high so bad. I want to feel good again."

"You were feeling pretty bad when you were drinking, weren't you?" I heard no judgement in her tone, all matter of fact.

"But I was thinking if I just drank a few, like two or three beers, that's all, it would take the edge off and give me a little break." As soon as I heard those words, I remembered every time I had ever made that promise. Hundreds of times.

"Some people can use alcohol like that. They have one or two glasses of wine to take the edge off. Do you think you'll be able to stop after a few beers?"

I stared up at the ceiling, the phone pressed to my ear. "I'll probably end up in some stranger's bed, wondering in the morning how I got there. Probably end up pregnant or with HIV. Or both."

"That sounds pretty scary." There was a beat of silence between us. "Can you tell me about the looking crappy part. Why does it matter how you look on campus?"

This was a huge, broken part of myself that I wanted to fix, but there was a wall I had not been able or willing to break down or scale or even peek through. Turning my sights inward, I thought about men watching me or wanting me and how that propped me up and made me feel valuable. In contrast, I wondered why a woman would want to talk with me. I didn't have anything to offer women. Only when a man wanted me—or, in Dad's case, when he wanted to be around me—did I feel even remotely okay about myself. Without a man cherishing me, I was worthless. Having a man want me, having a man pursue me, was how I kept myself from coasting into that nothingness.

"It's like that's all there is of me, my appearance, my body. The best part of me is how I look. If I don't look good, then I'm . . . no one. I don't matter. I'm nothing."

"Have you ever offered anybody anything else?"

My throat grew tight, straining against the words that were choking me, threatening to erupt. I squeezed my eyes shut to stop the tears that were sprouting there. "I don't have anything else," I whispered.

She let my words settle there between us for a few beats. "I believe you do. You have so much more to offer. All women do. You just need to find it."

28

THE SPACE BETWEEN US

*S*omething in me broke free after I reached out to Miriam that day. I began to share more truthfully what had been going on in my life, expecting her to be shocked by how bad my drinking was, but she listened as she always had with no sign of alarm. She probably knew I had been lying all along. I finally told her about Dad's smuggling and providing me with cocaine. The more I opened up to her, the less alone I was.

Miriam and I talked often about my relationship, or lack thereof, with Dad. With defeat, I slowly accepted that I wasn't going to have a father, ever. It was too late, I was twenty-two. For years, I had tormented myself trying to figure out what I had done to make Dad stop loving me. I came to understand the connection between seeking Dad's love and seeking approval from men, using the latter to make up for the lack of the former. Apparently, this behavior was not, Miriam assured me, pathological but was quite common in women who were abandoned by their fathers. Seeing this connection diminished the charge, the sense of power, I kept seeking from a man's attention. My new insight did not, however, diminish my radar for men who lusted after me (or lusted after women, in general—the type of men who could so easily be had). As hard as I tried to turn off my lust detector, to lower that antenna, I couldn't. This awareness had become instinctive and instantaneous. All I could do was try to ignore the signals and, by all means, not take action on them.

I began exploring what I wanted to do with my life, even simple activities I never experienced because I couldn't leave the bar or my apartment or my attic. Since I was working at the athletic club, I decided to try the sports they offered. Racquetball required a partner, which I didn't have, so I only knocked the ball around the court a few times. Next was an aerobics class, but I was far too uncoordinated. Jogging on the indoor track gave me painful shin-splints. Then I started swimming, which was instantly familiar and gratifying. I swam a few nights each week, and one of the lifeguards helped me improve my stroke, allowing me to gain both speed and strength.

One evening, I dove into the pool, and all my worries, loneliness and social struggles of the day slipped off as I glided through the water. Finding a rhythm between my stroke and my breath, I became entranced by the sunlight dancing on the bottom of the pool. The image transported me back to my childhood, to Miami, safe and secure, splashing in our pool with Dad, Mom and Rick. Everything had been good then. I had been taken care of and loved, always, even by Dad. Especially by Dad. Ours had been a genuine and deep connection. The certainty of that connection was visceral. It was in my legs treading the water behind me, in my arms plowing through the water—kick, pull, glide—then and now, as a child and as an adult. My body slid through the water. My heart pumped blood through my veins and into my lungs and muscles. My body was strong. I was strong. As long as I could tap into this place inside of me, I might be okay. I could learn to take care of myself.

I began to rebuild myself from the inside out, developing interests and pursuing activities I had only dreamed of when I was getting loaded every day. After I quit smoking, I built up to swimming several miles per week. Next, I took long bike rides in the rural areas around our condo. Having never played sports, I was surprised at how much fun they were, even though they were all solitary activities. Miriam and I talked about me finding a woman at work or college who I might invite to go bike riding, but I explained to her that women didn't like me.

She raised her eyebrows. "None of them?"

I scanned my recent interactions with women, which weren't many, and shook my head. "There's some older women at the hospital, secretaries and nurses, but they're motherly type women. They won't go riding with me. Women my age just don't like me."

"How do you know that?"

"They don't talk to me."

"Do you talk to them?"

"Hmm. Not really. What would I say to them? 'Want to go for a bike ride?'"

"That's a good start. It helps to have some common interest, something to chat about."

"What do *you* talk to women about?"

"Lots of things. I ask other moms about their children or ask my colleagues about work. With my closest friends, we mainly complain about our husbands." With that statement, she tossed her head back and laughed. That gesture and her levity formed a picture of something I wanted: a lightness about being close with another woman, close enough to confide in her.

"I haven't had a close female friend for years. There were girls I used to get stoned with in high school. But we didn't talk about stuff. We weren't ... "

"Intimate?"

I must have been staring at her blankly because she elaborated.

"*Emotionally* intimate."

"Blech. I hate those words. They make me think of passive, weak, needy people who are about to get their hearts broken."

"Okay. How about letting it all hang out? Just being yourself.

Letting someone see you for who you are. No worrying what they think about you. No wondering if they think you're pretty."

My childhood friend Diana came to mind, causing a pang of sadness. I wanted that kind of friendship again, wanted it almost more than anything I ever wanted from a man. "I don't know how to do that. How do I get that kind of friendship with a woman?"

"Well, you start by getting acquainted with her. Over time you take small risks, gradually showing more and more of who you are. And if she continues to accept you, and you like her, you open up a little more. You learn to trust each other and share more of yourself over time. You make a connection."

She made it sound so simple, but letting other women see me, deep down, would allow them to discover that I was a drunk, a druggie and a slut. "What if they don't like me? You know, the real me."

"Then that friendship isn't for you. Sometimes you can get hurt or rejected. That's painful. But trusting someone doesn't mean they'll never hurt you. It just means if they do hurt you, you'll talk about it and try to work it out. You'll give them a chance to repair things."

I gazed out at my sycamore tree. It was a giant watchman waiting for me in the parking lot each week when I pulled up, waiting for me outside Miriam's window whenever I felt exposed. "I don't let myself get hurt like that."

"How do you manage that? Never getting hurt?"

There she goes again, asking me a question she already knows the answer to. "By not letting anyone in. I just don't let anyone get that close."

"You have a tender spot, a wound, from the abandonment and rejection you experienced from your dad when you were so young. It'll take some time, but it will heal. And you'll always be choosy about who you open up to. But you can't have any real closeness without taking some risks. With men or women."

"All this applies to men too?"

"Pretty much. The physical attraction adds another dimension.

For you, it'll work better if you postpone the sex long enough to develop a friendship and some trust first."

"Well, I pretty much always skipped that part. But that's all men ever wanted. The sex."

"All of them? Lawrence stayed with you for how long?"

"Eighteen months."

"Just for the sex?"

I pondered that for several seconds and was stumped. "I have no idea why he stayed. Early mid-life crisis?"

"What about Brad?"

"Oh, he definitely wanted more than sex. Way more. I felt so bad about how I treated him, because he did want more than sex. That was an all-time low for me." I always wished I could've called him and apologized, but he was seriously involved with someone else by then. Never seemed like a good idea to open an old wound just so I could say I was sorry.

"How long does that take, you know, to become friends and trust a guy? Before having sex? I mean, I've waited, like, a couple of weeks before."

She shrugged. "Months. Maybe several."

I raised my eyebrows in disbelief.

"Some people wait until they get married." She grinned.

I waved that idea away with a brush of my hand. "Well, it's way too late for that now."

We both broke out in laughter. I think I even tossed my head back as I did so.

29

COMING CLEAN

*W*hen Katherine called me at work, it took me a few seconds to realize who it was, as I hadn't spoken to her or Dad in several months. And they never called my work number.

Fear shot through me when she explained Dad was in the hospital. I wasn't ready for Dad to die, we had so much unresolved shit between us. I still wanted him to someday, somehow, be a father to me. Expecting it was a heart attack, just like Grandma and Grandpa had had in their forties and fifties, I hoped it wasn't a massive one. I set the stack of mail I had been sorting on my desk and eased into my office chair so its squeaking wouldn't block out any of her words.

"He had an operation. His esophagus was tearing away from his stomach from all those bad ulcers he's had for years." I replayed in my mind a lifetime of his Rolaids. "But it's not healing, and they don't know why. He hasn't been able to keep any food down for a week. They've got him on a feeding tube, but he's looking pretty thin. And it's painful, I guess. He says it's like a constant searing pain in his belly."

"What can I do? Should I fly down?" Dad wasn't likely to be using in the hospital, but he'd done crazier shit than that before.

Rick and Vanessa had been trying to get off all the coke since their son was born, but it'd been a struggle for them, so I wasn't sure they were clean either. I was torn between an obligation to see Dad and not wanting to risk being around any cocaine. The whole scene down there was shaky ground for me.

"No. Your dad didn't even want me to tell you. Said you'd try to come down here, and he didn't want that. Truth be told, he hardly wants *me* in the room with him. He's that miserable. He just wants to be left alone. But I wanted you to know." There was a pause over the line. "He thinks he's dying."

"Is he?"

"No. The doctors don't know what's wrong, and he's in a lot of pain. But he's got a feeding tube in and he's on IV fluids, so the doctor assured me he's not dying."

She let out a heavy sigh. "The doctors are putting a scope down his stomach, then we'll know more. I forget what it's called, but I guess it lets them see inside his esophagus and stomach. Let's see if he doesn't improve after they figure out what's goin' on inside there. I just thought you should know what was happening."

A few days later, Katherine phoned me at home early in the morning. "It doesn't look good." Her voice wavered. Not a good sign. "Now he's throwing up blood. He's so thin and still can't eat. They took out his feeding tube so they could insert that scope. I guess the area of the surgery, that area where they tried to reconnect the stomach and the esophagus, isn't healing up like they expected. They don't know why."

I dropped into a kitchen chair, the wooden slats hard against my spine. Mom came in and started a pot of coffee. Her curly perm was flattened on one side of her head, and her cheek was creased from her pillow.

"What are the doctors gonna do next?"

When Mom heard me say this, she mouthed the words, "Your dad?"

I nodded.

Mom poured me a cup of coffee, stirred in lots of milk and sugar the way we both liked it, and slid it to me. She gave my shoulder a squeeze before sitting down across the table.

"They took him by helicopter to a different hospital with specialists. They're running all kinds of tests. He's in so much pain, and now with him throwing up blood, they don't want to put the feeding tube back in yet. He's still on the IV fluids, the kind with sugars in it, so he won't starve. But he asked me to get your granddaddy in there last night to"—there was a catch in her voice—"to pray for him."

Out of the blue, the thought popped into my mind that he was still using coke in the hospital. As unbelievable as that seemed, he never went long without using cocaine. Even if he wasn't using in there, I had no doubt he'd snorted right up until the morning he was admitted. I recalled the sensation of cocaine draining down the back of my throat—I could taste the bitterness—and then of it being swallowed. Swallowed. My pulse quickened. Even in the few years I had used blow, and Dad had abused the stuff way worse and longer than I had, I often had sores inside my nose. Especially on the soft, moist septum, which would crack, bleed, scab over then open up again. They were basically ulcers in my septum that sometimes festered for weeks.

I tipped the phone away from my head, covered the mouthpiece with my hand and whispered to Mom. "Now he's throwing up blood. What if it's from all that coke? That it's eating away at his stomach?"

"I don't know much about what cocaine does to the body. Or about GI surgery. I'm just not sure."

"Are you still there?" Katherine said.

"Yeah, I'm here. Uh, just a second."

Hand over the mouthpiece again. "Should I tell her? About all Dad's using?"

Mom shrugged. "It definitely couldn't hurt for the doctors to know. At this point, he doesn't have anything to lose."

My stomach knotted up, and I stared at Mom, who gave me a

reassuring nod. I took a quiet deep breath. "Okay, sorry. I'm back. Hey Katherine? I want to tell you something."

"What?"

"Um, I'm not sure this has anything to do with Dad being sick, but he's ... " *He's never gonna forgive me.* Never snitching on other smugglers was one principle in which Dad took great pride— honor among thieves and all that.

"He's what?"

This probably has nothing to do with his stomach. Mom was watching me, her face concerned but neutral. She would support me whether or not I told Katherine. One more deep inhale. "He's an addict. A cocaine addict. This is none of my business, telling you, but if he's really that bad and he's still using coke in there, or at least right before he was admitted, then the doctors should know. It might not even be related, but what if that's causing the bleeding? It can't hurt for them to know ... if you decide to tell them."

The phone line buzzed between us for several seconds. *What the hell have I done?*

"How long? How long has this been going on?"

"Years. Since he got out of prison. I know for sure he was using last year, because I used with him."

I could feel her fury coursing through the phone line and hoped I wasn't destroying their marriage. In the next moment, I realized the absurdity that *I* could destroy their marriage.

"I knew it. I just knew it. I found some white powder last year, and he told me it was Rick's. Said he was trying to help him straighten up, so he took it from Rick. I didn't want to believe it was your dad's, you know? I just didn't want to believe it. It was in a small red—"

"That was his." My heart was racing, either from her agitation or from the visceral memory of flaky cocaine crystals in that maroon disk.

"How much does he use?"

"He has a huge habit. Huge. Last year, he was snorting several grams a day."

"I don't know what that means. How much is that?"

"Let's see. It's thousands of dollars-worth of cocaine. Each day. He was snorting lines all day long, maybe a dozen, maybe more. I'm not sure what he's doing lately, but I bet it's the same. I'm sorry if I did the wrong thing, telling you. I don't want to hurt you or—"

"No, I'm glad you told me. I am *so* glad."

When I hung up Mom said, "Well?"

"Hope that was the right thing to do. If he died and I hadn't said anything, I'd always wonder if I should have spoken up."

"You did the right thing. It's about time she knows about all his lies. And who knows, you might have saved his life."

Katherine called me a few days later to tell me she'd confronted Dad and insisted he tell the doctors everything or he'd never see her again. I cringed to hear she told him that I was the one who blew his cover. But he would've known anyway that it was either Rick or me. Who else?

"He told the doctor everything, right there in front of me. They transferred him to the drug and alcohol unit. He's been there two days and was finally able to keep down the first solid food he's had in over a month. A buttered English muffin." She laughed, and I heard the joy and relief in her voice.

"That's great news. So, what are they doing different? Like, what was wrong with him?"

"Well, they didn't put the feeding tube back in. They think that might have been irritating the area of the surgery. And they put him on an antibiotic, something for bacteria that grows in the gut."

"Is he pissed at me?"

"No. He said he's glad it's all out in the open now. Says he was sick and tired of all the secrecy and the lying. I'm glad it's all over now."

Sure, I thought. Just like that, and it's all over? This is one naïve woman. She has no idea what or who she's dealing with.

When Dad telephoned a couple of weeks after he had been discharged, he never said a word about my conversation with Katherine. I was indignant, expecting he would at least thank me, because I might have saved his sorry ass. Instead, he told me how he had turned his life around, how he wasn't smuggling anymore or using that "nose candy." He told me he felt like a million bucks, even though he barely had a penny to his name after all the medical bills.

All I wanted to say was how fucking glad I was he had made such a good decision, and all on his own, without any help from me. I wanted to call bullshit on him, because it couldn't be that easy for him to walk away from the coke. It had taken me the better part of a year to begin repairing the wreckage of my life—brought about in part by him. "Good for you," I said. "I turned my life around too."

"I'm glad to hear that."

I waited for him to ask me how I had turned things around, or what I was doing with my life now, or how I was, but he blathered on about his latest scheme to make a killin' with a hotdog stand as soon as he found the perfect location. That sounded like a lame idea to me, but I supposed anything was better than smuggling uncut Colombian cocaine from Miami to a small town in North Carolina while on parole and married to a high school teacher. (Actually, by then she had become a school counselor. That degree might come in real handy for her in dealing with Dad.)

His story smacked of more lies to me. I speculated he was only laying off until things cooled down with Katherine. And if he *had* walked away from it all, he wouldn't stay away for long. He was too hooked on not just the cocaine, but the smuggling, the money and the thrill.

In the end, it didn't matter if Dad was still using or not, because I didn't dare visit him. I had way too much to lose.

CHOOSING SIDES

A few months after Dad, miraculously, turned his life around, he called to tell me Grandpa was in the hospital and not expected to live much longer. If I wanted to see him one last time, he told me I better get down there.

"Let me ask you first Dad, are you still using? Because I quit and don't want to start again. I can't start again."

"What are you talking about? That nose candy? Haven't touched the stuff in months. You don't have to worry about that no more. I told you when I got out of the hospital, I left all that behind me."

Just talking about cocaine with Dad gave me butterflies in my stomach. Not from anxiety but from anticipation—that was hardwired into my brain and body still. Deep in my soul and my heart, I never again wanted to touch that spectacular, magical, maniacal powder. But my body, and occasionally my brain, still lusted for cocaine. My body was still having a love affair with cocaine and had been patiently waiting to see this long-lost lover again. "Well, I want to come see Grandpa, but I can't be around that shit anymore."

"I'm tellin' you, you won't have any problem with that here anymore. I promise you that."

Yeah, right. As soon as I got to Dad's, I planned to find out where the recovery meetings were.

Down in North Carolina, Dad, Rick and I visited Grandpa in the hospital every day. Between visits, we hung out at Dad's condo. Rick and Vanessa came over with their children, and we splashed around the pool and barbecued at the clubhouse. While Rick was cooking burgers on the grill, I went over to chat.

He talked about how they were trying to raise their kids in a better environment now. "We're stayin' away from the coke. It's been several months now. We still smoke weed and drink a few beers now and then, but we're keepin' our noses clean. That shit almost killed us."

"I know. Vanessa was skin and bones when I last saw you two. You guys look great now. It's been close to a year without any drugs for me. I don't drink either. What about you and Dad? You get along better now, living so close and all?"

He shrugged. "He don't call me much. Not since I stopped dealin' for him. Tells me he walked away from it all after that ulcer surgery. Who knows? He's been lyin' to everyone his whole life. I don't even know if he *knows* how to tell the truth."

A small shudder ran down my back, remembering that phone call to Dad when the cops were sitting outside my apartment and I needed help getting rid of his cocaine, but all I got was his I-don't-know-nothin-about-it line. "He's an expert at being anyone he thinks people want him to be. Probably why he was such a good smuggler. And a narcotics agent. It's all a cover. I have no idea who he is. Katherine doesn't either probably. Hell, he doesn't even know who he is."

After we ate, everyone went swimming except Katherine and me. At one point, Dad grabbed my hands and pretended he was going to toss me into the deep end with all my clothes on. I squealed, "No, no, no!" while everyone else laughed. Katherine snapped a picture of Dad threatening to toss me in the pool. In the snapshot, Dad and I are both smiling. Rick was standing nearby watching and laughing. There we were, all three of us, goofing around the pool the way we had two decades earlier. As if we'd been doing that all our lives.

I made sure I was never alone with Dad for long, and when we were, our conversations were stilted and brief. Without the drugs, we didn't have much to say to each other. I kept waiting for an apology, or at least an acknowledgement that what he had done was wrong. That conversation never happened.

When I returned home, I received a short letter from Dad. Seeing his handwriting on an envelope again after so many years, gave me the same joy I had experienced as a kid, anticipation and hope coursing from my fingertips to my chest. The note read:

I know nothing I say or do can make up for not being there in the past. 'I'm sorry' isn't enough. I can't change the past. But I want us to have as good a relationship as possible in the present. You have a right to be skeptical of me. But with time you will believe that I have changed. My life now is no longer a big scam.

That was the apology I had been waiting for? Indignation flared inside me. I had tried for years to stop hoping for anything from him, and yet, reading his words, my old hope fluttered. Followed instantly by me admonishing myself for being so stupid. I was furious at him for stirring up all my old fantasies and at myself for letting him. I envisioned ripping the paper into tiny pieces but couldn't shake the preciousness of a letter from Dad. "This is un-fucking-believable," I mumbled. "He can't send me a seven-sentence letter and expect me to forgive him."

Obviously, he couldn't change the past, but he could at least acknowledge what he had done wrong. If he thought not being there in the past was his worst offense, he was in serious, deep denial. As much as I recognized how drugs had lowered my values, allowed me to behave in ways I never thought I would, Dad had crossed way over the line. What we did, using cocaine together, wasn't a simple now-that-you're-all-grown-up-let's-have-a-drink-together. He was allowing, no supporting, my drug abuse. Dad's unlimited cocaine had brought me to my knees. And I know it nearly destroyed Rick too. He had almost died one day from freebasing coke for too many days in a row: no food, no sleep, hunched behind his couch, flinching and peeking out at every noise while he continued to smoke that shit. I doubt Dad even knew about Rick's trip to the emergency room with convulsions that day.

Dad was right. His seven-sentence "sorry" wasn't enough. If he truly wanted us to have a good relationship in the present, he was going to have to put in some effort. How the hell could I possibly come to believe he had changed when he never reached out to me? Since I had stopped going to North Carolina almost a year earlier, he had contacted me exactly twice: once to tell me he was out of the hospital and once to tell me Grandpa was nearing the end of his life. The man who helped to create me, who helped bring me into the world, barely acknowledged my existence.

Unearthing my Roman Meal bag of letters that I had been squirreling away since I was a child, I read every note and card. Then, I pulled my Dad-scrapbook off the bookshelf and flipped through each page, reading the yellowed newspaper articles about Dad and looking at the photos. The old pain of abandonment washed over me. After the waves of grief subsided, I carefully put all the notes back in the bag, including the new one, and wrote a terse letter back stating that it wouldn't be so easy for him to waltz back into my life after being gone for most of it. Too much had happened, I wrote, and he didn't even know me.

A couple of years went by with Dad and I barely talking. He called when Grandpa died and once on my birthday. I always called him on Father's Day, his birthday and Christmas. That was the extent of our communication, which was okay with me. I had my hands full catching up in college and hanging out with friends in recovery—some were even women!

When I received a call from Katherine, I was certain the news wasn't good—her speech was too steady, forcibly calm. Dad had

had a massive heart attack and was scheduled for a triple bypass surgery in two days. I had a sinking sensation that time was running out, for him and for us. How long could his body hold out after all the years of abuse? Driving through the night, I hoped he would still be alive when I got there. I just wasn't ready to say good-bye yet.

When I arrived at the hospital in the morning, Katherine was there along with Rick and Julie. I hadn't seen my half-sister since she was a toddler, during the Orlando visit that I later learned had been when Dad's trial was held. I'm sure she didn't remember me. While I expected to feel anger or jealousy toward her, I never expected to be overwhelmed with empathy.

She was clearly uncomfortable sitting next to all of us. The strain in her voice as she talked with Dad was all too familiar. She was me, a decade earlier. I tried to make conversation—I'd gotten pretty good at befriending women by then, even had a female biking buddy—but she was only a teenager, and I was a complete stranger to her. After a few bumbling exchanges, during which she seemed to become even more uncomfortable, I focused on Dad. As I watched Julie interact with our father, it occurred to me that in a few years, Julie would be the age I was when I first used drugs with him. In her clamoring for his attention and love, in her idolization of him, I saw myself. In her, I saw the inevitability of what had happened between Dad and me. I had craved his love so fiercely, there was little I wouldn't have done to recapture it. As a teenager, I had needed my father as desperately as I needed a shot of tequila or a drug, longing for the glow of his adoration to warm me, to make everything okay, to make me whole again. Time after time, I attempted to connect with Dad and was offered only cocaine. My father had been no more capable of loving me than I had been capable of drinking and using in moderation.

The tension was palpable as the four of us sat around Dad's bed that day, knowing he would be having open-heart in twenty-four hours, while he cracked jokes and made light of the somber situation. In the evening, the others went to grab a quick dinner, and I stayed in the room. Thinking he was dozing, I studied him. His hair was thinning, and his belly was bigger than when I'd last seen him. The vertical crease between his eyebrows had grown deeper. It was quiet in the room, and then I heard his feet shifting back and forth underneath the stiff hospital sheets.

"Are you in pain?" I whispered.

He shook his head. "No. Why?"

"When I'm sick or in pain, I shake my feet like that. Nervous habit. It kind of distracts me from whatever's hurting."

He looked over at me and gave me a weak smile. "How about when you're scared?"

I scooched my chair closer to the bed and rested my hand on top of his. "Especially when I'm afraid."

He took a deep breath, stared at the ceiling for a few seconds then closed his eyes. I watched his chest to make sure he was still breathing, though his heart monitor was still beeping. It was just so rare, if ever, that I had seen my father lying motionless.

When visiting hours were over, we all said goodnight to him, and I was bombarded with things I wanted to say to him, things I wanted him to know, but when my turn came, all that came out of my mouth was, "I love you, Dad." I bent down and pecked his cheek. "I'll see you tomorrow after your surgery." He smiled, but I saw nothing but fear in his eyes. He didn't think he was going to see tomorrow.

Early the next afternoon, I arrived at the hospital before the rest of my family. I didn't expect Dad would be allowed visitors yet, but after a few minutes in the waiting room, a nurse said I could go in and see him.

I walked quietly into his room and felt weak in the knees at the sight. He was pale. From the waist down, he was draped in a sheet and a thin, woven hospital blanket. Wires from various machines were threaded through his hospital gown and a thick bandaging covered his chest. As I tiptoed closer to his bed, I could smell the betadine they had painted on his chest—its scent medicinal and iron-like. That's good, I thought. Sterile is good. The heart monitor beeped slow and regular, a comforting sound.

I sat down next to his bed, and the cushion on the chair released a soft whoosh. He rolled his head in my direction and opened his eyes halfway. His voice broke when he said, "What day is it?'

"Tuesday. You had your surgery this morning. You're in the recovery room."

His eyes clouded over with confusion, and he lifted his hand off the bed. Expecting he was going to wave me away, out of his room, I was surprised when he extended his hand toward me. I wrapped my hands around his. As pale and cold as he looked, his hand was surprisingly warm. That's good. His circulation is good. He gave my hand a squeeze. I had forgotten how large his hands were.

"Your bypass surgery went really well. No complications or anything."

He nodded and let his eyelids close.

I scrutinized his breathing, the rise and fall of his chest exaggerated by the thick gauze padding taped to it. The steady beep of the monitor was hypnotic. This was the closest I had felt to him— genuine closeness, not cocaine-induced closeness—since I was little. My love for him poured out of me like a Miami rain shower —not the torrential, hurricane storms that knocked branches against our house, rattled our front door, sprayed rain through our window slats and bent palm trees into stooped, stick figures with wild hair whipping around their heads. No, this love was a springtime shower that started with hardly a warning, steadily drummed on our roof, drenched everything in seconds and formed great big puddles and sometimes a rainbow. One of those gentle Miami showers that stopped as suddenly as it started.

After Dad's surgery, we both went on with our lives again, distant and aloof. Once in a while, I visited Dad and Katherine and my brother's family. As we moved further away from our drug use, talking about that time in our lives, about those events, became easier. We talked about our previous drug use briefly and always respectfully, acknowledging that those were scary times. But Dad and I could not overcome the unfamiliarity between us. The past lay between us, insurmountable.

Dad seldom called me, unless he was back in the hospital with chest pain or GI troubles. As my birthday neared each year, I hoped to hear from him, then became mad at myself for having such childish, wishful thinking. When my birthday came and went with no communication from Dad, anger boiled up in me despite all my self-talk about not expecting a call. As the years went by, that jolt of anger softened into sadness and then into a wistful twinge. The anger was softened by the fact that Bob, my self-appointed godfather, sent me a birthday card and flowers *every* year, even when he was travelling in Australia and once while he was sailing partway around the world. Floyd always remembered my birthdays too, calling to tell me how much he loved me and how proud he was of me. Those two men were the best fathers I never had.

At this point, I accepted my estranged relationship with Dad and no longer yearned for him to be part of my life. I no longer wanted anything from him. The more I understood how I had changed under the influence of drugs and alcohol—I hardly recognized the person I had been several years earlier—the more I accepted that Dad had done the same. When he was using drugs, he lost himself, nothing mattered as much as the cocaine, and he had become disconnected from everybody, including me. I had a vague sense of having a father, but it became more and more nebulous until Dad was only a collage of memories from my childhood, a bread bag of letters, a dusty album of yellowed newspaper clippings and photos.

THE THINGS I CARRY

*T*he summer before graduating from college with a degree in environmental sciences, I took a job working as an Idaho wilderness ranger. An ex-boyfriend had introduced me to backpacking in the Appalachian Mountains the year before, and I was hooked and eager to try hiking in the rugged western mountains. There was something freeing about carrying everything I needed on my back, stripped down to the bare essentials. And the solitude of being out in the wilderness, sometimes not seeing other people for days, was peaceful. After all my years of isolation, being alone was much easier than being with people; I suppose it always would be.

Mom was excited about my new job away from the psych hospital where I had been working for seven years, assuring me I was going to have a blast. Bob fretted and gave me all kinds of advice, but I wasn't sure if he was exaggerating, which he often did, or if he was genuinely worried. He insisted I take his .38-caliber pistol.

"I'm not allowed to carry a weapon," I explained during my last visit to his cabin before I left for Idaho.

"So? Don't tell anyone."

"I've got a bear bag. I've backpacked in bear country—"

"Child, this gun is *not* for the wild animals. It's for the wild men that might be out there. Humor me, will you? Just take the thirty-eight."

The memory of Mark crossed my mind. "Okay. I'll take it."

"Thank you. Now, come out and refresh your shooting skills. I'm not sure if you've shot anywhere else recently, but you haven't shot out here since you were a bratty teenager. Christ, that was, what, like ten years ago?"

"Let's see, I was fourteen or fifteen the last time I shot a gun. Back when you and Mom were still dating."

"Ah, yes, before she made the worst decision of her life and broke my heart."

I let out a scoffing laugh. He handed me a box of .38 rounds and motioned for me to follow him out to his shooting range. The hundred or so acres that surrounded his cabin were forested and hilly except for a flat acre with no trees right behind the cabin. Where the hills rose steeply from that level ground, he had set up a target practice area: a wire for hanging bull's-eye sheets and big tree stumps where he could prop empty beer cans.

After he acquainted me with his .38, I took aim and fired at the aluminum cans he lined up on a log. After a few practice shots, I plucked all three of them right off.

He beamed at me. "Not bad. Not bad at all."

I reloaded the gun. "Well, I did grow up shooting guns with my dad."

"That's right! I forgot he was a cop before he was a criminal. Well, at least he taught you something worthwhile." I had never thought of those early gun skills as worthwhile.

Bob sent me off with his pistol, a pile of Army ready-to-eat meals, a pad of notepaper and a pencil. Standing beside my car before I left his cabin, he said, "If you don't write to me at least every two weeks, I will drive out there to check on you."

"Is this crazy? Driving all the way across the country to work in the wilderness? It's so far, and I've only backpacked a few times in my life. I don't know a soul out there . . . "

"It's not crazy at all." He embraced me in a reassuring hug. "It's gonna be the adventure of a lifetime. Be smart, be safe and you'll be fine. And for Christ's sake, stay away from any drugs. And all the men, stay away from them too. I still say you should consider a convent."

"I'm not Catholic, and it's way too late for that anyways."

"Oh, Jesus wept. Don't tell me that crap. Let me pretend you're still an innocent child."

As I drove down his long, gravel driveway, he waved good-bye and hollered after me, "Love you, kid." And I knew he did.

Miriam and I had an emotional good-bye. As we sat across from each other, I saw in her face the tenderness she felt for me. I reminisced about how hard it had been to sit in that room years earlier and make eye contact with her. So much had happened in that small space between us—I had become a completely different person.

We laughed about that first appointment when she assumed Lawrence had referred me to her professionally. "See that relationship with him wasn't all bad, was it? He sent you to me," she said, smiling.

"Guess that was the best thing he ever did for me, huh?" I glanced at the big sycamore tree outside her window and smiled. "I am so nervous about doing this. It's so far from home, and I'll be working with a bunch of strangers. I don't want to end up sleeping with any men out there or drinking again."

"It'll be difficult, but you're ready. And you can always call me. Anytime. If you don't drink, you'll be okay. And you know how to avoid the old behavior with men now too."

I'm sure I did, because by then I had truly dated men and had even had a couple of longish-term relationships. But when she said it as if there were some simple steps I needed to take or not take, I couldn't for the life of me think of what those steps were.

She used her measured speech, the way she did when she was about to reveal some important truth. "It's all about good boundaries. Once you start offering more than friendship, getting physical, it's very difficult to step back from that. If you just don't cross that line until you have a connection, it's much easier."

I nodded. "It's kind of like drinking. Once I take that first drink, then I'm off and running and there's no stopping me."

"Exactly. And if you make friends with the women too—you know how to do that now—well, that will be—"

"Less complicated."

"Exactly. And more fun. And you won't be lonely. *Right*?" That inflection at the end of one of her sentences had become a signal to me over the years. I took it to mean she thought I was smart and knew this truth already and was simply giving me a quick reminder. But on the precipice of this huge leap into the unknown, aware of all that was at stake for me, I doubted my ability to navigate the normal world. Inside Miriam's office and in recovery meetings, I was safe. In Idaho, where everything and everyone would be unfamiliar, I wasn't so sure I would be safe or that I could take care of myself.

"I guess. I'm really having second thoughts though. I'm not sure I'm ready for this."

"I think you're ready." She gave me that knowing smile. "Do you remember what you were like when you first came to see me? You were so scary."

"Scary? Because of all the drinking and drugging?"

"Well, that *was* scary." She shook her head. "But you were so . . . disconnected. From everyone. You didn't have any healthy connections to anyone. I didn't think you'd ever let me in."

"I wasn't *that* bad, was I?"

"You were. And you had only a shred of self-esteem." She held up her index finger and thumb with a small space between them. "If it wasn't for that shred, I don't think you would've made it. You know where you got that tiny bit of self-esteem from don't you?"

"No. Where?"

"From your mom. She did something right."

*A*s I drove across the country alone, to a place I had never been before, to work with complete strangers, I experienced surges of doubt. They weren't bowling me over though and in between were rushes of excitement. By day two of my four-day drive, my anticipation about the adventure ahead pushed aside any residual anxiety. I listened to music, chatted with folks at gas stations and gawked at the scenery in parts of the country I had only seen in magazines and movies. I began to see my journey as symbolic of the last several years of my life. I was leaving behind my familiar surroundings, my comfort zone, for something different and, hopefully, better. The person I used to be could never have done what I was doing. Not in a million years.

I stayed in cheap hotels in Iowa and Montana. The tiny rustic towns dotting the expansive western states were charming, as were the rugged men with their cowboy boots, hat-tipping and "yes, ma'am." To save money, I stocked up on groceries and avoided eating at restaurants. That also kept me away from any bars I might stumble into. I didn't want to drink, but the delusion popped into my mind, unbidden, that I could drink one measly shot of tequila and who would know way out there in the middle of the country? That lovely notion was followed by a chilling image of me drunk with a stranger in a run-down motel, my meager savings spent and no way to get to Idaho or back home. I remembered where my drinking and drugging career took me: hunkered in my attic off and on for days, hiding from the cops who were supposedly watching Rick's house, vacillating between feeling connected to Dad and suspecting I was a toss-away pawn in his high-stakes smuggling game, but as long as I snorted a line or drank a beer every hour or so, everything was fine, my life was fine. *Yeah, I'm steering clear of any and all bars today.* All I have to do is not drink today, I reminded myself. Staying sober was similar to steering clear of seductive behavior with men: Not this time. Not today. About face. Good-bye. Some other time. Maybe tomorrow.

My first weekend in Idaho, I found a recovery meeting. Connecting and being honest with others who were also staying clean and sober had become fundamental to my continued recovery, to my life. I couldn't live in total isolation and loneliness anymore. Time alone was fine, but it was crucial for me to stay connected to people who I knew and trusted. In fact, whenever I found myself wanting to hide the real me from those closest to me, that was an indication I needed to do the exact opposite. Those were the times I made myself go to a meeting or call another person in recovery or reach out to a girlfriend.

Four days after I left Ohio, the mountains where I was to work rose into view, jutting up from a sweeping glacier-carved valley. I pulled my car off the road to gawk at them, having never seen anything so magnificent. The mountains were a mix of icy, snow-covered peaks, jagged gray rock outcroppings and lower elevations of coniferous forests, some still blanketed with snow and some a dark green army of spires.

My stomach tightened when I turned into the Forest Service workstation where I was to report. I checked in at the office, one of several wooden structures sunbaked to a pale, splintery gray. A chatty woman named Michelle greeted me. While I signed some papers, she asked where I was from and told me she was volunteering there for the summer with her seven-year-old son. She left her husband at home to fend for himself, she said, throwing her head back in laughter. That gesture reminded me of Miriam and her solidarity with woman. I smiled at her and said, "Sounds like you got the best part of that deal. Can't wait to meet your son."

Michelle took me to the women's bunkhouse and introduced me to the other two women with whom I would share living quarters for the summer. I tried to keep my face relaxed and open, despite the perspiration breaking out under my arms, and came up with a list of questions to keep the conversation going.

At nine the next morning, we all reported to the middle of the compound to get oriented. As soon as I saw a few of the men I would work with, a thrill flashed through me, followed immediately by fear. Living and working in close proximity to rugged, healthy, good-looking men all summer was more of a temptation than I believed I could handle. If I reverted to my old behavior, flirting and getting seductive and—*Wait a minute. I can do this. I know how to do this now.* I reminded myself about keeping good boundaries and befriending the men in the same way I was going to become friends with the women.

Everyone was helpful, familiarizing me with the work center and what each of our jobs would entail. Of the three wilderness rangers with whom I would work all summer, of course, two had to be the handsome men there: Charlie and Greg. Heidi, our supervisor, was a short, powerhouse of a woman with blonde hair and freckles all over. I couldn't imagine how she survived the sun —my shoulders and nose were already hot and tingly. The sun was much more intense at that altitude and without the hazy humidity of the Midwest. And it was only June.

The second day, I took my breakfast out to the stoop of my cabin to eat. The cool morning air was permeated by a pungent, herb-like aroma. After eating, I walked over to the scrappy, woody bushes that surrounded the work center and carpeted the foothills. I pinched off a few of the pale greenish-gray leaves and crumpled them under my nose. It was sage and was definitely the source of the aroma.

As I took in the jagged mountains, someone behind me said, "Morning." I turned to see Greg walking up to my cabin. He followed my gaze to the peaks. "Breathtaking, isn't it?"

I opened my mouth to respond but couldn't find the words. I could see in my peripheral vision that he was watching me, waiting for a response. "I've never seen, or smelled, anything like this." I looked back at him. "It's magical."

"Wait 'til you get up in those mountains." He ticked his chin toward the icy peaks. "You'll never be the same." His face was ruddy and slightly weathered, as if he spent a great deal of time outside.

"When do we go up?"

"After the snow melts in the lower elevations." He scanned the peaks. "I'd say about two weeks, now that the days are warming up. There'll still be snow on the trails, but we'll be able to get to some of the lower lakes and train you and Charlie."

Charlie walked up then and stood next to us, a big grin on his face, sipping on a mug of tea. "Well? What do you think about this place?" He was puppy-dog cute and had the loping gate of a big puppy too, long legs and big feet with clunky hiking boots.

"I love it here. Nothing like this in Ohio, that's for sure."

"Work-day today. Pack lunch and *lots* of water," Greg said over his shoulder as he and Charlie headed to the garage. Greg had perfect legs: not too hairy, chiseled muscles all the way up to a great ass. *No, no, no. I am not flirting with any of these men. I am not crossing that line.* I reminded myself I did not need to act on my desire for a man, or as Miriam had once put it, why ruin a perfectly good fantasy?

The first week, we all received training and worked on the low-elevation campgrounds that campers could access by car. The work was tough: digging post holes, building fences, relocating fire pits, digging drainage ditches. The other women were bigger, or at least sturdier, than me, but I was able to keep up, thanks to all the weightlifting and swimming I had been doing. We all did our share and worked well together, and the work was a welcome focus for me, allowing me to begin connecting with the group over shared tasks. While my awareness of the men was palpable and hard to ignore, I focused my attention on the women, pursuing the connections I had learned to build and come to need. With these women, I laughed and bantered as we all sweated and struggled together, and the comradery helped me focus less on myself and more on the joy of my adventure, my new friends and my long journey to get there.

My first night camping at an alpine lake was 7,400 feet above sea level, the highest I had ever been while still standing on the planet. As the freezing-cold water numbed my sore, blistered feet, I surveyed my surroundings. The sun was scorching and relentless, but the air was cool, especially where my shirt was plastered against my back with sweat. The lake was a deep blue, fading to turquoise in the shallows, and at the outlet, was a dam of sun-bleached logs. On the lake's surface was a mirror image of the craggy, snow-capped ridge—a stoic, ancient sentry—dominating the far side of the lake. Sub-alpine fir, which I was tickled to be able to identify from a forestry class I had recently completed, were straggly and widely spaced at that elevation, and once warmed from the sun, released a spicy, citrusy aroma (no book could ever teach you that). My physical and mental exhaustion dissipated as a peaceful contentment filled me, heightened by the amazement of the arduous journey I had taken to get there. This was a long way from The Bottoms.

That summer, I experienced many firsts. A swath of stars across the sky that, though millions of light years away, appeared so close it seemed I could reach out and touch them. Wind that howled like a wild animal through the mountains and trees. Dozens of lakes frigid with snowmelt, each a different shade of milky turquoise, that beckoned me to slip in—and jump right back out! An eagle that swooped over my head as I crested a mountain pass. A growing comprehension that the planet and the forces on it, the entire universe, had been here long before I ever existed and would be here long after I was gone. The wilderness put my life into perspective and made me right-sized. All my struggles, pain and anguish, as well as all my joy and triumphs, paled in comparison to that vastness surrounding me. My life was one miniscule part of this world, a brief blip. I would be just a brief blip. My time on this planet and my influence over it would be but a speck. But instead of making anything I did while alive seem insignificant, my new awareness of how fleeting life was made life that much more precious. When I had been gripped by addiction, there were times I hadn't wanted to live, days when I no longer wanted to walk on this planet. Now, stretched out before me was more opportunity than I could embrace in one lifetime. I was bursting with an urgency to begin living my life.

My wilderness experience would catapult me into action so that within three years I would obtain a graduate degree and launch a career in the nascent field of environmental mediation, helping parties to resolve natural resource disputes collaboratively rather than suing each other. Little did I know how my hard-won skills at disarming tense situations and angry people would serve me in this line of work!

Each week, I headed into the wilderness for five days at time. Alone. All four rangers covered different territories each week. Everyone I met out there was friendly and interesting, but there was one encounter that made me grateful I carried Bob's gun.

As I began my trek into the wilderness one week, I chatted with a man who was on his way out. As I set up camp that evening on a ledge perched above a lake, that same man came around the edge of the lake, scouting for a campsite. When we had crossed paths earlier, he was only a mile or so from the trailhead, almost done. But this lake would've been a strenuous five-mile hike back into the mountains that he had just come down from. Backpackers can't easily change plans like that, heading back into the wilderness, because we carry the minimum amount of food needed for precisely the number of days we'll be in the backcountry. My gut told me the man came back looking for me. I recalled he had asked if there were other rangers hiking with me. My body and brain went into hyperalert mode. I set my gun on the ground in easy reach and where it was visible. A deterrent, I hoped. But in my memory, I glimpsed Dad with his snub-nosed pistol, always readily available but always concealed. Instead, I tucked the gun in my food bag right next to me.

As the man's boots crunched through the brush below my campsite, Dad materialized again, scanning the water around our sailboat then jumping into motion the instant he spotted that shark. I scrutinized the terrain around me, identifying another route I could take down off the ledge if the stranger cornered me up there.

Despite having my gun close at hand, fear shot through me

when I saw his head, then his shoulders, emerge from below the ledge where I was perched. Dad was beside me again, this time behind me in the junkyard telling me to line up the gun's front and rear sights with our target. This guy was close enough I wouldn't have any trouble shooting him, could easily hit his shoulder or leg. That would stop him but not kill him. Dad's words echoed in my mind, "Never point a gun at someone unless you plan on shooting them." Then Mark's face appeared at the end of a shotgun. My heartrate accelerated as if I had been running. *Oh, please, please, just leave me alone.*

"Hey," he said, "it's you again. Remember, we passed on the trail earlier? I was just out exploring around the lake, looking for huckleberries."

"Still too early for them at this elevation. They don't ripen until August this high up. Thought you were heading out of the wilderness today?" Dad again, this time at the fairgrounds, focused, telling us where and when to meet back up with him then talking all calm and cool with the drug dealers. I recalled where the nearest campers were set up, perhaps close enough to hear me if I screamed.

"Well, I figured I had enough food to eke out one more night up here. It's just too beautiful to leave." He smiled at me.

I didn't return his smile. "Wow. You're dedicated. Hope you weren't relying on the berries for food."

He picked up a rock and began tossing it from hand to hand. "Do you want to eat together? I can bring my dinner up here." Plunk, plunk, plunk with the rock.

I wiped my palms on my shorts. "I already ate, and I have some work to do still." I pointed at my pad of paper.

He made some more small talk, until I said I hoped he enjoyed his second, last night out here, then picked up my notepad and began scribbling.

As I watched him weave his way back down toward the lake, and my heartrate returned to normal, I was struck by a new realization. A few years earlier, I would've been flirting with that man, trying to win him over. Hell, if I had been drinking, may even have had sex with him. All my focus on men—approval-seeking, flirting, seducing, fucking—was how I tried to feel cherished . . . loved . . . and that had gotten all tangled up with trying to feel safe. Yet the very behavior I used to stabilize my world made me unsafe and, certainly, made it impossible to experience any love. But all that time, I had spot-on instincts about people, especially men. Instincts I could have relied on to stay safe. Instincts I would now trust. As I watched that man walk out of my campsite, I understood that I had always known how to take care of myself. My father had taught me how.

In my weekly letter to Bob, I told him that he was right, as usual, there are a lot of creeps in the world and having his gun was reassuring, and no, I hadn't needed to use it. I wrote a letter to Dad that week also, the only one I wrote to him that summer. I expressed my gratitude for all the ways I was just like him and thanked him for all the lessons he taught me over the years.

A few weeks later, I was surprised to see Dad's familiar handwriting on a slender box in the mail. I wasn't surprised his handwriting still gave me a tug of emotion. Inside the box was a clever, compact, folding handsaw with a sturdy oak handle that was hinged to fold over and cover the gnarly steel teeth. Dad wrote that he had it custom made for stowing in my backpack. In his brief note he also said he couldn't imagine what I had ever learned from him that would help me in the world but hoped the folding saw would come in handy out there in the wilderness.

I carried that small piece of my father with me on every trip I took that summer. And every journey I have taken since.

EPILOGUE: THE LIGHT OF DAY

When I was clawing my way out of Dad's drug smuggling world, the illusory hope for his love called to me still, just as the cocaine and alcohol had. But I also carried a fear that if I went near him, I would end up like so many times before, right back in his auction barn snorting lines all day. After I stayed away from him and the coke for several years, those beasts no longer nipping at my heels, I ceased to be plagued by dreams of a father who cherished me. What never went away though was a curiosity, a fascination, about how all of this had happened to my father—and to us. I didn't dare get close enough to ask him until I had rebuilt myself from the ground up, until long after I had married a fellow recovering addict, established a successful career and was teaching university classes on conflict resolution.

In my work world, as with Dad, I maintained a rigid boundary between my new life and my past. With my colleagues, I never mentioned the self-destructive, drug-addicted woman I had been. There was no way I would let my past collide with my present.

Then I began working with high school students whose parents were drug addicts. Helping those teens understand that they could choose their own paths helped me to see how far I had come. And seeing how my journey could help others heal allowed the line between who I had been and who I now was to soften and blur. I came to accept that I was both a strong, independent businesswoman and a former drug addict; a trustworthy wife and a previously promiscuous woman; a healthy adult and, once, a lost, fatherless child.

What I still could not reconcile though was how a doting, protective father and narcotics agent walked out on his family, without so much as a glance back, and dove head-first into a world of drug smuggling. This question began to burn inside me. By then, I was certain Dad was no longer abusing drugs. So, finally, I asked him to tell me his story.

To my surprise, he agreed.

In the summer of 2002, Dad and I sat in his living room grappling for something to say to each other until I turned on my tape recorder. Over the course of several days, he described what it was like working undercover narcotics on the streets of Miami in the 1970's. He detailed the increasing difficulty of shedding his identity as a drug smuggler every night, and how booze was the only thing that took the edge off and helped him unwind before coming home. Then, how the booze became necessary to do both: be a drug dealer every day and come home every night and be a decent husband and dad and teach Sunday school on the weekend. He explained how he slowly lost himself, sinking deeper and deeper into his alter-identity until he had no idea who he was. Then, how easy it was to cross that line and become a drug smuggler, a real one, because as an undercover narcotics agent, he'd basically been a smuggler for years.

As my father's story unfolded, the fragments of fantasies and lies I had told myself about him dissolved, and I saw him for who he truly was. He had been a great cop and a great dad, a corrupt cop and a cold, rejecting father, a drug addict and a dangerous father—he was all of those things. As the truth came to light and filled the spaces where before there had been only questions and endless longing and crushed hopes, my complicated relationship with Dad came into sharp focus. He gave me all the love he had ever been capable of giving. I was never going to win him over again as I had when I was a child. And thankfully, I didn't need to anymore. I had barely survived the charm and the hell of my father, and yet some of my greatest strengths came from doing so.

While my quest had always been to piece together the story of my father, what I finally found entangled in his story was my own.

ALSO BY LYNN WALKER

Lynn Walker will soon be publishing the story of her dad's infamous life as a Miami undercover narcotics agent-turned-drug smuggler, which she wrote in close collaboration with him. Stay tuned for release date:

www.LynnWalkerMemoir.com

social media: @WalkerMemoir

IF YOU FEEL INSPIRED BY THIS STORY...

please tell a friend about *Midnight Calling* and post a review on Amazon, GoodReads or your favorite online bookstore.

IF YOU NEED HELP:

• Find an anonymous recovery meeting for drug or alcohol addiction, many are now held virtually.

• Domestic Violence Hotline: 1-800-799-7233 or text "START" to 88788

• Runaway Hotline: 1-800-786-2929

• Planned Parenthood: 1-800-230-7526 or text "PPNOW" to 774636

• Suicide & Crisis Lifeline: dial 988